FLEET AIR ARM
Carrier War

FLEET AIR ARM
Carrier War

The History of British Naval Aviation

Kev Darling

Pen & Sword
AVIATION

First published in Great Britain in 2009 by
Pen & Sword Aviation
an imprint of
Pen & Sword Books Ltd
47 Church Street
Barnsley
South Yorkshire
S70 2AS

ISBN: 978 1 84415 903 1

A CIP catalogue record for this book is available from
the British Library

Typeset in Palatino by S L Menzies-Earl

Printed in the UK by MPG Books Group

Pen & Sword Books Ltd incorporates the imprints of:
Pen & Sword Aviation, Pen & Sword Maritime, Pen & Sword
Military, Wharncliffe Local History, Pen & Sword Select, Pen &
Sword Military Classics, Leo Cooper, Remember When, Seaforth
Publishing and Frontline Publishing.

For a complete list of Pen & Sword titles please contact:
Pen & Sword Books Limited
47 Church Street, Barnsley, South Yorkshire, S70 2AS, England
E-mail: enquiries@pen-and-sword.co.uk
Website: www.pen-and-sword.co.uk

Contents

Introduction

During its entire existence the Fleet Air Arm, the aviation wing of the Royal Navy, has frequently suffered from political interference. Having literally got off to a flying start as the Royal Naval Air Service the Admiralty was most upset to find the world's largest naval air wing being subsumed into the newly formed Royal Air Force in 1918. During the inter-war period the Royal Navy managed to hang onto its aircraft carriers although the aircraft it carried were under the control of the Air Ministry. Eventually the Admiralty managed to increase its influence over its own aircraft and the crews they carried. By the time hostilities erupted over Europe again in September 1939 the Royal Navy had fully regained control of both its ships and aircraft which, given the tasks that faced them, was the sensible option. Even though the Admiralty was now in control the major problems facing the carrier crews was the poor performance of the aircraft they were equipped with because they were designed for the warfare of a much earlier era. But, even though the fighter and attack units were equipped with obsolescent aircraft, through skilful flying and great bravery the crews managed to achieve some great feats of combat.

WWII brought a perilous period of existence for the Royal Navy when many of its fleet carriers were sunk. However, hasty conversions of merchantmen, the lend lease by America of the smaller escort, or jeep, carriers plus a speeding up of the building of replacement main and light fleet carriers meant that the navy was soon fully equipped again. Allied to the increase in carrier strength came a new crop of aircraft from both British and American manufacturers. With this new strength and the tide of war changing in the favour of the Allies the Fleet Air Arm and the aircraft carriers would finish their work in the Atlantic and then proceed into the Mediterranean and onto the Pacific and the war in the Far East. Here they would join up with the US Navy whose forces could only be described as massive.

When Japan finally capitulated in 1945 most people hoped that the threat of war would recede for many years. However, this was not the case as the power vacuum caused by the removal of conquerors and colonial powers would result in further conflicts. Again the Far East would figure greatly, this time it would be Korea where the Communists, both Russian and Chinese, would begin to flex their muscles. After nearly three years of fighting up and down the country a truce was finally achieved.

Nevertheless, Britain would find itself at war again in 1956 this time over the Suez canal which Egypt's President Nassar decided to sequester. Although a combined British and French force, with Israeli support, was making great headway against the Egyptian forces, pressure by the United States via the World Bank resulted in the operation ending prematurely.

After Suez the Fleet Air Arm and the Royal Navy were active participants in the Cold War as was the remainder of Britain's Armed Forces. This would change in 1982 when Argentina invaded the Falkland Islands in an effort to divert attention away from problems at home. After a massive effort the British Armed Forces successfully recaptured the islands. Again the Fleet underwent changes, this time the last of the vessels whose roots lay in the Second World War were finally retired and were replaced by three smaller carriers that were capable of operating both helicopters and Sea Harriers. Obviously machines as complex as aircraft carriers will eventually wear out so it is fortunate that the Royal Navy will receive the first of two new super-carriers within a few years. Not only will these new ships improve the capabilities of the fleet but the aircraft intended for deployment in these new vessels will also increase the effectiveness of the fleet. Should all this come to pass without too much political interference the future of the Fleet Air Arm looks good.

Obviously a work such as this could not be completed without the help of others therefore I would like to thank the staff at the Fleet Air Arm Museum, Yeovilton, Air Britain, the late and sadly missed Ray Sturtivant, John Ryan, Ray Harding and all at Aerophot.

Kev Darling, Wales 2009

Chapter 1

Aviation for the Navy – From the Start to 1939

W hen Admiral Sir John 'Jackie' Fisher, later Lord Fisher of Kilverstone, was returned as First Sea Lord in October 1914 at the age of 74, having retired for the first time four years earlier, he continued the process that speeded up the evolution of the Royal Navy, taking it to the pinnacle of its existence. It was only the requirements of the First World War and the forced retirement of the previous First Sea Lord, Prince Luis of Battenburg due to alleged German connections, that had seen Fisher recalled. His tenure of office ended on 15 May 1915 after a flaming row with Churchill over the Gallipoli campaign which Fisher strongly disagreed with. The irony of this was that Churchill also resigned when the campaign went disastrously wrong.

Contrary to the opinions of many critics that had been voiced strongly since the creation of the battleship fleet the Royal Navy was very much in favour of adopting emerging technology. However, they exercised some restraint until the technology was proven and thus numerous developments took some time to enter general naval service. Typical was the care taken over the deployment of breech loading guns, the gun turret and barbette to house them and the creation of hull forms and the finally revealed upper structures developed from these developmental evaluations. With Admiral Fisher in control, all of these developments plus others, such as the oil fired boiler and the turbine engine, came to fruition in the shape of the Dreadnought class battleship. Not only did this class of sea-going weapon render the remainder of the world's fleet's obsolete it instituted a global arms race with the British having the avowed intent of retaining 'the two power fleet'. This standard was

The confirmation that the carrier borne aviation was possible was provided by Squadron Commander E.H. Dunning who would land aboard the partly converted HMS *Furious* in August 1917. Unfortunately Dunning would be killed on 7 August when attempting to land aboard *Furious* again in Scapa Flow. (FAAM Yeovilton)

based on the idea that the soon to be named Grand Fleet should be stronger in numbers and firepower than the combined two numerically nearest fleets of the competing nations. While Fisher did reveal some strategic flaws, the best known being his support for the battlecruiser which mounted battleship guns over cruiser thickness armour, he was enthusiastic and supportive of other emerging technologies that could be of use to the Royal Navy in the future .

Although not a prime objective for Fisher the development of an aviation component for the Royal Navy received distant encouragement. The first use of any form of aviation by the Royal Navy occurred in 1806 when kites were deployed aboard HMS *Pallas* for the purpose of distributing propaganda leaflets. While these trials were successful the Royal Navy would not use kites in any form in future operations as they were, for all practical purposes, useless for daily use. Trials were also undertaken using a standard army spherical balloon during 1903-04 which confirmed the thinking of the time that such a shape would be uncontrollable whilst operating from the deck of a moving ship. Balloons would eventually find a place with the sea-going navy, however they would resemble floppy sausages in shape and were graced with a limited control range and were not powered thus they had to remain tethered to their carrier vessel.

The innovation that really sparked the development of naval aviation was the early aeroplane and it was an American, Eugene P Ely, who would lay his claim to fame on 4 November 1910 when he successfully piloted a Curtiss pusher-aircraft from a specially constructed platform on the forecastle of the cruiser USS *Birmingham*. Given that a previous attempt from the torpedo boat USS *Bagley* had ended in a crash this success was vital to the continuance of ship-borne aviation. Ely would also be the first to land an aircraft aboard a ship on 18 January 1911; the battleship USS *Pennsylvania* being the recipient. While the launch and landing trials were carried out under anchored and calm conditions it should be remembered that these were the infant days of aviation. Not only were the early aircraft difficult to fly but the skill needed to land such a delicate contraption aboard even a stationary vessel required exceptional skill and courage.

News of the American research had reached the Admiralty in 1909 and their response was to build the rigid airship *Mayfly*. After a series of flights, which ended in complete disaster in September 1911 when the

A Sopwith Camel departs the first aircraft orientated HMS *Ark Royal*. It was also one of the few aircraft carriers to utilise a mizzen mast for longitudinal stability. In 1935 the vessel was renamed HMS *Pegasus*, the name being transferred to the new fleet carrier HMS *Ark Royal*. (FAAM Yeovilton)

airship crashed, the Admiralty then turned their attention to fixed-wing aircraft with trials beginning in 1912. The pilot chosen to undertake these initial flights was Cdr Schwann who successfully lifted an Avro biplane from the water near Barrow-in-Furness. This was followed by Lt Cdr Sampson RN who flew a Short pusher aircraft complete with rigid buoyancy floats mounted under the wings and carried in the event of an unplanned water landing. The chosen vessel was HMS *Africa* which sported a steeply sloped launch ramp mounted on the bow. On 10 January 1912 a successful launch was undertaken while the ship was at anchor in Sheerness Harbour. On 2 May 1912 the pre-Dreadnought battleship HMS *Hibernia* was modified in a similar way to HMS *Africa* although the launch ramp was set at a shallower angle. Lt Cdr Sampson was again the chosen pilot and the aircraft was, as before, a Short Pusher. During these trials the *Hibernia* was steamed at 10.5 knots in Weymouth Bay. A third series of flights was undertaken from 4 July 1912 although this time the cruiser HMS *London* was the chosen carrier vessel. Again a launch ramp was mounted over the bow using the same pilot and aircraft

Even though it wears a Blackburn Aeroplane Company badge on the fin this is in fact a contract built Sopwith Baby. The floatplane was the alternative way for the navy to carry fighter aircraft aboard its capital ships. Instead of a flight deck aircraft could either be launched into the air from a turret ramp or craned off onto the sea, there to take off under its own power. (BBA Collection)

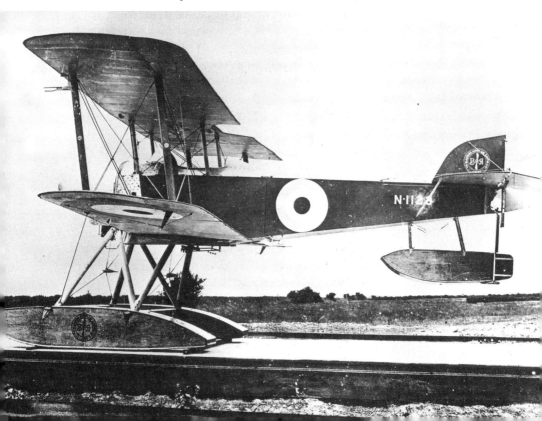

Not the recommended way to return to earth. As the launch comes alongside his stricken Camel the pilot reaches out to his rescuers. (Aerophot)

although *London*'s speed varied between 10 and 15 knots while the ramp was extended in length to 25 feet. While the use of such ramps was non productive from a combat point of view because they rendered the forward guns unusable, it did pave the way for further experiments in naval aviation. While these flight trials were being undertaken the army had set up the Royal Flying Corps which included in its constitution a Military Wing, a Naval Wing and a Central Flying School.

Naval flight training had initially begun in early 1911 when the Admiralty had accepted the offer of Mr. Francis McClean, later knighted, for the free loan of two of his privately owned aircraft for flight training purposes. The training took place at the Aero Club aerodrome at Eastchurch, Isle of Sheppey, this being possible as McClean was a member of the Royal Aero Club. Two of the first graduates were Schwann and Sampson both being trained by Mr George Cockburn. Alongside Schwann and Sampson Lieutenants Gregory and Longmore RN plus Lt Gerrard of the Royal Marine Light Infantry also qualified. However, they were not the first as Lt G C Colmore RN had qualified at his own expense in June 1910. By the end of 1912 the Royal Navy had 16 aircraft consisting of 13 land-based aircraft and three hydroplanes, later renamed seaplanes. The year 1912 was also the first time that the dropping of bombs was undertaken, the pilot again being Cdr Sampson. Radio communications were also trialled at this time and proved successful. All these innovations were matched by the establishment of coastal seaplane stations, the first being at the Isle of Grain. Further funding was included in the 1912 Naval Estimates which allowed for the establishment of bases at Calshot, Cromarty, Felixstowe and Great Yarmouth. When 1914 opened the RNAS had over 100 trained pilots and would later acquire all the available airships which would remain under their control until 1919. While rumblings of war spread across Europe during 1914 the RNAS continued its aviation experiments, the first was a one and a half pounder gun mounted in the nose of a Short Gun-Carrier piloted by Lt Hall. When the First World War finally encompassed Britain the RNAS had a strength of 78 aircraft which included 40 landplanes, 31 seaplanes and seven airships. Personnel strength consisted of 130 officers plus 700 Petty Officers and other ranks. During this conflict the RNAS fought at sea as well as on the Western Front. Their first raid was undertaken on 22 September 1914 when four aircraft from Cdr Sampson's Eastchurch squadron attacked targets in Germany. Following this raid the RNAS units undertook raids mainly against the Zeppelin sheds at Dusseldorf and Friedrichshafen. The home based units were mainly allocated to the air defence of Britain as the Royal Flying Corps was fully engaged over the Western Front.

While the Royal Navy was laying the foundations for the aircraft-carrier fleet another method was needed to launch aircraft. The solution was the flying-off platform fitted to ships as small as the light cruiser. Smaller vessels, such as the destroyers, sometimes towed lighters at high speed thus creating the wind needed to launch an aircraft. Aboard the lighter would be a single-seat fighter such as the Sopwith Pup which, when close to the launching point, would have its tethers cut and the aircraft would take off. The lighters had originally been built to move large flying boats across the North Sea and were sized accordingly at 58 feet long and 16 feet in the beam. The first take-off was undertaken by Lt Culley on 31 July 1918, a few days later he repeated the feat destroying a Zeppelin in the process. The first vessel fitted with a flying-off platform was HMS *Yarmouth*, the pilot was Flight Cdr Rutland who flew a Sopwith Pup off successfully in June 1917. This was followed by experiments using the battlecruiser HMS *Repulse* in October. Mounting the flying-off platform on gun turrets meant that the carrying ship only had to rotate the requisite gun turret into wind for the aircraft to take off. No landing on was possible therefore the launched fighter needed to find dry land for a safe touchdown. By the time the war ended in 1918 over 100 aircraft were carried aboard the ships of the Grand Fleet.

The first modern *Ark Royal* was purely a seaplane tender during the First World War. In the next conflict the vessel had been renamed *Pegasus* and was used as a catapult ship for convoy escort duties. (Terry Johns Collection)

Seen from the rear cockpit of a departing aircraft is HMS *Courageous*. Once a large light cruiser the vessel was converted into an aircraft carrier although its war service was cut short as it was sunk by U-29 on 17 September 1939. (FAAM Yeovilton)

HMS *Hermes* was the first aircraft carrier in the world built as such. Its lines reflect its intended role: that of travelling in concert with a cruiser force at speed. The vessel was later sunk by Japanese forces near Ceylon in April 1942. (Trevor Jones)

On 23 October 1912 the ship constructors Beardmores sent the Admiralty a proposal for a parent ship to carry naval aeroplanes that in turn was based on the concept put forward by the Marquis of Graham, an early aviation pioneer. The initial design featured a flat decked hull some 450 feet long with a beam of 110 feet. Mounted on each side of the central flight deck were island structures which were in turn connected by a flying bridge. The island structures contained the hangars, workshops and funnels. While this design was championed by two naval aviation enthusiasts, Rear Admiral Moore and Captain Murray Sueter, the Admiralty decided to reject the proposal until further experience had been gained in the operation of aircraft from ships. This was a fortunate decision because the placing of island structures aboard aircraft carriers had a profound affect on wind flow across the deck due to turbulence caused by the eddies generated by the islands and any landing aboard a ship such as the Beardmore proposal would have encountered severe turbulence. Further confirmation of this was discovered during early wind tunnel trials at the Admiralty test centre. Even so this design did lay the foundation for the aircraft carriers of the future.

While the Beardmore proposal never came to fruition the Admiralty was intrigued enough by the idea of a dedicated vessel for carrying aircraft that in 1913 Admiral Mark Kerr suggested the construction of a purpose-built aeroplane carrier. However given the risk that such a vessel might turn out to be unsuitable the First Sea Lord, Admiral of the Fleet Sir Arthur Wilson, proposed a safer option. This was to take the

Eclipse class cruiser HMS *Hermes* and fit it with two flying-off decks fore and aft, although the idea was that the forward platform would be used for launching and the rear for landing only. To move the aircraft from deck to deck it was decided to fit special cranes capable of moving the aircraft safely, however, this in turn would require the ship's superstructure be modified and this, in turn, would require the main mast to be removed. Having been chosen for this new role the 13 year old cruiser HMS *Hermes* underwent conversion during 1912 and was declared ready for naval manoeuvres during May 1913. When *Hermes* was first revealed it was obvious that the modifications were less than proposed as only one launching platform was fitted forward while the area originally proposed for landing was occupied by a canvas hangar while another readiness hangar was installed to the rear of the launching platform. Aircraft movement fore and aft was courtesy of specially designed derricks. Tanks were installed for the carriage of 2,000 gallons of aviation petroleum. During the first weeks of July 1913 two seaplanes were lifted aboard, these being a Caudron and a Short S64 better known as the folder due to its wing folding capability. During these trials a series of nine flights were undertaken, the first launch being the Caudron. Once the naval exercises had been completed a further series of flights was undertaken to prove the concept and the vessel. In July 1903 *Hermes* was

A Fairey Flycatcher of 402 Flight passes across the bows of HMS *Eagle*. Once intended to be the Chilean Navy *Admirante Cochrane* the partly built vessel was completed as an aircraft carrier. After adventures in the Mediterranean *Eagle* was sunk by torpedoes in August 1942. (Trevor Jones)

With HMS *Ark Royal* in the background a flight of Fairey Swordfish from No.820 NAS pass by. The Swordfish was a vital part of the carriers' armoury during its career. (NARA)

The Hawker Osprey was the first high speed two seat fighter reconnaissance aircraft. It was available with both wheels and floats the latter being deployed aboard capital ships and cruisers. (NARA)

part of the 'Red Fleet' under the command of Vice Admiral Jellicoe. During these summer exercises Borel No.48 was damaged during a gale and was replaced by Caudron No.55. It was on 28 July that *Hermes* launched its first aircraft, the Caudron, which departed courtesy of the forward rail assembly. *Hermes* would pay off into the reserve at Chatham in December 1913 having carried out 30 successful launches. Just prior to paying off, the vessel had been returned to standard cruiser configuration. However, HMS *Hermes* was recommissioned in August 1914 having had all its aircraft support equipment refitted and was used as a transport for RNAS aircraft during which period aircraft, equipment and personnel were shipped to France. While the presence of *Hermes* did little to enliven naval operations the ship and its crew had proven that it was possible for such a ship to undertake sustained shipboard naval operations. One obvious omission that was revealed in these trials was that aircraft engaged in spotting for the fleet had to be fitted with radio. As for HMS *Hermes* she remained in use as a seaplane carrier although her use during the Great War ended on 31 October 1914 when she was sunk by a German torpedo fired by U-27 off Ruylingen Bank.

Having first been conceived purely for the spotting role it was the development of the torpedo that could be launched from the air that gave the naval air wing its first offensive capability. This weapon, a 14 inch 80 lb-warhead lightweight torpedo, began trials in March 1914 and was assigned, after service clearance, to the Short Type 'C' aircraft that had flown a year earlier. On 1 July 1914 the naval air wing separated from the Royal Flying Corps to become the independent Royal Naval Air Service. To complement this change in circumstances the Admiralty established an Air Department under the command of Captain Murray Sueter. During the Naval Review at Spithead held that year on 18 July the RNAS was well represented with three airships and seventeen seaplanes on display. To emphasize the capabilities of the aeroplane a Sopwith Batboat flew around the anchored fleet with all lights blazing. When Europe descended into violence on 4 August 1914 the strength of the RNAS consisted of 17 airships, 52 seaplanes and 39 landplanes although not all were serviceable. To reinforce the spotting role of these early aircraft many of the seaplanes were equipped with lightweight radios that had a theoretical range of 120 miles. This line up made the RNAS the largest naval air force in the world.

The initial post war period was a trying time for the Royal Navy, the RNAS was absorbed into the newly formed Royal Air Force, much to the chagrin of the Admiralty and also removed from their control was the purchase and the provision of their own aircraft. By the end of 1919 the naval aircraft force consisted of one spotter reconnaissance squadron, one

Possibly one of the ugliest aircraft ever deployed aboard ship was the Blackburn Blackburn. Here N9982 of 422 Flight passes the camera and reveals its very blunt profile. (FAAM Yeovilton)

fighter flight and half a torpedo squadron. To these were added a seaplane and flying boat flight. Over the next 20 years the Admiralty and the Air Ministry expended much energy squabbling about who provided what for whom. Eventually, just before war broke out in 1939, the Admiralty finally regained control of its aircraft. During this period of naval aviation unrest some progress was made in giving the Royal Navy more control. The first step was taken in 1921 when the Admiralty gained agreement that the aircraft observers aboard the carriers' aircraft should be drawn from the ranks of the Royal Navy. Two years later a Committee of Inquiry recommended that as well as all observers being from naval ranks that at least 70% of pilots should now come from the same source. The following year the RAF naval air arm was renamed the Fleet Air Arm. In 1937 control of the Fleet Air Arm was finally handed over to the Royal Navy, the announcement being made in the House of Commons. As if to celebrate this the Royal Navy began establishing its own naval air stations at Donibristle, Eastleigh, Evanton, Ford, Hatson, Lee-on-Solent, St Merryn and Worthy Down. Aircraft strength, as ever constrained by budget cuts, grew very slowly during the inter war period. At the beginning of 1924 there were 78 aircraft in 13 flights, 10 months later there were 128 aircraft in 18 flights. In September 1930 there were 26 flights with 144 aircraft which increased to 156 aircraft in 26 flights. The unit size and designation changed to the 'squadron' with between 9-12 aircraft apiece. The only flights that would remain were those allocated to individual ships such as battleships and cruisers. The rearrangement saw 15 squadrons equipped with 175 aircraft although by the time war broke out again in 1939 there were only 20 squadrons with a total of 340 aircraft, 225 of these were available for carrier duty while the rest were allocated to individual ship's flights.

Following the success of the seaplane carrier HMS *Hermes* the Admiralty was convinced that the idea was worth pursuing therefore an £81,000 budget was set aside in the 1914-15 Naval estimates for another aircraft carrying ship. In this particular case the chosen vessel was a merchant ship hull that had just been laid down at Blyth in May 1914. Purchased on the stocks the nascent ship was named HMS *Ark Royal*. While hull construction continued as normal the remainder of the vessel was completely redesigned under the direction of J H Narbeth ably assisted by C J W Hopkins of the Department of Naval Construction. The naval requirements were specified by Captain Murray Sueter and his assistant Commander Malone, all four combining their talents to create a valiant first attempt at an aircraft carrier. One of the major alterations to the merchant ship design was the move of the engine room to the centre of the ship thus making room for a combined hold and hangar. This space was 150 feet long, 45 feet wide and with a height of 15 feet that could

In the background is HMS *Eagle* in the vicinity of Argentina in 1931 while the aircraft is a wheeled Hawker Nimrod assigned to No.803 NAS. (NARA)

accommodate 10 seaplanes. Access to the hanger was through a sliding hatch that was 40 feet by 30 feet in size, the housed aircraft being lifted clear by two steam cranes onto the upper deck. The cranes' other role was to recover aircraft from the water onto the deck. While an excellent idea on paper this was the only real weakness in the design as the cranes could not be used when the ship was rolling. To help counter the vessel's rolling tendency and to increase the draught a considerable amount of water ballast was carried and was located slightly higher up the ship which helped improve stability.

A secondary use for the water ballast was to surround the compartment where the aircraft petroleum store was housed thus reducing the fire risk for the ship. To complement the hangar space a part of the ship was given over to workshops and storerooms to support the aircraft carried. Also, and so that engine runs could be carried out in relative peace, there was a space under the bridge that protected both the aircraft and crew during testing. The forward part of *Ark Royal* was given over to a flying-off deck which allowed the seaplanes to take off using a wheeled trolley. To assist in these take-offs the ship was equipped with bow trimming tanks that allowed the bow to be trimmed down thus increasing the slope. Except for the movement of stores and other ship's items the flight deck was kept clear thus the anchor and cable gear were stowed on the deck below, a change from the normal forecastle practice. Just to prove that the Admiralty had not completely lost its love of sail the *Ark Royal* was fitted with a mizzen mast whose sail could be hoisted to stabilize the vessel longitudinally. As this was an early carrier built to a budget the *Ark Royal* was only capable of 11 knots which frequently relegated her to depot ship status as the main battle fleet normally travelled at 20 knots. This was a complete contrast to later times when the battleships would have to be extensively modernised to keep up with the fleet carriers. In order to get the most from the *Ark Royal* the Admiralty despatched the ship to the Dardenelles to assist in that ill fated and ill conceived campaign and returned to British waters towards the end of the war. Unlike many of her contemporaries the *Ark Royal* was retained for service between the wars and was mainly engaged on catapult development trials and a seaplane landing mat called the Hein Mat. In December 1935 the ship was renamed *Pegasus* so that the *Ark Royal* name could be applied to the newly built aircraft carrier. As for the *Pegasus* it was equipped with Fairey Fulmar fighters serving on convoy duties until 1941 after which it was employed on secondary tasks. After the war the vessel was sold off for civil use and finally scrapped in October 1950.

Following on from the *Ark Royal* the Admiralty purchased the Cunard liner *Campania* that had earlier gained fame for its high speed Atlantic

The Fairey Seafox entered service with ship catapult flights in 1937. The type will always be associated with the Battle of the River Plate. The Seafox was finally retired in 1943. (NARA)

crossings at the turn of the century. By November 1914 this famous vessel was withdrawn from use and was scheduled for scrapping when purchased by the Admiralty. Originally planned for use as an armed merchant cruiser because of her high speed the *Campania* was converted for aircraft support work. Initially fitted with a launching ramp over the forecastle and aircraft stowage aft this initial arrangement was less than satisfactory. Further conversion work was undertaken at the Cammell

Not quite as ugly as the Blackburn Blackburn, the Avro Bison would also not win prizes in a beauty contest. However in the early years of carrier aviation it was adequate for its task of fleet spotting. (FAAM Yeovilton)

One of the first torpedo carrier aircraft purchased by the Air Ministry on behalf of the Royal Navy was the Blackburn Dart which served between 1926 and 1935. (NARA)

Laird yard at Birkenhead during 1915 and into early 1916. The applied modifications included an extended downwards sloping platform that required the funnels to be diverted from fore and aft to each side of the superstructure, an enlarged hatchway for hangar access and improved aircraft handling derricks. The masts and superstructure were cut down to increase clearance further and improve aircraft handling. *Campania* was ready for service in April 1916 and was equipped with Fairey Campania patrol seaplanes which had been specially designed for the aircraft carrier. Launching of these aircraft required the use of a trolley while landing was on the sea with recovery undertaken by derricks. *Campania* had one more claim to fame being one of the few designated fleet vessels to miss the Battle of Jutland in 1916 due to a communications breakdown, whether Admiral Jellicoe's staff had forgotten about the ship or were deliberately late in signalling we will never know. *Campania* came to an unfortunate end when she collided with both the battlecruiser HMS *Glorious* and the battleship *Royal Oak* in the Firth of Forth after the ship's anchors dragged during a gale. Other vessels requisitioned by the Admiralty included the *Empress* gained from the South East and Chatham Railway, *Engadine* also from the SECR, *Ben-My-Chree* an Isle of Man steam packet, plus *Vindex* and *Manxman* also from the same source. *Engadine*'s claim to fame was that it was the only aircraft-carrying vessel to take part in the Battle of Jutland. During this operation *Engadine* launched a Short Type 184 which successfully spotted the German High Seas Fleet cruiser screen, but was unable to communicate this information to Admiral Jellicoe and the Grand Fleet due to radio problems.

Having begun the development of the aircraft carrier with the *Ark Royal* the next stage was to design and build bigger and better vessels. These would be based on the three battlecruisers that Admiral Fisher had sneaked through the budget as 'large light cruisers' in the 1914-15 naval estimates. The first of these ships, HMS *Furious*, was launched in August 1916 and was ready for sea in June 1917. Although *Furious* was intended to carry a pair of 18 inch guns the forward turret was deleted prior to installation and replaced with a sloping launch-platform. Under the platform was housed an enclosed hangar with space for eight seaplanes, workshops, petrol stowage for 1,200 gallons and ammunition stowed in the original magazine. Access to the aircraft was through a hatch in the after end of the deck, the aircraft being brought up into the daylight by a pair of derricks. Deck landing trials using wheeled aircraft were undertaken during mid 1917 using a Sopwith Pup although the pilot involved, Squadron Commander Dunning, would be killed during his third touchdown having managed two successful attempts previously. In light of this accident it was recommended that the ships aft end be rebuilt to accommodate a landing–on deck. As with the forward deck it was intended that a hangar be placed underneath thus doubling the available

The Blackburn Baffin was another stalwart of the FAA torpedo force. Only 29 aircraft were built, the rest being converted from the earlier Ripon. The type remained in service until replaced by the Shark in 1937. (NARA)

The Fairey Seal would be the type that replaced the Fairey IIIF in FAA service. A development of the earlier aircraft it would serve from 1933 until replaced by the Swordfish in 1938. (NARA)

aircraft complement. These modifications were carried out from November 1917 and *Furious* was released for service duties in mid 1918.

Although adding an aft deck had seemed like a good idea the currents and eddies generated by the remaining superstructure made landing on *Furious* a hazardous affair therefore in 1921 it was decided to rebuild the ship completely with a full–length carrier flight–deck. The use of a single flight-deck for arrival and departure operations was not fully adopted during these modifications but a separate flying-off deck was retained at a lower level over the bows. Two innovations introduced during this conversion included the rounding down of the trailing edge of the deck and the first examples of arrrestor wires. The use of a round down had been the result of experiments by the National Physical Laboratory which revealed that this would steady the airflow coming off the trailing edge of the deck thus improving the chances of a safe landing. *Furious* would be further modified in 1932 when the lower flying-off deck was deleted with the ship retaining the upper deck only. After a full period of war service *Furious* was sold off for scrapping in 1948.

Constructed at the same time as *Furious* were two other similar ships that were launched in 1916 as large light cruisers. At the completion of war service both vessels were tied up to await their fate. Initially it was suggested that both be cut up under the auspices of the Washington Treaty of 1922, however the success of *Furious* in the carrier role led the Admiralty to suggest that both be converted to fast carriers, *Courageous* and *Glorious,* thus giving the Royal Navy three fast, 30 knot, carriers. Unlike *Furious* both *Courageous* and *Glorious* were razed down to hull level and a complete new set of upper works was installed. In contrast to *Furious* both ships were built with an island from the outset into which was integrated the funnel. Few modifications were carried out after entering service however *Glorious* did have its flight deck extended in 1935. During the second world war both carriers were sunk, *Courageous* being torpedoed while *Glorious* was sunk by the German battlecruisers *Gneisenau* and *Scharnhorst.*

Also destined to serve during the 1939-45 war HMS *Argus* began life as the Italian *Conte Rosso* whose construction was suspended on the outbreak of the Great War. Laid up for two years at the Beardmores yard the Admiralty initially wanted to rebuild the vessel, by now named *Argus,* as a seaplane carrier however Beardmores suggested strongly that the best proposal was to complete *Argus* as a flush deck carrier. Although *Argus* saw little wartime service it did find useful employment as a test bed for the National Physical Laboratory where it was fitted with a dummy island and smoke generators. The experiment carried out aboard *Argus* was in connection with the construction of HMS *Eagle* and was intended to produce the best shaped island-airflow characteristics.

Argus was followed by HMS *Hermes* which was a significant vessel for the Royal Navy as it was their first purpose designed aircraft carrier. Ordered in 1917, launched in September 1919 and commissioned for sea duty in 1924 HMS *Hermes* would remain virtually unchanged for the next fifteen years. Unlike the following carriers *Hermes* was based on the cruiser hull form as its intended role was to act in concert with a cruiser force which required the ability to steam at high speed over long distances. The primary strength deck for *Hermes* was the main deck above which was built the hangar surmounted above which was the full length flight deck. Mounted on the starboard side of the ship was the island integrated into which were the funnel, bridge and flying bridge. The flight deck itself featured a rise on the rear section of the deck and a considerable round down, both of which had been developed by the National Physical Laboratory and considerably improving the stability of aircraft landing on. Access to the hangar was through a single lift, later increased to two, while arrestor wires were stretched longitudinally along the deck to retard landing aircraft. While it looked the part *Hermes* was a very unstable ship and its fuel oil capacity depended on the specific gravity of the oil being carried and required that certain tanks be emptied first while others were flooded to maintain stability. During the inter-war period *Hermes* had a second lift installed forward while the arrestor wires were changed to the more familiar and effective transverse type. In contrast to later carriers *Hermes* was considered a small vessel and was thus restricted to carrying 12 aircraft by 1939. While *Hermes* put in some sterling service during the early part of the Second World War its cruiser-like protective armour would finally be its undoing as it was sunk by its Japanese counterparts while operating off Ceylon on 9 April 1942.

The vessel that followed *Hermes* into service was HMS *Eagle* which was based on the battleship *Almirante Cochrane* that was being built for the Chilean Navy. Construction of this ship and its sister was duly suspended in 1914 although only one would see service during the conflict as HMS *Canada*. In contrast the ship that would become *Eagle* would remain incomplete on the slips at Elswick awaiting a decision as to its fate. The initial idea of completing the vessel as a battleship for onward sale to Chile was soon discarded as was the plan to complete it for the same purpose for the Royal Navy because after the Battle of Jutland it was obvious that the German High Seas fleet was of little threat to the Royal Navy. Thus the Admiralty decided that the ship would be finished as an aircraft carrier. Initially *Eagle* was to be completed in a similar manner to *Furious* with a landing–on and launching deck either side of the superstructure. After the airflow problems experienced by *Furious* the *Eagle* was completed with a single piece flight deck with an island offset to starboard. *Eagle* was finally completed at Portsmouth Dockyard entering service in 1924. HMS *Eagle* was sunk by torpedoes from the U-boat U-73 on 11 August 1942 whilst acting as a launch pad for the Malta fighter reinforcements undertaken as part of Operation *Pedestal*.

Possibly one of the most famous aircraft carriers ever built was HMS *Ark Royal* which was designed from the outset as a large fleet aircraft carrier. Ordered in 1935 from Cammell Laird this ship would incorporate all the lessons learnt from the previous conversions while landing the constructors and designers with new problems. Stability was a major issue and therefore the hull was designed to compensate for the weight of the island on the starboard side. The location of the island on this side of every aircraft carrier was down to the direction of piston engines which in the main rotated to the left thus placing the superstructure away from the direction of rotation and ensuring the safety of the personnel commanding and controlling the vessel. The only fault in the entire design was the location of the machinery spaces which were placed abreast of each other. Exhaust for the boilers was through the funnel on the port side while the air and ventilation intakes were located on the other side of the ship. Unlike earlier carriers the hull of *Ark Royal* was

A Fairey IIIF floatplane is launched from a capital ship of the Royal Navy, one of the roles assigned to the type. Eventually it was replaced by the Seafox and the Swordfish. (FAAM Yeovilton)

well armoured whilst the main strength deck was the flight deck and not the lower set main-deck as in previous vessels thus giving increased rigidity to the hull. Access to the hangar below the flight deck was via three lifts located in offset positions from the centreline. Other innovations fitted to *Ark Royal* were a pair of hydraulic catapults and to bring aircraft landing-on to a halt a series of transverse arrestor wires were installed. Another change from previous ships was that the island was more compact which reduced the airflow impact across the deck. In service *Ark Royal* gained fame when one of the ship's Blackburn Skuas shot down a German flying boat while the ships biggest claim to fame was the attack on the *Bismarck* in May 1941 when one of her Swordfish launched the torpedo that began the great battleship's downfall. Having gained success in the Atlantic *Ark Royal* was despatched to the Mediterranean to join Force 'H' where operations also took in the eastern Atlantic. On 13 November 1941 HMS *Ark Royal* was torpedoed by U-81 while cruising off Gibralter. While the hull had reasonable armour protection and was well divided internally the engine room vulnerability

Fairey Swordfish K5949 makes a left wheel first landing aboard *Ark Royal*. Of note are the bomblet and smoke dispensers beneath the lower wing. (Martyn Chorlton)

was its downfall. Once the ship's list had been slowed the crew were confident that the carrier could be saved however water was still entering via the machinery space intakes which would eventually flood the starboard side thus causing the ship to capsize.

Having set the benchmark for carrier design the *Ark Royal* was followed down the slips by two further types of aircraft carrier. The first would be the *Illustrious* class of fleet vessels which consisted of four vessels, the name ship plus *Formidable*, *Victorious* and *Indomitable*. As these ships were built under the auspices of the Washington Treaty they were limited by their maximum allowable tonnage therefore only a single hangar deck was incorporated into the design unlike *Ark Royal* which was double decked. The reason for the reduction in storage was the need to incorporate extensive armour protection and matching anti-aircraft armament. While the deck was armoured to help protect the ships vitals the two lifts were not armoured due to the weight penalty; however, armoured screens were provided in the hangars themselves. This amount of protection, both passive and active, was found to be very effective when the Royal Navy faced the Japanese kamikaze in the Far East. From the outset the ships were fitted with a single hydraulic catapult on the port side of the flight deck while the aft end of the deck had six arrestor wires with protective barrier nets available to protect aircraft ranged forward from the antics of the aircraft landing aft. HMS *Illustrious* and *Formidable* both commissioned in 1940 while *Victorious* and *Indomitable* were available in 1941. During their working lives all four ships had their flight decks lengthened while their anti-aircraft complement was considerably increased in the light of combat experience. Radar became a permanent feature on these ships covering air warning, height finder and gunnery control. After war service *Illustrious* remained in use as a trials carrier before paying off in 1954, *Victorious* was rebuilt for further service and remained in use until 1967 while *Formidable* and *Indomitable* were retired in 1947 and 1953 respectively.

In 1944 two further ships similar to the *Illustrious* class were commissioned these being *Indefatigable* and *Implacable*. Both served with the British Pacific Fleet before being retired in 1954 and 1955 respectively.

Following on from the Fleet carriers came the *Colossus* class and these were designated as light fleet-carriers. In contrast to their heavyweight cousins this class were scaled down *Illustrious* ships that utilised merchant ship design hulls. To enable quick construction no armour protection was fitted while the anti-aircraft armament was limited to light weapons only. *Colossus* commissioned in 1944 while *Glory, Venerable, Vengeance, Ocean, Perseus* and *Pioneer* entered service in 1945 the latter two being reworked as maintenance ships. In 1946 HMS *Theseus* and *Triumph* were available while *Warrior* would become available in 1948. Very little war service was seen by this class, most earning their crust during the Korean War, laughably called a police action by the United Nations, and the Suez conflict.

With their demise the Royal Navy was still in possession of *Victorious, Eagle* and *Ark Royal* which were later supplemented by *Albion, Bulwark* and *Centaur* completed during 1953-54. Only the first three would be considered for jet operation as they were of a size and capacity for such usage. The two most important changes applied to the carriers were the angled flight deck invented by Captain D R F Cambell DSC RN, this first being applied to HMS *Centaur*. The next innovation that altered carrier capability was the mirror landing aid developed by Commander H C N Goodhart RN which overcame the deficiencies posed by a deck landing officer trying to control numerous aircraft landing with the aid of bats. Such a method of control was a necessity as the speed of aircraft had increased from the 60 mph of the biplane Fairey Flycatcher to the Sea Venom approaching at approximately 140 mph. The appearance of jet aircraft in the FAA inventory also changed the method of approach practised by naval pilots. Initially aircraft approached using a steep curving approach towards the round down however jet aircraft were far happier undertaking a flatter approach path as visibility was not so obstructed by an engine or forward fuselage. This method of landing allowed for a constant speed approach and negated the need for flare out and cutting of the engine until the landing was safely completed. A further aid developed to help the pilot was the audio airspeed indicator that was heard in the pilots earphones. Use of this aid allowed the pilot to concentrate upon the mirror landing aid without being distracted by the need to scan the instrument panel gauges.

While the British shipyards were frantically building various fleet carriers the shortfall in air cover for both surface ships and convoys needed to be addressed rapidly. The answer was the escort carriers which were rebuilt or requisitioned merchant ships. Initially these ships carried part of their normal cargo, however this idea was soon dropped for more warlike stores for the ships and the carried aircraft. The British shipyards did their best to assuage the requirements of the Admiralty but the burgeoning needs of the various fleets at sea meant that all facilities were stretched to the limit. To fill the gaps the Admiralty turned to the United States, with their massive industrial capability, for assistance. The result was a fleet of ships based on merchant ships' hulls. In contrast to the bigger carriers these vessels were nearly 50 per cent shorter, slower due to having only a single shaft although they did have good anti-aircraft armament and reasonable-sized hangars complete with access lifts. In contrast to the British built ships those from America came equipped with wooden flight decks, a vulnerability that their major fleet carriers would regret in the war against the Japanese in the Pacific. Eventually 34 of these useful ships became available from 1943 proving their usefulness in the air defence, anti submarine and transport roles. After hostilities ended most of these ships were returned to the United States where most were converted into merchantmen for a second useful career. While the purpose of the aircraft carrier was to promote naval warfare over longer ranges it should be remembered that full development took no more than ten years to create the prototype of the ship that commands the oceans today.

The same could not be said of the aircraft that these ships carried. Initially under the auspices of the Admiralty and the RNAS naval aircraft kept pace with those of the land based RFC. The RNAS had come into official existence on 1 July 1914 a situation which pleased the Admiralty as the naval wing arrangement within the RFC had been very unpopular with the Navy. Having proven that naval aviation was at least possible the Admiralty set about creating operating bases. Having got off to a good start the RNAS continued its training and development programme which saw over 100 trained pilots being available at the beginning of 1914.

Developed as a rival to the Fairey Swordfish the Blackburn Shark would leave front line service before the start of the war. This aircraft K4352 740 was flown by No.820 NAS when photographed. (FAAM Yeovilton)

Aircraft delivered to the Admiralty during the 1918–1939 period included the Fairey Flycatcher biplane. Designed from the outset as a fleet fighter the Flycatcher was a ruggedly built little machine which was easy to fly, good for aerobatics and most importantly easy to land aboard an aircraft carrier. This machine introduced many original features including flaps that ran along the entire trailing edges of both wings, the outer sections also acted as ailerons, this innovation allowing the Flycatcher to achieve exceptionally short landing and take-off runs. It was also the Flycatcher that introduced the hydraulic wheel-brake system that was used in conjunction with the fore and aft arrestor wires favoured aboard carriers at that time. Flycatchers entered service in 1923 finally leaving in 1934 being superseded by Hawker Nimrods.

The arrival of the Nimrod in naval service gave the fighter squadrons a much needed increase in speed over the Flycatcher. Although the Nimrod closely resembled its land based counterpart the Fury there were significant changes under the skin in that the wings were of greater span and flotation boxes were built into the wings and fuselage. While this made the Nimrod slower than the Fury it was still a speedy machine. The first production machines had no arrestor gear fitted however this omission was rectified in the Mk II when a hook was fitted under a

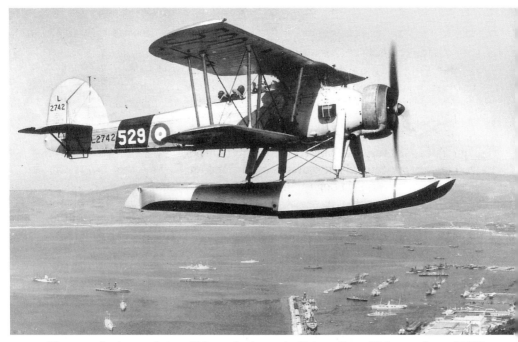

Photographed overflying Valetta harbour is Fairey Swordfish seaplane L2742 assigned to No.701 Catapult Flight. (FAAM Yeovilton)

strengthened fuselage. Aircraft manufacturers Glosters provided the next aircraft type for the naval fighter squadrons: the Sea Gladiator. This was another land-based design adapted for life aboard ship. To that end the aircraft's structure was strengthened to absorb the punishment of landing and the drag forces associated with the arrestor hook. Other extras were the catapult launching hooks and the collapsible dinghy carried between the undercarriage legs. The Sea Gladiator entered service in December 1938 and remained in front line use until 1941. The Sea Gladiators claim to fame came in mid 1940 during the defence of the island of Malta in the Mediterranean when a depleted but valiant fighter force fought off the combined air forces of Germany and Italy.

The arrival of the Fairey Fulmar into naval service gave the fleet fighter force an aircraft that mounted eight machine guns and was powered by a Rolls Royce Merlin. Although it was on a par with its land based counterparts, the Spitfire and Hurricane, it was slightly slower due to its being a multi place monoplane as an observer was carried as well as a pilot. Designed and flown under great secrecy the Fulmar first appeared in public in January 1937 and the type entered service in June 1940 with No.806 NAS later to embark aboard HMS *Illustrious* during the Malta convoy runs. During 1941 a further five squadrons formed on the type of which No.805 NAS was land based at Dekheila in Egypt. During the following year another six squadrons received the type but this was the peak of its career. Replaced mainly by the Supermarine Seafire the greater majority of Fulmars had been relegated to second line duties by April 1943 although a specialist night fighter unit retained the type until March 1945. In addition to providing air support for the vital Malta convoys the Fulmar also played its part in the shadowing of the *Bismarck*. Even more perilous duties awaited the Fulmar squadrons when the convoys to north Russia began. Not only were day fighter versions taken to sea there was also a flight of night fighter Fulmars frequently deployed. During its frontline service the Fulmars successfully shot down 112 enemy aircraft between September 1940 and August 1942 which was nearly a third of the Fleet Air Arm's total air to air victories throughout the war.

It would be the arrival of the Sea Hurricane that would introduce the single-seat monoplane fighter into naval air service that was on a par with its land based counterparts. As before, the standard Hurricane design was reworked to cope with the rigours of deck landings and take-offs although the most obvious change was the installation of an arrestor hook. The Sea Hurricane would be one of the few shipboard fighters never to be fitted with folding wings although such a conversion had been schemed by General Aircraft Ltd in consultation with Hawkers, the former being responsible for upgrading standard airframes for naval use. While it was intended to deploy as many Sea Hurricanes on board carriers as possible the lack of available flight decks meant that another temporary measure had to be employed. This took the form of the Catafighters this being a Hurricane mounted on either a merchantman or a warship within the convoy. While this was a useful temporary measure the guaranteed loss of an aircraft and the potential loss of an experienced pilot meant that the arrival of the escort carrier could not come soon enough.

While the catapult-armed merchantman was in use it proved successful in keeping away the snooping Focke Wulf Fw200 Condor reconnaissance aircraft. Fortunately for the Sea Hurricane pilots their aircraft were soon fitted with a pair of 45 gallon overload tanks which gave them the option of returning to friendly territory if within range. The arrival of the escort carrier meant that a measure of anti-submarine protection could be given to each convoy while the Sea Hurricane pilots had the welcome advantage of returning to the postage stamp carrier deck tossing about on a grey ocean.

Sea Hurricanes were deployed on the Russian convoys where they provided much needed air support to beat off the attacking *Luftwaffe* aircraft operating out of Norway. In warmer climes the Sea Hurricanes were fully employed providing support to the convoys battling their way through to Malta although not without the loss of HMS *Eagle* sunk by a U Boat's torpedoes on 11 August 1942. Although the Sea Hurricane did not have the racy looks of its erstwhile land counterpart, the Spitfire, the skill, determination and courage of its pilots ensured that the convoys they escorted reached their destinations with minimal losses. The Sea Hurricane remained in front line service with the FAA until mid 1944 having been fully superseded by the Supermarine Seafire and aircraft acquired from the United States.

Operating alongside the Sea Hurricane were the first of the American fighters to join the Fleet Air Arm , the Grumman Martlet. Featuring the short dumpy fuselage and retractable undercarriage that had characterised the company's earlier biplane fighters the Martlett was a monoplane mounting four 0.50 inch calibre machine-guns in the wings. The Martlets replaced the Sea Gladiators in FAA service where its folding wings were seen as a bonus aboard the smaller British carriers. The Martlet entered service in September 1940 opening its score sheet by shooting down a German aircraft on Christmas Day of that year. The next batches of aircraft supplied to the Royal Navy were designated the Mks IV and V and differed from the earlier machines in that they were supplied under the Lend Lease arrangement, the earlier fighters having been purchased outright. These versions started to enter service in July 1942. The Grumman Martlets and Wildcats remained in front line usage until the end of the war after which the Lend Lease items were either junked or returned to the United States. While other American fighter types did serve with the Fleet Air Arm their use would be curtailed at War's end which meant that the Fleet Air Arm would have to rely on British built resources such as the Supermarine Seafire and the Fairey Firefly.

With the disappearance of the greater majority of the American Lend Lease aircraft the Royal Navy was thrown back on British manufacturers for their fighting machines. Initially the Seafire was retained as the Fleet Air Arms front line fighter however its inherent weakness around the tail to fuselage interface meant that on operations the numbers available fell rapidly. Hawker would later combine the roles of fighter and attack aircraft together in the Sea Fury fighter bomber that was capable of taking on contemporary jets and shooting them down. When the FB.11 came into use it added the carriage of rocket projectiles and bombs to its repertoire allowing it to attack different types of targets. The jet age arrived with a spread of aircraft from Glosters with a handful of Sea Meteors, de Havilland with the Sea Vampire and the more successful Sea

Venom plus Supermarines with the Attacker. These machines were configured as fighters, the attack role being retained by propellor driven machines such as the Blackburn Firebrand and the Westland Wyvern. It was the arrival of the Hawker Sea Fury that finally combined the fighter and bomber roles carrying out both successfully during the Korean war. The Fleet Air Arm finally went supersonic with the Supermarine Scimitar that was also the first carrier-borne aircraft capable of carrying a nuclear weapon for attacking enemy warships. The fighter component aboard the Royal Navy carriers was eventually shouldered by the de Havilland Sea Vixen which in its latter days became a bit of a maid of all work adding such extras as in-flight refuelling to its repertoire. The Fleet Air Arm and the Royal Navy achieved its ideal solution aboard the Ark Royal when the bomber component was fulfilled by the Blackburn, later Hawker Siddeley, Buccaneer S.2 while the fighter and reconnaissance roles were covered by the anglicised McDonnell Douglas Phantom FG.1. Also deployed aboard the *Ark Royal* were Westland built Sea Kings, one of the most efficient anti-submarine aircraft ever built.

It was in the post-war period that another airborne resource increased in importance: the Airborne Early Warning that was designed to give increased radar coverage for the carrier and its supporting vessels. The initial type used to carry the radar in its familiar bulge was the Grumman

With HMS *Ark Royal* behind Swordfish I L9781 650 assigned to No.810 NAS prepares to enter the approach leg prior to landing. (FAAM Yeovilton)

Thundering past the fleet anchored in Gibraltar harbour is Swordfish floatplane L2749 529 of No.701 Catapult Flight which is throwing up a fine spray. (FAAM Yeovilton)

Avenger which was followed by another American type the Douglas Skyraider. The final conventional type to carry the AEW radar was the Fairey Gannet AEW.3, although this, with the Phantom and Buccaneers, would soon return to land when the *Ark Royal* was retired in December 1978.

This was not the end of the Royal Navy airborne component as a new group of through-deck cruisers entered service from 1980. Unlike their forebears these vessels are only capable of operating V/STOL aircraft such as the Harrier and the full range of naval helicopters, these mainly being Sea Kings which included the AEW variant. Sea Kings are currently being replaced by the Westland Merlin. Alongside the three small carriers the navy still retained HMS *Hermes* as a commando carrier although it was later fitted with a ski ramp which allowed it to operate Harriers. *Hermes* was eventually sold to the Indian Navy while the other vessels are awaiting replacements capable of operating the Joint Strike Fighter. The JSF or F-35 will be the primary aircraft aboard the two new CVF (Carrier Vessel Future) on order for the Royal Navy although their delivery is still a few years in the future.

Chapter 2

The Fleet Air Arm in the Atlantic

When war erupted over Europe in September 1939 the Royal Navy had finally regained control of its air assets and was in possession of the following aircraft carriers: *Argus, Ark Royal, Courageous, Eagle, Furious, Glorious* and *Hermes*. The most modern of these was HMS *Ark Royal* which had been launched in April 1937 and commissioned in November 1938: she later became the Flagship Rear-Admiral Aircraft Carriers, Home Fleet. At the outbreak of hostilities the carrier was operating two squadrons of Blackburn Skuas, Nos 800 and 803 NAS plus Nos. 810 and 820 NAS equipped with Fairey Swordfish while a single Supermarine Walrus was carried for reconnaissance and Air Sea Rescue purposes. Operating alongside *Ark Royal* was HMS *Argus* which had joined the fleet in 1918, by 1939 this, the first full length deck carrier, was equipped with No.767 NAS which flew Swordfish. *Argus* was sent to the Mediterranean for use in the deck landing training role. The next three aircraft carriers began life as light battle cruisers: *Courageous, Furious* and *Glorious*. HMS *Courageous* had been winched into Devonport dockyard in 1924 for conversion to aircraft carrier status and recommissioned for its new role in 1928. The aircraft assigned to this vessel included two squadrons of Swordfish: Nos. 811 and 822 NAS whose role was that of anti-submarine patrols. HMS *Courageous* played only a small part in the Second World War and was sunk by torpedoes fired by the German Navy Submarine U-29 whilst traversing the south western approaches of Britain, nearly 50 per cent of the crew were lost when the carrier was sunk. HMS *Furious* was very much the prototype fleet carrier and joined the Home Fleet fully reconstructed in 1925. By 1939 the air group consisted of No.801 NAS with Skuas plus two squadrons equipped with Swordfish: Nos. 816 and 818 NAS. HMS *Glorious* joined the Mediterranean Fleet after reconstruction in 1930, nine years later this carrier was operating the Gloster Sea Gladiator with No.802 NAS and No.825 NAS was flying the Fairey Swordfish. Another vessel that started life in another role was HMS *Eagle* that had originally been laid down as the battleship *Almirante Cochrane* for the Chilean Navy although its construction was suspended when the Great War broke out in 1914. The carrier was equipped with Fairey Swordfish operated by

The Blackburn Skua was slightly more successful than the turret fitted Roc fighter as it was designed and built from the outset as a fighter bomber. It was a Skua that claimed the honour of shooting down the Fleet Air Arm's first victory in WW2, a Dornier flying boat. (Will Blunt Collection)

Nos 813 and 824 NAS as part of the Far East Fleet. Also part of the Far East Fleet at various times was HMS *Hermes* which had been designed and built from the outset as an aircraft carrier although its form was based on the cruiser type hull. As completed it was fitted with a lift for moving aircraft off the flight deck to the hangar below. At the outbreak of war this vessel was operating the Fairey Swordfish, the unit being No.814

NAS, as part of the Channel Force in support of the British Expeditionary Force in France. The final flight deck available to the Royal Navy was HMS *Pretoria Castle* which had originally been launched as a passenger liner in October 1938 but was requisitioned at the outbreak of war for use as a trials and deck-landing training carrier.

The war that started to engulf the world in 1939 was the strongest test of carrier warfare and the aircraft it carried up to that date. It would also reveal that naval vessels of all sizes were not safe anywhere that land or sea based aviation could reach. Initially the Admiralty decided that the best way to utilise their carrier assets was in an offensive role instead of using them to protect the convoys that were vital to Britain's survival. The first patrols despatched by the Admiralty involved *Ark Royal* and *Courageous*, complete with escort screen, that travelled around the coast of Britain following up reports of submarines. This mad adventurism was soon highlighted when, on 14 September, close to the Hebrides HMS *Ark Royal* was nearly torpedoed by the German submarine U-39. Twelve days later on 26 September the carrier was attacked by a *Luftwaffe* aircraft piloted by Lt. Adolf Francke who claimed to have sunk the *Ark Royal*, on the back of his report the pilot was promoted and awarded the Iron Cross for his efforts. On 17 September 1939 the foolishness of this idea was emphasised by the loss of HMS *Courageous* which was sunk by torpedoes launched by the submarine U-29 when the carrier was cruising off the south of Ireland. While the loss of a carrier this early in the conflict was a blow, the effort that the Royal Navy made to cover great areas of ocean gave the German forces much food for thought as they would be unsure where the carriers were. This would be a factor in the loss of the so called pocket battleship *Graf Spee* off Montevideo. Having been driven up the River Plate by a force of British cruisers the captain of *Graf Spee*, Captain Langsdorff, was worried that the *Ark Royal* would come to finish off his damaged vessel, the irony is that the carrier was hundreds of miles away assigned to the Mediterranean Fleet.

HMS *Ark Royal* was recalled to the Home Fleet in April 1940 after the German invasion of Norway. Restored and rearmed the carrier departed for Norwegian waters with Nos. 800 and 803 NAS equipped with Skua and Roc aircraft whilst the other two units, Nos 810 and 820 NAS, were equipped with Fairey Swordfish. The first strike launched by the carrier was aimed at the German cruiser *Konigsberg* which had been damaged during the attack on Bergen on 9 April and was tied up in the harbour awaiting repairs. On 10 April the Royal Navy launched seven Skuas of No.800 NAS led by Captain R T Partridge RM and another nine Skuas of No.803 NAS led by Lt W P Lucy both groups having been launched from *Ark Royal*. Each aircraft was armed with 500 lb armour-piercing bombs

The Blackburn Roc was an attempt by the Admiralty to introduce a turret fighter to the FAA. However the Roc was too slow and the turret fighter concept suffered from an inability to track and predict the actual and potential positions of a target. (BBA Collection)

plus a maximum load of fuel. This mission was right at the limit of the aircraft's range. Fortunately the weather was clear thus the crews were able to spot the *Konigsberg* quite easily. The aircraft were well into their dives before the surrounding anti-aircraft guns opened fire. All fifteen bombs were released and the three bombs penetrated the ship's deck causing massive internal explosions. The remainder of the bombs landed close by the ship causing possible further damage below the waterline. Blazing strongly the cruiser would be rent by a massive explosion that broke the vessel in half, both ends sinking quickly. Only one Skua was lost on the run home to base. While this had proven the value of the dive bomber against naval targets and would hasten the introduction of this method of attack into the air forces of other nations, it was strange that the Royal Navy would leave themselves without such a weapon after the withdrawal of the Skua in 1941 and the introduction of the Fairey Barracuda in 1943.

The only other carrier available to assist in countering the German invasion was HMS *Furious* which at the time was refitting on the Clyde.

The refit was completed as quickly as possible and the carrier put to sea with a load of RAF Gloster Gladiators and Hawker Hurricanes aboard. Once these had been flown off the *Furious* air group consisting of No.801 NAS with Skuas and Nos.816 and 818 NAS finally arrived. While the air group carried out reconnaissance, strike and fighter missions, the lack of a dedicated air defence fighter quickly became obvious as the *Luftwaffe* assault on the Royal Navy ships was so intense that the light cruiser *Curlew* and the destroyers *Gurkha* and *Afridi* were sunk, as was the French destroyer *Biso*, the Polish destroyer *Grom* plus the sloop HMS *Bittern*. Other ships damaged during these attacks included the battleship HMS *Rodney*, the carrier *Furious*, the anti-aircraft cruiser *Curacoa* plus numerous other vessels all of which fired much ammunition in their defence although it was not enough to deter the German assault. Even in these circumstances there were stalwart efforts to save vessels as shown by the cruiser HMS *Suffolk* which limped home with the quarterdeck awash.

Given the limited number of naval assets available to the C-in-C of the Home Fleet, Admiral Forbes, it is to his credit that he authorised the deployment of the carriers *Ark Royal*, *Furious* and *Glorious* to provide as much air cover as possible over the land forces and any ships at sea. Even this had its limitations as both *Furious* and *Glorious* were used to transport RAF fighter squadrons to Norway. In between ferry operations HMS *Furious* found time to launch an attack on the German heavy cruiser *Hipper* on 11 April utilising its Swordfish. By the time the aircraft arrived

Pounding through a heavy sea is HMS *Furious* that began life as a large light cruiser in 1917. Converted into an aircraft carrier in 1925 the vessel served with distinction until withdrawn from use in October 1944. (BBA Collection)

While the crew aboard the aircraft carriers were entirely male it was not unusual to see females engaged in aircraft work. Here a group Wrens prepare to load a torpedo under the fuselage of a Swordfish. (NARA)

at Trondheim the German cruiser had already sailed and the Swordfish returned to the carrier. The following day the same force was sent to attack targets at Narvik although on this occasion bad weather foiled their mission. In the meantime *Ark Royal* provided coverage for both land and sea forces and would find itself involved in the evacuation of British forces from Narvik. *Ark Royal* would have one last bite of the cherry when it launched a strike against enemy warships in Trondheim on 13 June. During this attack *Scharnhorst* was hit by one 500 lb bomb although the damage was minor. Two Skuas were shot down and the crews became prisoners of war.

Increasing the number of RAF aircraft to provide cover for British troops became a priority during the Norway campaign. To that end HMS *Glorious*, which had returned to the Home Fleet with *Ark Royal*, was selected to transport these reinforcements to the operations area. On 21 April 1940 the carrier disembarked Nos 812 and 825 NAS equipped with Fairey Swordfish to make room for the 18 Gladiators of No.263 Squadron RAF which were landed onto the carrier by naval pilots. *Glorious* still retained Nos 802 and 823 NAS equipped with Sea Gladiators and Swordfish respectively although the situation changed again when *Glorious* arrived at Scapa Flow on 22 April. A further change of units saw No. 823 NAS replaced with Nos.804 and 803 NAS which operated the Sea Gladiator and Skuas respectively. Operation DX began the following day when *Glorious* and *Ark Royal* departed from Scapa Flow to undertake their duties around Norway, the most vital of which was flying off the

RAF Gladiators to Lake Lesjaskou. *Glorious* would remain with *Ark Royal* for four days before departing for Scapa Flow although not before transferring four Skuas to the other carrier. Having arrived at Scapa Flow the carrier was quickly refuelled and embarked Nos. 802 and 804 NAS with Sea Gladiators plus No.823 NAS with Swordfish. By 1 May *Glorious* had returned to Norway although the vessel's duties had changed to that of covering the withdrawal of British forces from Norway. Having arrived the C-in-C Home Fleet ordered the carrier to return to Scapa Flow to collect more RAF fighters. Having dispensed with its Skuas to *Ark Royal* the carrier made haste to Britain picking up the Hawker Hurricanes of No.46 Squadron before setting sail in company with HMS *Furious* on 14 April. The carriers arrived off Norway three days later and the Walrus of No.710 NAS were disembarked, however, the Hurricanes remained aboard as the bad weather precluded their flying off. After four days of trying to launch the visiting Hurricanes the carrier needed to withdraw to Scapa Flow to refuel and arrived there on 23 May. *Glorious* reached Norway on 24 May and flew off the cargo of Hurricanes two days later and they all made a safe landing at Bardufoss. The *Glorious* air wing would achieve a success on 28 May when three of No.802 NAS Sea Gladiators shot down a Heinkel He115 floatplane which had been shadowing the fleet. *Glorious* again returned to Scapa Flow for refuelling on 30 May and left the following day in company with *Ark Royal* to take part in Operation Alphabet, the evacuation of British forces from Narvik. The carrier had only half an air wing embarked as room had to be left for any recovered RAF aircraft. While *Ark Royal* carried out the required air support missions, HMS *Glorious* managed to recover ten Gladiators of No.263 Squadron and seven Hurricanes of No.46 Squadron and this was the first time a high performance fighter had landed on a British carrier. Having collected all possible RAF aircraft by 7 June orders were issued for *Glorious* to depart the area that day making best possible speed. Although the carrier had started life as a light battlecruiser and had the powerplants and hull developed for that kind of ship its lack of available offensive aircraft and defensive armament and light hull-armour would lead to its downfall. In the late afternoon of 8 June HMS *Glorious* was south west of Narvik at 60 degrees 45' N 04 degrees 30' E when the carrier plus the escorting destroyers *Ardent* and *Acasta* were intercepted by the German battlecruisers *Scharnhorst* and *Gneisenau* which sank all three vessels by gunfire, the destroyers putting up a valiant fight to protect the carrier. For whatever reason Captain G D D'Oyly-Hughes did not turn the carrier into wind to launch scouting aircraft preferring to make a high speed dash to Scapa Flow. *Scharnhorst* was the first to open fire at 28,000 yards scoring hits on the bridge and flight deck with the first

Complete with a load of smoke bombs and 60 lbs rockets this Swordfish of No.842 NAS prepares to depart from HMS *Fencer* on another anti submarine patrol. (Rick Harding collection)

salvo. Such was the accuracy of the German gunfire that *Glorious* was soon brought to a standstill and then rolled over to starboard and sank. The two escorting destroyers headed towards the German attackers laying down a smoke screen in an attempt to cover *Glorious*. HMS *Acasta* even managed, in the finest traditions of destroyers everywhere, to launch a torpedo which hit *Scharnhorst* but with little damage. This gallant action ended with both ships sunk, the German vessels departed at speed making no attempt to pick up survivors. Eventually search vessels collected 42 survivors from *Glorious*, two from *Ardent* and a single seaman from *Acasta*.

After the disasters of the Norway operations the Royal Navy needed some good news, not only to improve the morale of the service but that of the country. Although some periods of excitement occur in service lives much of it is tedium coupled with heightened tension. Thus the aircraft carriers were employed in escorting convoys across the Atlantic and to Malta, the Royal Navy having finally decided that convoys were the best way to get vital supplies to needy recipients. Then HMS

Victorious, which had been launched in September 1939 and commissioned in May 1941 and under the command of Captain H C Bovell CBE, joined the available aircraft carriers. Having been employed in shipping crated Hurricanes to Malta *Victorious* was at Scapa Flow preparing to depart for Malta when intelligence reports indicated that the German battleship *Bismarck* was loose in the Atlantic. On 22 May 1941 *Victorious* was assigned to the Home Fleet and was allocated No.800Z NAS with Fairey Fulmars and No.825 NAS with Swordfish.

The *Bismarck* plus the heavy cruiser *Prinz Eugen* had originally undertaken working up exercises in the Bay of Danzig before departing from Gotenhafen (Gdynia) on 19 May under the command of *Kapitan sur See* Ernst Lindemann to take part in Operation Rheinubung (Rhein Exercise), the intention being to cause serious disruption to the convoys supplying Britain. Intelligence sources reported that both vessels had departed the Baltic which rang alarm bells at the various Ministries. The first response was from Coastal Command which launched every available aircraft towards the Norwegian coast on 20 May. Their intensive flying bore fruit when both vessels were spotted at Korfjord just south of Bergen. In an attempt to confirm that these were the ships that the Royal Navy and RAF were seeking Cdr G A Rotherham was flown off in a Martin Maryland towards Norway. Although the aircraft flew into bad weather and later heavy anti-aircraft fire enough of a cloud break revealed that both ships had sailed. The Maryland crew tried in vain to radio the news back to the Admiralty but the primary radio had failed, fortunately, this aircraft was fitted with a target-towing radio system and this was used to send the signal. Although the German ships had slipped their shadowers the greatest ship hunt had just begun.

Powered by early versions of the Merlin engine, the Fairey Fulmar could best be described as a workmanlike machine. Based on the earlier Battle bomber this multiplace fighter featured good range and heavy firepower courtesy of the eight Browning machine guns mounted in the wings however it was let down by its limited top speed. (Will Blunt Collection)

Caught posing in front of their Hurricane these pilots and their aircraft were based aboard a MAC ship involved in defending convoys. Fortunately this situation did not last long given the danger although this limited defence was effective. (Rick Harding Collection)

The *Bismarck* and the *Prinz Eugen* had been spotted by patrolling aircraft on 23 May thus it was possible for the cruisers, *Norfolk* and *Suffolk*, to pick up the vessels on radar in the Denmark Straits and continue to shadow them until heavier units turned up. This would be the ill fated HMS *Hood* which was sunk by the *Bismarck* on 24 May after the *Hood* was hit by plunging fire that set off explosions in the magazines leaving only three survivors. Also damaged in this engagement was the new battleship *Prince of Wales* which had not even completed its work-up and still had dockyard mateys aboard. Although damaged *Prince of Wales* did manage to score two hits on the German battleship. While the damage overall was superficial the shells had hit part of the fuel system isolating 1,000 tons of vital fuel. It was obvious that the intended rampage through the Atlantic by the German force was no longer possible, therefore Admiral Lutyens ordered both ships to make for the French coast. During this run south the German vessels were shadowed by the *Prince of Wales* and by both cruisers and aircraft of Coastal Command. The German commanders were not aware that HMS *Victorious* plus escorts were within striking range and that the carrier was preparing to launch an air strike. This involved the Swordfish of No.825 NAS which launched in the evening of 25 May in terrible weather conditions. This was not the preferred option for the commander of the *Victorious*, Captain H C Bovell, who had wanted to delay the launch until the weather improved, however *Bismarck* had made a turn towards the two British cruisers to cover the escape of the *Prinz Eugen*. This change of course opened the distance between *Victorious* and *Bismarck* and, therefore, Admiral Curties, the commander of the 2nd Cruiser Squadron, decided that the air attack must go ahead without delay. Nine Swordfish led by Lt Commander Eugene Esmonde, who had survived the sinking of the *Courageous*, were launched from the carrier accompanied by three Fairey Fulmars for spotting and shadowing purposes. While Esmonde was an experienced pilot the remainder had little experience, some had only been aboard the carrier for a week and the average number of landings for these pilots was three, all in fair weather. Departing into a strong north-west wind and a 30 feet sea swell the Swordfish settled down for their 120 mile trip. Although the weather was deteriorating rapidly the aircraft were fitted with AirSurface Vessel (ASV) Radar that had just been cleared for service use and this allowed the aircraft to detect the *Bismarck* at a greater range than normal. A visual sighting of the *Bismarck* was made at 20 miles distance and the Swordfish climbed into the cloud to avoid any visual sighting by the battleship lookouts. As the Swordfish approached they

On a wet flight deck the ground crew await the pilot's signal that he is about to start the engine of his Sea Hurricane. Although it is not possible to read the aircraft's codes clearly it is highly likely that these are No.800 NAS machines aboard HMS *Indomitable* preparing for another patrol. (BBA Collection)

Preparing to land at Yeovilton after a training flight is Sea Hurricane II V7438 Y1-C of No.759 NAS. Although it was replaced by the Seafire, the Hurricane still had a vital role to play in the training field. (Rick Harding Collection)

were detected by the *Bismarck* radar which immediately placed the gunnery crews on alert. Dropping out of the cloud cover the biplanes began their attack runs. The ship's defensive guns opened up spitting lethal death in all directions, however the slow Swordfish initially threw the accuracy of the German gunners. They would recover quickly enough to score four hits on Esmonde's aircraft and drive another away from the group. Seven of the remaining Swordfish attacked the port side of the battleship diverting fire and concentration away from the other side of the ship. This distraction allowed a single unobserved Swordfish to launch its torpedo which struck the starboard side causing a column of smoke to rise from the rear starboard quarter. Having struck a blow against the *Bismarck* the Swordfish turned towards the *Victorious*. In order to aid his inexperienced crews in making their night landings Captain Bovell turned on all the carrier landing lights plus the main searchlight shone along the deck. Admiral Curties ordered these lights to be switched off, however, the gallant captain, alert to the needs of his aircrews used a very bright signal lantern to make a signal that not only illuminated the deck but helped guide the aircraft back on deck. All nine Swordfish landed safely but only one Fulmar returned, the other two were lost.

Bismarck managed to elude the pursuing cruisers for more than 24 hours but then the battleship was spotted by a searching Catalina of No.209 Squadron on the morning of 26 May. The battleship was heading towards Brest at best speed and the vessel's gunners were reported as very aggressive as the Catalina found out when it flew too close. By this time *Ark Royal* was coming into range having steamed with Force H at full speed from the Mediterranean. The Catalina was later relieved by a pair of Swordfish launched from *Ark Royal*. It would be from *Ark Royal* that another strike was launched, however the vessel attacked was the cruiser HMS *Sheffield* which had been detached to shadow the German vessel closely. Fortunately the cruiser captain was able to manoeuvre his vessel out of trouble and the torpedoes, fitted with magnetic pistols, exploded harmlessly. Having battled their way through a rising gale the 14 aircraft made their way back to the carrier. The second strike was launched in late evening, but this time the torpedoes had been fitted with contact pistols and their depth setting had been reduced. Yet again the weather was poor, however, the *Bismarck* was sighted again and the aircraft began their attack runs. While the *Bismarck* gunners put up a relentless barrage in defence of their ship one Swordfish from No.810 NAS managed to launch a torpedo that hit the rudders jamming them hard over. While the ship's engineers and divers struggled to clear the damage the battleship was forced to steam in circles and was harried all the time by ships from the 4th Destroyer Flotilla. On the morning of 27 May 1941 the Royal Navy battleships HMS *King George V* and *Rodney* opened fire on the crippled warship stripping much of the upper deck bare. By now the ship was unable to fight and the order was given to abandon ship and it was left to the cruiser *Dorsetshire* to administer the coup de grace.

After the sinking of the *Bismarck* HMS *Victorious* returned to the Clyde to complete its work-up before resuming its career in the Mediterranean. HMS *Ark Royal* returned to its role as an escort carrier. Units aboard at this time included No.807 NAS with Fulmars while the Swordfish squadrons swapped from Nos.825, 816 and 812 NAS to Nos. 820, 818 and 810 NAS. During its wartime career *Ark Royal* had led a charmed life even though the German broadcaster Lord Haw Haw had claimed on a number of occasions that the carrier had been sunk. Some of these stories had a small basis in fact, the first occasion was on 26 May when the carrier plus the battlecruiser HMS *Renown* passed across the bow of U-556, fortunately the submarine had expended its complement of torpedoes. However, this would change on 13 November 1941 when the carrier was escorting another convoy to Malta. Crossing the path of the German submarine U-81 the carrier was struck by a single torpedo. In all reality the damage control organisation should have saved the vessel, however, the design of the propulsion rooms meant that as soon as the engine intakes became submerged the ingress of water could not be

This overview of HMS *Stalker*, a member of the Attacker Class escort carriers, shows how short the flight deck is and the location of the deck lifts. *Stalker* joined the Royal Navy in December 1942 and took part in operations in both the Atlantic and Pacific. Returned to the USN in December 1945, the carrier was rebuilt as a merchant ship remaining in use until scrapped in 1975. (BBA Collection)

This Grumman Wildcat AJ148 was on the strength of No.888 Sqdn which flew operations from HMS *Formidable* during operations in the Indian Ocean. The type was delivered to the Royal Navy under Lend Lease. (United States Navy)

stopped even though the pumps were running at full power. Every effort was made to keep *Ark Royal* afloat although they ended in failure when the ship slid below the waves. Fortunately only one life was lost, all the other men were taken off by the escort vessels.

While the fleet carriers caught many of the newspaper headlines they also provided much needed defence for convoys crossing the Atlantic. Unfortunately the need to pursue German raiders would leave many of these vital lifelines unguarded and, therefore, another form of protection was required. Thoughts turned in two directions: the first was to create the merchant aircraft carrier, a vessel that could carry both defensive aircraft and a useful load of supplies, the second was the escort carrier, a smaller aircraft carrier derived from an American merchant-ship hull. As these ships were based on already available designs their construction would be a much quicker process than starting from scratch. However both these options were not immediately available therefore another solution was needed. This would be the CAM (Catapult Armed Merchantman) ship. These vessels were standard merchant vessels that had a rocket powered catapult on the forecastle, the aircraft being a single Hawker Hurricane Mk.1A, nicknamed Hurricats or Catafighters, flown by volunteer RAF pilots.

These ships were put into service during 1941 and were part of the Naval Service and designated auxiliary fighter catapult ships. The purpose of these fighters was to chase off any lurking *Luftwaffe* reconnaissance aircraft such as the Focke Wulf FW 200 Condor. The downside of this defence method was that it was a one way trip for the fighter. Once the shadower had either been shot down or chased away the pilot either had to ditch or make landfall at the nearest friendly base. Obviously this was expensive in aircraft and sometimes in pilots, an even more precious asset. During the period of the CAM-ships some 35 vessels made 175 voyages over a period of two years. From this small but vital fleet 12 ships were lost, they made eight launches, shot down six enemy aircraft all for the loss of one pilot. Ships known to have undertaken this role included the SS *Ariguani, Maplin, Patia* and *Springbank*, the latter two were lost undertaking convoy duty. The first successful shoot down by a CAM ship Hurricane occurred on 3 August 1941 when Lt R W H Everett RNVR was launched from the SS *Maplin* to chase a shadowing FW200 Condor. The pilot managed to get close to the *Luftwaffe* machine before the crew noticed him, however, by then it was too late. Accurate shooting saw pieces fly off the German machine although the pilot had his own concerns as the Hurricane's canopy and windscreen had become covered in oil. Originally intending to bale out Everett noticed the FW 200 crashing into the sea while closer observation of his engine and its

One of the most efficient aircraft developed by Grumman was the Avenger , a very efficient attack aircraft. Here three aircraft fly in formation during a training flight. (Will Blunt Collection)

instruments showed that the powerplant was running fine. Remaining in the cockpit Everett decided to ditch being picked up by a boat from HMS *Wanderer*.

It was the escort carrier that would make the greatest difference to both the convoy defence and various offensive operations. While fleet carriers were nearly 700 feet long and carried an average of 40 aircraft their smaller siblings averaged some 450 feet with a complement of aircraft that varied between 15 and 20 depending on role. These smaller vessels also had a secondary role as an aircraft ferry for which up to 70 aircraft could be carried. While smaller than the fleet carriers these vessels also featured a deck lift for access to the hangar below, an catapult for launching aircraft, a full range of arrestor wires and extensive anti-aircraft armament. Four classes of escort carriers were purchased from the United States: the *Archer, Attacker, Avenger* and *Ruler* classes. The *Archer* class was a single vessel purchased by the Admiralty from the Sun Shipbuilding and Drydock Corporation prior to Lend/Lease arrangements and these vessels were converted to escort carrier standard by Newport News before entering service. After commissioning this vessel was originally employed on convoy escort duty to South Africa and back before taking over the North Atlantic run. It was during one of these voyages in support of a convoys that one of the embarked Swordfish from No.819 NAS attacked and sunk U-752 on 23 May 1943 using rocket projectiles, a first in anti-submarine warfare. The *Attacker* class of 12 vessels, known to the US Navy as the *Bogue* class, began to enter service in 1942 after being accepted from the builders, Western Gas and Pipe in San Francisco or Ingalls Shipbuilding of Pascagoula. Prior to deployment these carriers underwent some modifications to suit them for Royal Navy service, some modifications, such as communications, were required for operational use while others were for safety reasons. The main areas covered by these modifications included the hangars which received improved fire suppression and containment while the aviation-fuel store protection was completely revamped as the previous arrangements were deemed inadequate. This class consisted of *Attacker, Battler, Chaser, Fencer, Hunter, Puncher, Pursuer, Ravager, Searcher, Stalker, Striker* and *Tracker*. Of these only *Chaser, Fencer, Puncher, Pursuer, Searcher, Striker* and *Tracker* would see any significant period of service on the North Atlantic convoy routes the others being deployed to either the Mediterranean or Indian Ocean areas. As the war moved further east so many of these escort carriers followed the war.

The *Avenger* class of carriers was built by Sun Shipbuilding and completed by Bethlemen Shipbuilding and consisted of three vessels, these being the name ship plus *Biter* and *Dasher*. HMS *Avenger* was commissioned in March 1942, however, its career was short; it was sunk by a torpedo on 15 November launched by U-155. HMS *Biter* was a far luckier ship. Commissioned in April 1942 the carrier initially deployed to the Mediterranean but then returned to Britain for modification as Anti-Submarine Carrier in April 1943. Reflecting this change in role No.811 NAS, a combined unit operating Swordfish and Grumman Wildcats, was embarked on the vessel which became part of the 5th Escort Group. During its first voyage aircraft from the carrier sunk the submarine U-203 after the submarine had first been driven to the surface with depth charges from HMS *Pathfinder* and *Biter* and in the following month aircraft from *Biter* finished off U-89. Biter then returned to the Clyde in October 1943 and became part of the 7th Support Group. Further convoy coverage in company with HMS *Tracker* occupied *Biter* during the early months of 1944 when one of the Wildcats shot down a Junkers Ju290. The career of HMS *Biter* ended in August 1944 when it was badly damaged in a fire while awaiting work at Greenock. Although *Biter* would not see any further Royal Navy usage the carrier was eventually repaired for service with the French Navy. HMS *Dasher* also had a fairly short naval career. Commissioned in July 1942 the carrier initially served in the Mediterranean before returning to Britain in November 1942. After working up at Scapa Flow in February 1943 the carrier embarked No.891 NAS with Sea Hurricanes and No.837 NAS with Swordfish before departing to escort convoy JW.53. HMS *Dasher* sank on 27 March 1943 following a massive petrol vapour explosion and a subsequent fire which erupted during aircraft fuelling operations. Such was the force of this explosion that the ship sank in three minutes: there were only 149 survivors.

The final class of American-built escort carriers, the *Rulers*, consisted of 21 vessels and were constructed by the Seattle-Tacoma Shipbuilding Corporation. Ships in this class included *Ameer, Arbiter, Atheling, Begum, Emperor, Empress, Khedive, Nabob, Patroller, Premier, Queen, Rajah, Ranee, Reaper, Ruler, Shah, Slinger, Smiter, Speaker, Thane, Trouncer* and *Trumpeter*. Commissioning of these vessels began in June 1943 and ended in February 1944. Of this class only HMS *Emperor, Nabob, Queen, Rajah* and *Trumpeter* would see service in the Atlantic while the remainder would be deployed to the Indian Ocean or to the British Pacific Fleet.

The Royal Navy deployed other escort carriers, many of which had originally been merchant vessels. The first of these was HMS *Activity* which had originally been laid down as a fast, refrigerated ship before being purchased by the Admiralty. Although hampered by a small hangar and limited stowage for aviation fuel this vessel found its niche in escorting convoys to Russia because it was felt that its riveted hull would be better able to withstand the sub-zero temperatures of the region. *Activity* finally commissioned for service use in January 1944 with No.819 NAS and its mix of Swordfish and Wildcats aboard. The first convoys escorted by *Activity* went to Gibralter although by March the carrier had embarked No.833 NAS with its particular mixture of aircraft departing almost immediately for Russia. After a sequence of convoys to either Gibralter or Russia HMS *Activity* was redesignated as a ferry carrier for use in the Far East as part of the Fleet Train and arrived in Ceylon (now Sri Lanka) in January 1945. HMS *Audacity* was another ship that started its career as a merchant vessel, albeit as the German cargo liner *Hanover*. Captured by the Royal Navy in March 1940 the vessel was converted for escort carrier use during 1941. Assigned No.802 NAS with Grumman Martlets, later Wildcats, the carrier sailed as part of convoy OG.74 for Gibralter and its aircraft shot down an FW 200 Condor during the voyage. The return convoy was uneventful but the next outbound trip in October saw the *Audacity* fighters shoot down a further Condor and chase off another. On 14 December 1941 HMS *Audacity* departed for Britain as part of Convoy HG.76 although there were only four flyable aircraft available. This was one of the hardest hit and most well defended convoys of the war. The escort commander was Commander, later Captain, F J Walker aboard HMS *Stork* and he masterminded one of the most successful defensive efforts ever undertaken by an escort screen. During the fighting that lasted four days two Condors were shot down,

With a battleship of the King George V class in the background, the deck handling party move this unidentified Seafire into position for takeoff. As this was before the take off, flap setting modification was introduced. The famous shaped wooden blocks are between the flaps and the wings. (BBA Collection)

a further three were damaged while the Martlets spotted and assisted in the destruction of eight U-Boats for the loss of one Martlett. *Audacity* finally ran out of luck on 21 December after seven days at sea. Against the advice of the convoy commander the captain of *Audacity*, Commander D W MacKendrick, decided to take the carrier to the starboard side of the convoy. Hit by three torpedoes fired by U-751 the carrier began to sink as the engine room flooded. Even so, as the ship was settling on an even keel the defensive guns were able to open fire on the U-Boat which had torpedoed them.

The next three British built carriers, although not given class status, were very similar in design having been laid down as merchantmen. Construction had been stopped in 1941 as the need for escort and anti-submarine vessels was deemed of greater importance. The first of the vessels was HMS *Campania* which commissioned in February 1944. After the usual range of defect repairs after its shakedown cruise the carrier was ready for use with the Swordfish, Fulmar night-fighters and Wildcats of No.813 NAS being assigned to it. After escorting various convoys to Gibralter *Campania* entered Scapa Flow being transferred from Western Approach Command to the Home Fleet in the process. On

This Seafire III, LR642 8-M, of No.807 Sqdn noses over amidst a pile of spinning debris aboard the escort carrier HMS *Hunter*. A not an unusual occurrence with this type. (Rick Harding Collection)

16 September 1944 the carrier, plus other convoy escorts, took up their positions around convoy JW.60, Operation *Rigmarole* that was taking much needed supplies to Northern Russia. On the return voyage, escorting convoy RA.60, the carrier aircraft sank the U-Boat U-921. After returning to Scapa Flow *Campania* sailed in company with *Fencer* and *Trumpeter* to provide cover for minelaying operations outside Trondheim before returning to Scapa Flow immediately afterwards. A further convoy to northern Russia, JW.61A or Operation Gloden, departed in November, the carrier brought back RA.61A on its way back to Scapa Flow although some storm damage was suffered en route. The return journey, RA.62, Operation Acumen, saw the carrier's aircraft sink U-365, otherwise the trip was uneventful. Repairs in the Clyde shipyards kept the carrier out of use until January 1945. The carrier's first task was to sail in company with *Nairana* and *Trumpeter* to undertake anti-shipping strikes off Norway. Having returned to Scapa Flow *Campania* returned to escorting convoys to Russia before changing its task to that of trooping to Trinidad. Between September and December 1945 the carrier, minus aircraft, sailed between the Clyde and Trinidad on trooping duties before

being placed in the reserve at Rosyth. *Campania* was considered for conversion to ferry carrier status in 1947 for manning by the Royal Fleet Auxiliaries, although in the event no further action was taken. In 1959 the ship was converted for use as an exhibition vessel continuing in this role until it was converted for use as the HQ vessel for the British atomic bomb tests off the Monte Bello Islands. In early 1953 *Campania* was returned to the reserve at Chatham and finally despatched to Blyth for breaking up in late 1955.

HMS *Nairana* was commissioned in November 1943 before being declared ready for service on January 1944 at which point No.835 NAS with its Swordfish and Sea Hurricanes was embarked. Convoys to and from Gibralter followed, that of March 1944 being of note when two Junkers Ju290s were shot down. *Nairana* joined the Russian convoys in October 1944 remaining on this duty until February 1945. The carrier would see no further war service and was transferred to the Royal Netherlands Navy as the *Karel Doorman* in March 1946. The last vessel in this group was HMS *Vindex* which commissioned in November 1943 and was ready for service in December. The carrier's first mission was to undertake an anti-submarine sweep in the Atlantic with No.825 NAS, with a mix of Swordfish and Sea Hurricanes, aboard. During this sortie the carrier's aircraft sank U-653. Further anti-submarine sweeps in May saw the *Vindex* Swordfish sink U-765. The *Vindex* airgroup was obviously very good at sinking submarines because they disposed of U-354 in August and U-394 in September. After returning to the Clyde for repairs the carrier celebrated by colliding with the *Queen Mary* which necessitated further repairs. Convoy duties started in October with No.811 NAS in place of No.825 NAS aboard, although the latter would return in December staying aboard until No.813 NAS returned in April 1945. *Nairana* entered the Clyde in May 1945 for reworking as a replenishment carrier for the British Pacific Fleet (BPF) Fleet Train. The carrier departed in July with No.1790 NAS and its Firefly night fighters embarked although these would be landed at Sydney when humanitarian aid was loaded for the relief of Hong Kong. This was the destination for the carrier for the next two months as supplies were shipped in while Prisoners of War were brought to Australia. In September 1947 *Vindex* was finally withdrawn and sold-on to Port Line for merchant service.

The use of the carriers plus their dedicated escort groups meant that for the hunted U-Boats life became difficult as the easy pickings faded away. With the ability to launch aircraft to range far and wide around the convoy meant that the chances of a submarine being able to get close to ships under guard was drastically reduced. Such was the sinking rate of the U-Boat fleet that Admiral Doenitz withdrew the submarines from the North Atlantic during April and May 1943. The Germans then decided to concentrate their efforts in mid Atlantic. In June Admiral Doenitz ordered the U-Boat fleet to fight on the surface after the success of U-758, however this was a misguided order as the loss rate increased. Consequently, Doenitz was forced to withdraw the submarine fleet again leaving just four on station. The Battle of the Atlantic had begun as soon as war had been declared in September 1939, although it was more like a war within a war. The defeat of the submarines was crucially down to the efforts of the various anti-submarine aircraft operating from both shore and sea. During this battle the losses to U-Boats included 63 ships totalling 359,328 tons in February 1943, during the following month the losses increased to 108 ships totalling 627,377 tons. In contrast the Axis forces would lose 71 submarines.

While the smaller escort carriers concentrated on protecting vital convoys their larger siblings were involved with preparing for more headline grabbing events. Having been involved with sinking the *Bismarck* the Home Fleet carriers found themselves involved in chasing the remaining capital ships of the German fleet. Having escaped from home waters the two German battlecruisers, (battle cruisers in name only due to their main guns' calibre) had undertaken a sortie into the Atlantic during which they sunk 115,600 tons of Allied shipping. Aware that British naval units were on the hunt the *Gneisenau* and *Scharnhorst* had finally entered the fastness of Brest on the French coast on 22 March 1941. After the sinking of the *Bismarck* the heavy cruiser *Prinz Eugen* had arrived there on 1 June. Unfortunately for the German Navy placing all these major vessels in one place made them prime targets for the aircraft of Bomber Command. Having sat in Brest for over six months Adolf Hitler decided that all three ships would better serve the German cause in home waters as the German intelligence service had deduced, incorrectly, that the Allies were preparing to invade Norway. Hitler gave his Admirals an ultimatum, move the ships or they would be stripped of their armament and left as hulks. It was also decided that the quickest way to get the ships home was through the English Channel. On the face of it given the narrowness of the channel between France and Britain this was madness, however, just for once the Navy and the *Luftwaffe* decided that co-operation was vital to complete this operation. The initial preparation involved extensive sweeping for mines, an operation that ran continuously, until the ships were ready to leave. Escorting the heavy units would be ten destroyers plus an outer screen of E Boats. Air cover would be provided by the *Luftwaffe* which would deploy 280 fighters

Against a background of a fleet carrier, possibly HMS *Victorious*, and two battleships of the King George V and Queen Elizabeth class respectively, pilots aboard one of the light fleet carriers discuss their next mission while their Seafires are prepared for flight. (Ray Sturtivant)

including Messerschmitt Me109s, Messerschmitt Me110s and Focke-Wulf FW190s as a constant cover during the move. This air cover increased to a maximum when the ships reached the narrowest point of the channel. To hide this increase in operations the Germans used every trick possible to camouflage their activities. Thanks to diligent intelligence the Admiralty discovered, in January 1942, that the Germans were preparing to put to sea, not only was the strength of the escort known, the route and air cover strength was also correctly estimated. The only thing that was incorrect was the time of departure. From the beginning of February the Admiralty increased their patrol and surveillance of Brest but even so the submarine HMS *Sealion* missed the German fleet leaving in the late evening of 11 February, no-one had thought that Admiral Ciliax would be bold enough to run out during daylight. The patrolling Lockheed Hudsons also missed the ships moving as their radar systems were malfunctioning. It would be reconnaissance Spitfires that finally spotted the moving ships and made a hasty signal to the Admiralty as soon as possible. Admiral Ramsey, Flag Officer Dover, initiated the first operations, all of which, in the event,

Fairey Barracuda II BV858 reveals the details and panel lines of the types under surfaces. Although it was developed as a torpedo and dive bomber the Barracuda also saw service in the parachutist delivery role courtesy of a pair of underwing drop pods. (BBA Collection)

were piecemeal, although their avowed intent was to inflict some damage to the ships.

The first attack was undertaken by No.825 NAS which launched six Swordfish led by Lt Cdr Eugene Esmonde; this squadron having moved from Lee-on -Solent to Manston in preparation for this attack. Such was the shortness of time that the briefing was extremely hasty and thus only a single escorting Spitfire squadron had joined the Swordfish in time to begin the attack. Two further units arrived later but, having missed the Swordfish, they proceeded towards the last known position of the German ships in order to engage the German air cover. Two further squadrons of Spitfires arrived much later. Having missed the initial formations these units proceeded towards Calais although for them there was no trade. The first decoy attack was mounted by five motor torpedo boats from Dover although they never came close because they were driven off by extensive gunfire from both the escorting vessels and the supporting German fighters. The MTBs stayed in the vicinity to give cover for the Swordfish. The first wave of Swordfish was led by Lt Cdr Esmonde although this gallant airman was shot down before making his attack run. All of the remaining aircraft made their attacks through intense gunfire and determined runs by the German fighter escort which initially was thrown by the slow speed of the old biplanes. Eventually all six Swordfish succumbed to the virulent defensive fire although two had managed to launch their torpedoes, unfortunately both missed. In recognition of his determination and leadership skills Lt Cdr Esmonde was awarded a Victoria Cross posthumously, his body was recovered from the river Medway on 29 April.

Having avoided the initial attempts of the British forces to sink them the German ships continued on their journey towards home. The first stroke of luck from the Allies point of view was when the *Scharnhorst* struck a mine close by the Schelde estuary which brought the ship to a stop. The German Admiral decided to transfer his flag to one of the escorting destroyers, however his sojourn was short lived as this ship suffered a premature shell explosion which necessitated a transfer to another vessel during which the motor launch was attacked by a patrolling Dornier Do217. To add insult to injury the Admiral was annoyed to see the *Scharnhorst* passing him at 25 knots. While the RAF was equipped with the Bristol Beaufort there were not enough available at any one airfield to make a concerted attack on the German fleet, thus their pinprick sorties did nothing to damage the vessels and at least two experienced crews were lost. The RAF had some success as *Gneisenau* hit a mine which slowed it down somewhat, while *Scharnhorst* hit a second mine causing further damage. *Scharnhorst* limped into Wilhelmshavan early on 13 February while the other two reached the mouth of the Elbe later that day. All three ships would have a less than successful further war: *Gneisenau* was hit by aircraft of Bomber Command while in the Kiel floating dock which resulted in its refit being abandoned, the vessel ended its days as a disarmed hulk. *Scharnhorst* was later sunk by the Home Fleet on Boxing Day 1943 near North Cape while *Prinz Eugen* would end its days as a target at Bikini Attol during the atom bomb tests.

With the German battleship *Bismarck* sunk and the two battlecruisers out of the picture, the German navy was left with one major unit: the *Tirpitz*. Launched in 1939 this vessel was the sistership of the *Bismarck* and had ended up being based in Norwegian waters. Although Hitler had lost faith in the navy he recognised that *Tirpitz* was still a vital asset in the war against the Allies and, therefore, he ordered that the battleship be used for limited sorties against Allied convoys. Operation *Sportpalast* began on 5 March when the *Tirpitz* plus destroyer escorts departed Norway with their object being to destroy the Russian convoys PQ.12 and QP.8. PQ.12

had departed for Murmansk from Iceland on 1 March 1942 while the return convoy departed at a similar time. Arriving off Bear Island the battleships plus escorts searched in vain for the convoys, their only trade being a single merchantman. Heading south towards Bear Island was the fleet carrier HMS *Victorious* which had been informed of the presence of *Tirpitz*. Aboard the carrier Admiral Tovey ordered that a patrol of six Albacores be flown off to search for the battleship and its escorts. A further strike force of 12 Albacores armed with torpedoes was launched an hour later led by Lt Cdr W J Lucas. One of the patrolling Albacores spotted the German battleship which at once turned away and headed off at full speed towards its base at Vestfjord. The strike force of 12 Albacores was vectored onto the escapees and finally caught up with them in mid morning. Splitting into two separate forces the Albacores attacked the *Tirpitz* from both sides. However the squadron was not practised in such attacks and their torpedoes were launched from too great a range thus the warship escaped unharmed. Although the battleship escaped, the attack did mean that Hitler would not allow the vessel to proceed to sea if there was any chance of aircraft being in the vicinity.

In June 1942 *Tirpitz* put to sea again as part of Operation *Rosselsprung*, the intention being to attack convoy PQ.17 which had departed Iceland on 27 June 1942. The Germans detected the convoy on 1 July and the *Tirpitz* consequently departed Trondhiem for Altenford. The Admiralty, unaware of the German restriction on exposing *Tirpitz* to danger, ordered that the convoy to scatter. This was the biggest mistake ever made as German submarines and aircraft successfully sank 24 of these vital merchantmen. As for *Tirpitz* the battleship made one sortie on 5 July before being ordered back to port by Admiral Raeder. The next convoy, PQ.18, was delayed until September as ships were needed for Operation Pedestal. PQ.18 started its journey on 9 September just off the coast of Iceland escorted by the carrier HMS *Avenger* which carried 12 Sea Hurricanes and three Swordfish. On 12 September the torpedo bombers of *Luftflotte* V from Norway penetrated the defence screen and sank eight merchant ships. After this the Sea Hurricanes fought off further attacks with greater success and the convoy did not lose another ship until the Kola Inlet was reached. During this persistent air battle the Sea Hurricanes shot down five German aircraft and damaged 20 more in return for four Hurricanes shot down (although three were shot down by the convoy's defences). Also in this convoy was the CAM ship *Empire Morn* whose Hurricane shot down two Heinkel He115 torpedo bombers. During 1942 German aircraft sank 32 vessels, but no more were lost until 1945 when a single vessel was sunk. The escort carriers *Activity*, *Nairana*, *Vindex* and *Campania* plus *Tracker*, *Fencer* and *Striker* were very successful

One of the most effective multi place fighter bombers was the Firefly which replaced the company's earlier products in Fleet Air Arm service. (FAAM Museum)

against the U-Boats in these northern latitudes sinking seven and sharing three more, courtesy of their anti-submarine Swordfish which could operate in virtually all weathers. Even so 80 of these venerable machines were lost escorting the convoys, mainly in landing mishaps, and even those that did return successfully frequently required their frozen crews to be bodily lifted out of their cockpits. *Tirpitz* would make only one other sortie out of its northern fastness to bombard the island of Spitzbergen with its main armament. Although the *Tirpitz* would never venture out to sea again its continued existence meant that vital resources were being diverted to monitor it. Various attempts by both the RAF and miniature submarines were made to sink it however none were successful.

In the summer of 1942 the Fleet Air Arm began an intensive campaign of air strikes in an attempt to sink the *Tirpitz*. The primary strike aircraft for these attacks was the Fairey Barracuda which had first seen service in the Salerno landings. An ungainly looking aircraft, the Barracuda was not overly popular with its crews as many of its faults still needed ironing out. The fighters involved in escorting the strike force included the Supermarine Seafire, Vought Corsairs and Grumman Hellcats, the latter pair being of American manufacture. Both types were large, rugged, well armed and well armoured. The first operation launched against the

Tirpitz was codenamed Operation Tungsten which began on 3 April 1944. The fleet carriers involved were *Furious* with Nos.801 and 880 NAS with Seafires plus Nos.830 and 831 NAS with Barracudas embarked and HMS *Victorious* equipped with the Vought Corsair operated by Nos.1834 and 1836 NAS while Nos.827 and 829 NAS flew the Barracuda. Accompanying these ships were four escort carriers namely the *Emperor, Pursuer, Searcher* and *Fencer*. HMS *Emperor* was operating as a fighter carrier thus Nos. 800 and 804 NAS with Hellcats were aboard while *Pursuer* was flying another Grumman product the Wildcat being flown by Nos.881 and 896 NAS. The *Searcher* was also another fighter carrier with Wildcats flown by Nos.882 and 898 NAS, and HMS *Fencer* was given the essential role of anti-submarine carrier and thus No.842 NAS was aboard equipped with a mix of Swordfish and Wildcats. The first attack began in the early hours of the morning which caught the *Tirpitz* unawares as the crew were occupied in preparing the battleship to go to sea. The fighters' escorts strafed the anti-aircraft positions and the superstructure of the *Tirpitz* while the Barracudas undertook the bombing using a mixture of 500 and 1,000 lb bombs. Fourteen direct hits were achieved and two very near misses caused by 40 Barracudas. Attacking aircraft losses were kept to two Barracudas over the target, one en route back to the fleet and a single Hellcat. In return the *Tirpitz* required three months of extensive repairs plus 438 personnel needed replacing.

A second series of strikes codenamed Operation Mascot were launched in mid July 1944. Only the fleet carriers were involved in this mission: *Formidable, Indefatigable* and, of course, *Furious*. *Formidable* had No 1841 NAS with Corsairs plus Nos. 827 and 830 NAS with Barracudas while *Indefatigable* had No.894 NAS equipped with Seafires and No.1770 NAS was flying the Fairey Firefly fighter bomber. The strike element was Nos.820 and 826 NAS equipped with Barracudas. The aerial strike force included 44 Barracudas, 18 Corsairs, 12 Fireflies and 18 Hellcats. Unlike Tungsten *Tirpitz* had 15 minutes warning and thus the battleship was able to create extensive smoke screens up to 800 feet and put up an extensive anti-aircraft barrage. Such was the intensity of the defensive fire that the Barracudas were unable to score any hits.

The final series of attacks were codenamed Operations Goodwood 1 to IV and were launched throughout August. As before, the three carriers from Mascot were involved plus the escort carriers *Nabob* and *Trumpeter*. HMS *Nabob*, although nominally allocated to Western Approaches Command, was attached to the Home Fleet for these missions and had No.825 NAS aboard equipped with a mix of Grumman Avengers and Wildcats. *Trumpeter* was also equipped with the same aircraft mix although the operating unit was No.846 NAS. Changes to the air wing of *Formidable* had also been undertaken with No.1842 NAS being added to the fighter strength while the Barracuda units had changed to Nos.826 and 828 NAS. While *Indefatigable* proceeded with the other ships *Formidable* was allocated to a parallel operation, Turbine, which was tasked with providing extensive fighter sweeps both before and after the Goodwood missions. During these missions 220 aircraft were involved although only two direct hits were scored against the *Tirpitz* on 24 August, one of these penetrated through the deck armour to the keel but failed to explode. However, many enemy aircraft were shot down but *Nabob* was torpedoed by U-354. Nevertheless, by careful management of the heavy flooding that ensued the damaged carrier managed to reach Scapa Flow. After examination the carrier was not fully repaired but patched up sufficiently enough so that it could be towed to a mud bank on the Firth of Forth where it stayed until returned to the US Navy for disposal.

While the *Tirpitz* had been damaged by the Fleet Air Arm attacks the battleship was still capable of sea duty although Hitler was reluctant to let such an asset be exposed to danger because it tied up a considerable number of resources by so doing. With the invasion of Europe well underway the destruction of the *Tirpitz* became a priority. Therefore, Avro Lancaster bombers of Nos 9 and 617 Squadrons were tasked with attacking the ship. On 15 September 27 Lancasters, 16 of which were carrying a 12,000 lb Tallboy bomb and the remainder had air-dropped mines, flew from Yagodnik in Russia. Although the smoke defences were set off by the *Tirpitz* defenders at least one massive bomb hit the bows of *Tirpitz.* The Germans decided not to repair the *Tirpitz*, but moved it to Tromso instead, although this was a mistake as the battleship was now in range of bombers launched from Britain. To that end on 29 October 12 Lancasters were launched and dropped further Tallboys which damaged the port propellor shaft rendering the vessel incapable of any further action without access to major dockyard facilities. The final attack took place on 12 November when 32 Lancasters were despatched and dropped 29 Tallboys. The result was two direct hits and a near miss to the port side. The result was extensive flooding in the *Tirpitz* and a massive explosion in an after magazine which was followed by the ship capsizing, most of the remaining crew were killed.

On 6 June 1944 the Allies launched the long awaited assault on Europe. As the distance was minimal between the airfields in England there was no real role for carrier borne aircraft. In fact, except for the *Tirpitz* operations, most of the fleet carriers plus many of the escort carriers were despatched to the Far East to join the British Pacific Fleet

Captured at anchor is the MAC *Empire McColl*. This vessel entered service in November 1943 using its embarked Swordfish in the ASW role. Decommissioned in May 1945 the vessel subsequently embarked on a career as a tanker with British Petroleum. (BBA Collection)

where the fleet vessels would undertake the attack missions while the smaller ships acted as part of the Fleet Train being used as spare deck space as and when required. Some carriers would remain involved in Western Approaches duties in support of convoys even though the U-Boat threat was much reduced. One of these escort carriers was HMS *Biter* which survived an attack by U-448, the submarine was eventually sunk by the escort HMS *Pelican*. Also retained was the *Campania*, *Nairana*, *Premier*, *Puncher*, *Queen*, *Ravager*, *Reaper*, *Slinger*, *Striker* and *Vindex*. Even this force declined as the U-Boat fleets were decimated thus many of these carriers were to enter the Clyde dockyards for preparation for service in the Far East.

Late in the war another type of carrier was to enter service: the Merchant Aircraft Carrier or MAC ships. The concept was developed by John Lamb of the Anglo-Saxon Petroleum Company whose proposal was to add a full length flight deck above a standard merchant hull. This concept meant that the hull would contain a bulk load, normally petroleum, while the flight deck would be home to a handful of aircraft there being no hangar facilities. Having overcome the Admiralties discomfort concerning the fuel cargo the decision to go ahead was made in September 1943. The first fuel tanker converted to MAC status was the MV *Acavus* which was commissioned in its new role in October at Falmouth. Given the absence of a hangar the aircraft complement was restricted to three Swordfish while the cargo load was reduced to 80% of maximum, the remainder being used for the stowage of aircraft fuel to Admiralty standards. To provide some weather protection for the aircraft on deck some collapsible wind breaks were fitted to the rear of the flight deck. Once the *Acavus* had completed its workup with No.836F Flight it was employed on convoys plying between Liverpool and Halifax, Nova Scotia. In March 1944 No.836F was replaced by No.836V Flight which remained aboard until the end of hostilities. The next ship supplied by Anglo-Saxon was *Adula* which became operational in March 1944 whose Swordfish Flight was No.836P. During the period July to December the Flight alternated with No.836G and this was the last incumbent until May 1945 when the vessel was returned to its owners. *Alexia* from the same source began its convoy escort duties in January 1944 with No.836F Flight aboard. Between May and December of that year No.836F alternated with No.836J Flight, however, No.836L Flight was embarked for the final convoy task in May 1945. In October 1943 No.836E Flight would embark aboard the MAC ship *Amastra* for convoy protection duties. During the period July to September this Flight alternated with No.836C Flight although as the war progressed the need for anti-submarine patrols decreased, therefore many of these MAC ships would end up carrying American aircraft and other stores on the flight deck. The final vessel from Anglo-Saxon was *Ancylus* which began operations in November 1943 with No.836G Flight aboard. As before there was an alternate Flight No.836D both of which were finally stood down in October 1944 as the vessel was used for transporting aircraft.

Another type of bulk ship that was converted for MAC duties was grain tankers. A total of 10 vessels was converted: the *Empire MacAlpine, MacAndrew, MacCabe, MacCallum, MacColl, MacDermott, MacKay, MacKendrick, MacMahon* and *MacRae*. The *MacAlpine* was the first MAC ship to be landed on when Lt Cdr Slater commanding Officer of No.836 NAS touched down on the deck at the beginning of May 1943. The permanent Flight initially was No.836B which alternated with No.836D Flight until the end of hostilities. *MacAndrew* began escort duties in August 1943 embarking No.836M Flight although this was replaced by No.836H in November. No.836R was also assigned to the vessel in June 1944 as the duty Flight until November when No.836B became resident.

No.836B was in turn replaced by No.836Z but this Flight left the aircraft in May 1945 as the vessels services were no longer required. The *MacCabe* had a fairly short career entering service in January 1944 with No.836N Flight embarked. The allocated Flight changed to No.836A in September and this Flight, in turn, was replaced by No.836H in May. This Flight's sojourn was brief as the MAC ship flew off its Swordfish in June. *MacCallum* began its convoy escort duties in January 1944 with No.836K Flight aboard. A month later this Flight was replaced by No.836R Flight which, in turn, was replaced by No.836T in June. No.836Y came aboard during July 1944 and remained there until February 1945 when No.836K was assigned and remained aboard for just three months before the ship was returned to civilian life. The *MacCall* joined the North Atlantic convoy runs in November 1943 with No.836A Flight aboard. In July No.836J became the resident Flight and was replaced, in turn, the following month by No.836E. Three months later No.836V took over the flying duties and remained aboard until January 1945. No aircraft were aboard until March when No.836Q was taken aboard for two months when the vessel was stood down from active service. In April 1944 the *MacDermott* with No.836K Flight aboard joined the other MAC ships for convoy duties. No.836N replaced the previous occupants in November until it too was replaced by No.836B in April 1945 although its tenure lasted only a month as the vessel was then paid off. Requisitioned from British Petroleum the *MacKay* entered service in October 1943 with No.836D Flight aboard. This unit remaining aboard until July when No.836W came aboard. Five months later No.836W was replaced by No.836R in December remaining in residence until the ship was paid off. In December 1943 the *MacKendrick* became available for escort duties with No.836M embarked. Four months later Flight No.836Z replaced No.836M which in turn was replaced by No.836L in January 1945. The last Swordfish Flight to embark upon the *MacKendrick* was No.836V Flight in March but it disembarked three months later when the ship was returned to its civilian owners. No.836J Flight and its Swordfish embarked upon the *MacMahon* in December 1943 and remained aboard until replaced by No.836B in April 1944. Six months later No.836G took over the anti-submarine duties until these were passed to No.836W in March 1945. This small unit's tenure ended in June when the ship was demobbed. The final vessel from this group to join the convoy escorts was the *MacRae* which started its new career in October 1943 with No.836C Flight aboard. No.836C was replaced by No.836L in May 1944 and this Flight, in turn, was replaced by No.836U some six months later. In March 1945 No.836D became the final Flight to embark remaining in residence until June.

Two other ships were also converted for MAC purposes: the *Miralda* and *Rapana*. The *Miralda* entered service in February 1944 with No.836Q Flight and its Swordfish aboard. On 21 June two of the Flight's aircraft attacked a U-Boat without discernible results, unfortunately both were damaged when landing although they were quickly repaired. No.836H Flight replaced No.836Q in August and was, in turn, replaced in February 1945 by No.836P. This unit would remain aboard until May when the vessel was decommissioned. The final MAC ship, *Rapana*, embarked No.836L Flight in August 1943 until it disembarked in February 1944. Over the following two months the *Rapana* would sail minus its aircraft complement but this was restored in October when the same Flight re-embarked. At the beginning of 1945 the vessel was demobbed. Although the Swordfish aboard the MAC ships had little trade to deal with their very presence acted as a deterrent to the few remaining U-Boats still operating in the Atlantic.

Chapter 3

The Fleet Air Arm in the Mediterranean

While the war in the Atlantic was grabbing many of the newspaper headlines there was another that was just as vital. This took place within the confines of the Mediterranean and was concentrated upon the island of Malta and its supply lines. This little pimple of rock was a thorn in the side of both Hitler and Mussolini. Keeping the supply lines open was vital to the survival of the island and the difficulty of their maintenance was very much allied to the successes or failures of the army on land. Heading the naval effort was Admiral Sir Andrew Cunningham, Commander of the Mediterranean Fleet. Initially this force had one carrier on strength: HMS *Eagle*. Originally designed for the Chilean Navy as the battleship *Almirante Cochrane* the partly complete vessel was taken over by the Admiralty in 1914. Unlike her sister ship, *Almirante Latorre*, *Eagle* was not completed until 1919 but was converted to full carrier standard in 1924. Prior to transferring to the Mediterranean the *Eagle* had been part of Force 'I' in the Indian Ocean before passing through the Suez canal in May 1940 to join Admiral Cunningham. Also joining the Mediterranean Fleet was the new fleet carrier HMS *Illustrious* which had been launched in March 1939, after working up with No.806 NAS operating Fairey Fulmars plus Nos. 815 and 819 NAS flying Swordfish. In August 1940 *Illustrious* departed Scapa Flow being escorted en route by the ships of Force 'H'.

HMS *Eagle* joined the Mediterranean Fleet in May 1949 undertaking its first patrols in mid June. Returning to harbour in Alexandria the Swordfish of No.813 NAS undertook an attack on shipping in Tobruk harbour sinking four vessels, including the liner *Liguria,* and damaging two others. After the joys and delights of attacking Italian shipping the *Eagle* was deployed to protect convoys of ships carrying evacuees from Malta to Alexandria. The next operation undertaken by *Eagle* was to help the surface forces take on the Italian Fleet off the Calabrian coast on 9 July 1940 where the aircraft undertook fighter cover, reconnaissance and spotting duties while some of the Swordfish of No.824 NAS undertook a torpedo attack with little success. The following day *Eagle* launched

Swordfish from No.813 NAS to attack shipping in Augusta harbour sinking a destroyer and badly damaging an oiler. The Italian air force would attempt to take its revenge on 11 July, however, the three Sea Gladiators assigned to No.813 NAS (this squadron basically was a Swordfish operator) managed to shoot down all the Savio Marchetti SM.79 bombers and three other Italian aircraft were reported as damaged. The other Swordfish unit, No.824 NAS, also undertook shipping attacks although this time the target was the submarine base in the Gulf of Bomba, not only were some of the submarines sunk, but the supporting depot ship was badly damaged.

The first combined operation involving *Eagle* and the newly arrived *Illustrious* was undertaken on 4 September 1940, the target being the Island of Rhodes. The target for the *Eagle* aircraft was the airfield at Maritsa where aircraft and facilities were attacked with some success by the Swordfish of No.813 NAS although four of the attacking aircraft were shot down by the defending Italian fighters. The *Illustrious* also hit targets on Rhodes, the Swordfish striking various targets while the Fulmars shot down three defending fighters. After this operation *Eagle* returned to Alexandria while its air group flew ashore and undertook an attack on

HMS *Eagle* began life as a battleship before requisitioning from the Chilean Navy. This side on view reveals its earlier antecedents which made it a difficult ship to keep in trim. Even so the carrier gave good service to the Royal Navy until sunk in August 1942. (Rick Harding Collection)

shipping at Bomba which caused some damage to a freighter. While in dock *Eagle* was attacked by Italian bombers but although the bombers missed their targets the close misses of the bombs caused some shock damage throughout the ship that eventually caused faults in the onboard aircraft fuel delivery system. While *Eagle* was in dock the *Illustrious*'s air wing undertook an attack on the harbour at Benghazi launching nine Swordfish of No.815 NAS and a further six from No.819 NAS. The first wave of aircraft attacked a destroyer and two merchant ships by dive bombing while the second group laid a minefield which took care of another destroyer, two merchant vessels and caused damage to a third. After attacking Benghazi the *Illustrious* covered two convoys to Malta carrying out an attack on Leros en route to Alexandria. Whilst in dock there was a fire in the hangar which caused some damage, fortunately the aircraft were all ashore.

Possibly one of the boldest moves embarked upon by the Mediterranean Fleet was undertaken on 11 November 1940. Known as Operation Judgement the target was the Italian Fleet at Taranto. Planning for such an attack had in fact begun in early 1938 the purpose being either to destroy or disable the Italian Navy. However as this fleet seemed reluctant to put to sea it would be the job of the Royal Navy and the Fleet Air Arm to take the war to them. The original date for *Judgement* had been set for 21 October, Trafalgar Day, but the fire damage aboard *Illustrious* needed repairing first. While *Eagle* was out of commission five Swordfish and eight crews from the air wing were transferred to *Illustrious* to increase this vessels available aircraft. Confirmation of the Italian Fleet presence in Taranto harbour was confirmed by Martin Maryland aircraft which undertook a reconnaissance flight on 10 November. Given this confirmation HMS *Illustrious* plus four cruisers and four destroyers set sail on Remembrance Day arriving at the launch point some 170 miles south-east of Taranto. At 20.57 hours the first strike of 12 Swordfish was launched led by Lt Cdr K Williamson. As predicted it was a fine night with a ¾ moon and light cloud at 8,000 ft which was good for the attacking force as it was unescorted, and for any alert defences. Of this first strike force six Swordfish were armed with torpedoes, four toted bombs while the remainder carried a mix of flares and bombs. The reconnaissance flights had shown that the harbour was well protected by balloons, nets, guard ships and extensive anti-aircraft guns. The pre-departure briefing for the crews meant that the torpedo-carrying Swordfish would attack the battleships in the outer harbour, Mar Grande, while the bombers were to attack the smaller vessels in the inner harbour, Mar Piccolo. Not long after 23.00 hours the flares were released by the two Swordfish. All the Swordfish had semi glided down from 8,000 to

4,000 ft opening their throttles up slowly until powering up at 30 ft to line up their torpedoes against the battleships. Although the Taranto defences had been given plenty of warning their fire was not accurate enough to stop the torpedo bombers nor the bombers. The second wave of Swordfish, led by Lt Cdr J W Hale, departed *Illustrious* at 21.23 hours, of these, five were carrying torpedoes, two had bombs while the remainder were again carrying a mix of flares and bombs. As this second wave approached Taranto they could see the harbour and its contents blazing nicely. Yet again the defences opened up with full violence and yet again the aircraft jinked their way through to hit the ships in the harbour plus the oil tanks on shore. Although the Italian defenders had put up an extensive defensive screen their efforts only resulted in the loss of two of the attacking Swordfish. The cold light of day revealed the battleship *Littorio* listing heavily after three torpedo hits which put the vessel out of action for over a year, the older battleship *Caio Diulio* had only suffered one hit, however, the flooding was so serious that the crew were forced to beach it to stop it floundering. A third battleship, the *Conte de Cavour*, was also struck and, although only one torpedo hit was registered, it was enough to cause extensive flooding that saw the ship settling on the bottom. Eventually it was raised although it would take no further part in the war. In the inner harbour the heavy cruiser *Trento* was badly damaged by bombs as were quite a few destroyers and oil tanks on the harbour side. When *Illustrious* rejoined the fleet Admiral Cunningham would signal 'Manoeuvre well executed'. A second strike had been planned for the following day but after the success of the initial attack it was cancelled.

Also giving the Italian fleet cause for concern was Force 'H' which was also operating in the Mediterranean. Centred around the carrier HMS *Ark Royal* this group had begun operations in June 1940 when *Ark Royal* had arrived at Gibralter with Nos.800 and 801 NAS flying Blackburn Rocs and Skuas plus Nos.810 and 820 NAS with Swordfish embarked. Force 'H' undertook its first attack on the French Fleet at Oran in July to keep these vessels out of the Mediterranean fighting. Having completed this operation the *Ark Royal* group turned their attention to the airfield at Cagliarion 2 August 1940, the intention being to keep the Italian air force on the ground while HMS *Argus* slipped by with a vital load of Hurricanes for Malta. Another airfield, this time at Elmas, was also attacked at the beginning of September in order that the carrier HMS *Illustrious* could pass through into the Mediterranean without being attacked by marauding Italian bombers.

The next task for Force 'H' and *Ark Royal* was Operation Menace, an attempt to turn the Vichy forces in Dakar on to the side of the Allies.

One of the most significant aircraft carriers to the Royal Navy was HMS *Ark Royal* which laid down the blueprint for the straight deck fleet carrier which continued in one form or another until catapult launched fixed wing aircraft departed the Fleet Air Arm. (Rick Harding Collection)

General de Gaulle had persuaded the British Government that either turning the Vichy forces or destroying their equipment to stop it falling into German hands were their only viable options. The core of these forces was the 95% complete French battleship *Richelieu* that had been operating in concert with the carrier HMS *Hermes* until the Vichy Government decided to throw in their lot with the Germans. Just as important was the fact that the gold reserves of the *Banque de France* and the Polish Government in exile were also in Vichy hands. While getting the Dakar forces on side was seen as a worthwhile object, the fact that *Hermes* had bombed the *Richelieu* and damaged it enough to stop it putting to sea was seen as a possible stumbling block. Also, in Dakar harbour were a handful of submarines and some small escort vessels. Further there were reports that three heavy cruisers, the *Gloire, Georges Leygues* and *Montcalm* were en route to Dakar. The *Gloire* was suffering engine problems and was intercepted by HMAS *Australia* and ordered to sail for Casablanca, although the other two cruisers and escorting destroyers managed to reach Dakar. In preparation for the landing of Free French forces the aircraft from *Ark Royal* dropped leaflets over Dakar on 23 September which was followed by the despatch of a pair of Free French *Caudron Luciolles* with de Gaulle's representatives aboard. As soon as these aircraft landed, their passengers and crews were taken prisoner. A further attempt to land representative ashore by launch was met by intensive gunfire. Obviously the Vichy French had no intention of joining the Allies and, therefore, stronger action was called for. During mid morning the French fleet attempted to leave harbour, although they quickly returned to port when fired upon by HMAS *Australia*. In return *Australia* was fired upon by the forts defending the harbour which in turn led to an engagement with the battleship *Barham* and the battlecruiser *Resolution*. A further attempt to secure Dakar for the Allies involved the destroyer *Rufisque* landing troops on a beach close by. Heavy gunfire met these landings and de Gaulle requested that the landings be called off as he objected to Frenchmen spilling French blood. After these aborted efforts the Allies used air and sea power to attack the harbour and its environs. Two submarines were sunk and a destroyer was damaged while the French defenders managed to hit both the *Barham* and the *Resolution* while *Ark Royal* lost nine aircraft. As the attacks were proving inconclusive the Allies decided to withdraw for the time being.

Ark Royal returned to Gibralter at the beginning of November losing No.803 NAS and its Skuas for the more capable Fairey Fulmars of No.808 NAS. On 9 November the *Ark Royal* air wing attacked the Italian airfields on Sicily in order to divert attention away from the *Illustrious* attack on Taranto. Eight days later the carrier provided coverage for *Argus* which was undertaking further resupply missions to Malta. On 27 November, off Cape Spartivento, Force 'H' intercepted an Italian naval force and launched an aerial attack against the two reported battleships. Although some hits were scored not enough damage was caused and the Italian force was able to withdraw at speed. *Ark Royal* had a quiet period until February 1941 when a torpedo attack was carried out on the dam at Tirso on Sicily after an earlier bombing attempt had failed. The Swordfish were back in action again a few days later acting as spotters for the *Renown* and *Malaya* while others attacked La Spezia and Pisa. On 22 March the *Ark Royal* was slightly damaged when one of the Swordfish crashed on take-off and its load of depth charges exploded. Although shaken the *Ark Royal* was deemed fit to continue its next task which was to ferry Hurricanes to Malta on 24 May. On the return trip to Gibralter *Ark Royal* was ordered to join the Home Fleet in order to join the hunt for the *Bismarck*. *Ark Royal* rejoined Force 'H' in October undertaking Operation Perpetual that saw the carrier taking RAF fighters to Malta. It was during the return voyage that the carrier was struck by a torpedo fired by U-81 thus a British naval icon disappeared under the waves.

With the continued resupply of Malta being successful and the Italian and Vichy naval units being trapped in their ports it was clear that Admiral Cunningham and Force 'I' had gained tactical superiority over the Axis forces. Not only were the Axis forces at sea proving ineffectual the Italian army had been stopped at Cyrenaica. Consequently, the Germans decided to transfer *FliegerKorps X* from Norway to Sicily in order to stiffen the resolve of the Italians. The first vessel to feel the might of this anti-shipping initiative was HMS *Illustrious.* Having sailed on 7 January 1941 to cover a fast convoy to Malta the carrier was attacked three days later some 75 miles from its destination. The first part of this attack saw a pair of Savoia Marchetti SM.79 bombers armed with torpedoes setting upon the battleship *Valiant.* An *Illustrious* fighter patrol was airborne at the time and they chased after the Italian aircraft which in turn allowed the German force of Junkers Ju.87 Stukas and Ju.88s to attack the *Illustrious* before it could launch further Fulmars. Fortunately *Illustrious* had been built with a strongly armoured deck and thus the six armour piercing bombs that hit the ship did limited damage. There were also three near misses. Even so the flight deck was pierced, the after deck lift was blown off its tracks, the hangar underneath was badly damaged and set on fire while the near misses caused some damage to the hull. Eventually the attackers were driven off and the fires brought under control and the wounded carrier was able to limp back to Malta under its own power and protected en route by the carrier's Fulmars which undertook constant patrols: the aircraft flying to and from Malta to refuel and rearm. With the convoy now vulnerable the Germans mounted a strong attack on the remaining ships during which the cruisers *Gloucester* and *Southampton* were badly damaged; the latter having to be sunk as it was unrepairable. HMS *Illustrious* was bombed again while in Valetta harbour but nevertheless emergency repairs were carried out and the carrier departed from Malta on 23 January arriving at Alexandria for further repairs on 25 January. These repairs were duly completed and on 10 March *Illustrious* sailed through the Suez canal en route to Durban. By 12 May the carrier was at Norfolk, Virginia where it would undergo extensive repairs and modifications over the next six months.

The removal of *Illustrious* for major repair left Force 'I' with HMS *Eagle* as the only available carrier. *Eagle* was not only elderly and unmodernized but its vital boiler clean, scheduled for May 1941 in Cape Town, had been cancelled as there were fears that *Bismarck* might break into the South Atlantic. Departing in company with the battleship HMS *Nelson* neither ship was engaged in sinking the German battleship, however the carrier's Swordfish found and sank the *Elbe,* one of the *Bismarck*'s supply ships. The

The Royal Air Force attempted to counter the Admiralties need for aircraft carriers and their fighters by proposing various floatplane versions of land based fighters. This is the seaplane Spitfire Mk.V W3760. While a capable machine, the idea of using the floatplane instead of the aircraft carrier thankfully died a death. (Will Blunt Collection)

Eagle and its consort came across the German supply ship *Lothringen* which surrendered to the British vessels. Having rampaged around the South Atlantic the *Eagle* then moved to St Helena for a more relaxed patrol but, unfortunately, a serious fire occurred in the hangar which destroyed 13 aircraft. Such was the seriousness of this conflagration that *Eagle* had to sail to the Clyde shipyards for major repairs and much needed modifications which included improved radar, improved anti-aircraft weapons and better stowage for aircraft fuel. By early January 1942 HMS *Eagle* was ready for operations again and embarked No.824 NAS with Swordfish plus No.813 NAS with a mix of Swordfish and Sea Hurricanes. On 23 February the carrier arrived at Gibralter where it joined Force 'H'. Over the next couple of months the *Eagle* was used to support convoys and ferry Spitfires to Malta and finally returned to Gibralter in April for minor repairs. At the beginning of May 1942 HMS *Eagle,* in company with the American carrier USS *Wasp,* proceeded towards Malta, both carriers flying off much needed Spitfires to that beleaguered island. On 11 June the *Eagle,* in company with *Argus,* took part in Operation *Harpoon,* both carriers being needed to support a vital Malta convoy. After two days at

Seen during its time engaged in RATOG trials is Swordfish III NR995/G which had been delivered in June 1944. After its trials service the aircraft was used by Nos.813, 838 and 836 NAS for anti-submarine duties. (Rick Harding Collection)

sea the combined Italian and German air forces launched a massive attack on the ships during which the carriers' fighters managed to shoot down nine confirmed enemy aircraft. Even though the Axis aircraft continued to attack the convoy the carriers and the escort group fought the convoy through with minimal losses. Returning to Gibralter *Eagle* underwent a period of rest and replenishment before joining up with the escort formed to support the largest convoy destined for Malta. On 10 August 1942, in company with the carriers *Indomitable* and *Victorious,* HMS *Eagle* departed Gibralter. Also in the convoy was *Furious* which was ferrying Spitfires. On 11 August 1942, in the early afternoon, the *Furious* was hit by four torpedoes fired by U-73. Two officers and 158 men lost their lives although there were 789 survivors, four Sea Hurricanes airborne at the time found sanctuary aboard other carriers. Fortunately for Admiral Cunningham the fleet carrier HMS *Formidable* had arrived to join the Mediterranean Fleet in March 1941, although the vessel should have arrived earlier but was delayed by German mines laid in the Suez canal. Given that this was a modern carrier commissioned in November 1940 the air wing was of similar modernity comprising Nos. 803 and 806 NAS equipped with

Fairey Fulmars, No.826 NAS with Albacores and No.815 NAS with the venerable Swordfish.

As the Royal Navy seemed to be able to run convoys through to Malta with minimal losses the German Navy High Command put pressure on their opposite numbers to use their battleships and other ships to intercept at least one of these convoys and destroy it. In response to these pressures the Italian Fleet put to sea and was spotted by a reconnaissance flight on 27 March which reported the vessels as heading towards Crete. In response, the Mediterranean Fleet put to sea the following day. The first aerial patrol launched by *Formidable* flew off just after dawn and came across the Italian Fleet some 100 miles to the north. The cruiser force of Vice Admiral Pridham-Wippell flying his flag aboard HMS *Orion* soon made contact with the enemy. In true naval fashion the cruisers pulled away in order to draw the Italian Fleet onto the heavy guns of the British Fleet. For their part the Italians took up the chase with great enthusiasm which put the British cruisers in great danger. Fortunately a strike from *Formidable* consisting of Albacores led by Lt Cdr Saunt arrived on the scene and set about attacking the battleship *Vittorio Veneto*. All the torpedoes fired missed the battleship which turned away, as did the three escorting heavy cruisers which had been attacked by Swordfish launched from Maleme airfield on Crete. While the first wave of attacking aircraft had missed the Italian ships the *Formidable* launched another wave of aircraft, however, before these aircraft found the Italians the RAF had launched an attack with Blenheims. Although no bombs hit the Italian ships they did cause some damage due to near misses. While the Italian Admiral aboard the *Vittorio Veneto* complained about the lack of reconnaissance and fighter support his opposite number aboard the *Formidable* was well furnished with both as the attacking SM.79 bombers discovered as another attack failed. Even as the Blenheims finished their attacks the *Formidable*'s aircraft began their assaults in order to keep the defending gunners aboard the *Vittorio Veneto* from shooting at the attacking torpedo aircraft. The Albacores therefore made their run-ins virtually unopposed scoring a torpedo hit right aft of the ship. The force of the impact was enough to slow the Italian battleship down temporarily although it soon picked up speed pulling away rapidly from the pursuing *Warspite* whose condensers had become contaminated with sand and mud particles. While the Royal Navy heavy units could not catch the Italian battleship the *Formidable* launched another aerial strike. This strike departed during the late afternoon and, although it missed the battleship, it torpedoed the cruiser *Pola* which stopped dead in the water. Instead of continuing back to port and safety, the Italian Admiral ordered the other two cruisers in the group, *Zara* and *Fiume*, to turn back and help the *Pola*. By the time these vessels had turned back it was dark and were, therefore, unaware that British heavy units were close by. Illuminated by the escorting destroyers' searchlights the two Italian cruisers were sunk by gunfire delivered by the battleships *Warspite, Valiant* and *Barham* as were two Italian destroyers plus the already stricken *Pola*. Thus ended the night battle of Cape Matapan.

On 20 May 1941 German forces launched a large airborne invasion to capture the island of Crete under the codename Operation Mercury. Crete was defended by a mixture of British regular army and Greek resistance fighters and both groups put up an admirable defence that caused great casualties amongst the attackers. As Crete was vital to the Allied cause Winston Churchill insisted that every effort be made to retain the island. However, there was a communications snarl up amongst the main commanders which allowed further Axis forces to land almost unopposed. In response to this increase in enemy forces on the ground Admiral Cunningham decided to commit increased naval forces in an effort to drive the invaders off Crete. Central to this effort was HMS *Formidable* which began operations in the early hours of 26 May. The first strike consisted of four Albacores escorted by four Fulmars, their target was the airfield of Scarpanto, the main base for the Axis air forces. During this attack six enemy aircraft were shot down as they headed towards *Formidable,* however, two attackers managed to evade the defensive screen and dropped two 2,000 lb bombs on the carrier while a third bomb caused severe underwater pressure damage. Fortunately for the Royal Navy *Formidable* had an armoured deck which kept the damage to a minimum. Nevertheless, the carrier had to withdraw and join *Illustrious* in the USA for repairs in the Norfolk navy yard in Virginia. The German anti-ship aircraft also attacked other Royal Navy vessels which had successfully turned back further seaborne forces attempting to land forces on Crete. The result of the German attacks was the loss of the cruisers *Fiji* and *Gloucester* and the destroyers *Kelly* and *Kashmir*. Other ships damaged in this engagement were the battleships *Warspite* and *Valiant*. Although the Allied forces resisted bravely they were gradually overwhelmed and eventually the Royal Air Force and navy units decamped to Alexandria while many of the army survivors and Greek resistance fighters disappeared into the hills where they caused destructive chaos until the end of hostilities. This was the last time that the German forces would launch such a massive airborne attack as Hitler had decided that the losses of such an operation were unacceptable amongst such elite troops.

While Force 'I' had taken a battering in the eastern Mediterranean Admiral Cunningham was fortunate that Force 'H' was still intact and

Unsung heroes of the defence of Malta were a small force of Fairey Albacore's. Manned by both RAF and FAA crews, these machines acted in the escort and anti-submarine roles. Here a mix of RAF and FAA personnel pose for the camera in front of their charge. (USAAF/NARA)

capable of controlling the western end of the sea. Although 1941 had ended disastrously 1942 began in a far better manner as the 8th Army successfully completed its attacks on Rommel's Afrika Corps, pushing the Germans back to the Libyan borders which saw the airfields in that country falling into Allied hands once again. As the land forces continued to pile success upon success the Royal Navy concentrated upon running convoys through to Malta. One of the first that sailed into Valetta harbour in January had been escorted most of the way by Beaufighters supplied by Nos. 252 and 272 Groups as there was a shortage of suitable naval vessels. This lack of vessels played into Axis hands as the Italian navy was able to escort a convoy to aid Rommel in North Africa with minimal British interference. Obviously the lack of escorts plus the increased boldness of the Axis navies meant that all the successes previously gained were under threat. Admiral Cunningham therefore ordered Force 'H' to start supporting convoys through to Malta on a regular basis. On 20 March a convoy escorted by ships under the command of Admiral

This view of a Fairey Albacore reveals its Swordfish antecedents, in fact the Swordfish would outlive its successor. (Rick Harding Collection)

Vian managed to outwit and outfight a stronger Italian force. Unfortunately, the exposure of the convoy to daylight saw two ships sunk and two survivor ships were sunk in Valetta harbour. It soon became apparent that sending supplies to Malta in such a piecemeal manner not only did little for Malta it was costing a great deal in equipment and personnel. This situation became a topic of conversation for the War Cabinet which decided that a major relief convoy must be fought through, hopefully intact, to Malta. On 10 August 14 merchant vessels, including the tanker *Ohio*, steamed westwards from the Straits of Gibralter heading in a westerly direction. The escorting forces included the battleships *Rodney* and *Nelson* plus the carriers *Indomitable, Eagle, Victorious* and *Furious*, the latter carrying much needed Spitfires, plus seven cruisers and 32 destroyers all under the command of Vice Admiral Syfret. Codenamed Operation Pedestal this would be one of the most spectacular convoys of the war.

Obviously such an assemblage of shipping could not go unnoticed and the Axis navies in the Mediterranean prepared their traps. The first trap was to spread a line of U-Boats across the perceived line of the convoy and their first success was scored by U-73 which fired four torpedoes at HMS *Eagle*, all of which hit the carrier causing it to sink in seven minutes with the loss of 200 crew. The next attack took place that evening when at least 35 Junkers Ju.88s from Cagliari, Sardinia, fell upon the ships. Fortunately, the aircraft from the remaining carriers were quickly airborne and with the assistance of the naval vessels' anti-aircraft guns drove the attackers away without loss. As the convoy got closer to Sardinia the severity of attacks increased and during the early morning of 12 March a large force of Ju.88s made contact. Over the next two hours over 100 aircraft attacked the convoy, and, although the Royal Navy ships suffered only minor damage, the merchantman *Deucalion* was hit by a bomb and had to be sunk. Having passed Sardinia, sinking the Italian submarine *Cobalto* on the way, the convoy came closer to Sicily which was the home of the *Luftwaffe* anti-shipping squadrons.

The first indication that the forces on Sicily were going to put extreme pressure on the convoy came on 12 August when the Italian submarines *Axum* and *Dessie* fired torpedoes at the ships. The unfortunate cruiser HMS *Nigeria* was the recipient of some torpedoes and the anti-aircraft vessel *Cairo* and the tanker *Ohio* received one each. *Nigeria* was forced to return to Gibralter, *Cairo* had to be sunk as it was too badly damaged to recover but the crew aboard *Ohio* put out the fires allowing the tanker to steam on. The escort was also running light as the major naval units had turned back before reaching the Sicilian Narrows. With the loss of *Nigeria* the convoy commander, Rear Admiral Burroughs, transferred his flag to the destroyer *Ashanti*. The next wave of attackers came from the air as 80 bombers and torpedo aircraft attacked and sank the merchantmen *Empire Home* and *Clan Ferguson* and damaged the *Brisbane Star* although it managed to keep going. By this time the convoy was in complete disarray dodging around the sea trying to avoid the rain of destruction falling from the skies. Eventually, some sort of order was restored before the convoy rounded Cape Bon where a waiting force of German and Italian E-Boats set about attacking the remaining vessels. During this assault a further four merchant ships were sunk and the cruiser *Manchester* was disabled by torpedoes and eventually scuttled. By dawn of 13 August the remaining ships of the convoy were on the last leg towards Malta, this was the signal for the Axis forces on Sicily to increase the strength of their attacks. The first wave of aircraft scored an immediate success when a bomb struck the petrol and ammunition stores on the freighter *Waimarama* which exploded and sank immediately. Yet again the *Ohio* was given special attention, the first attack was by a Junkers Ju.88 which crashed on the foredeck, and then a Ju.87 Stuka crashed on the poop deck. The result of all this aerial violence was that the *Ohio* came to a shuddering halt as the engines stopped. Another merchantman, the *Dorset*, was sunk while the *Brisbane Star* was damaged for a second time which slowed the ship even more. Eventually, the *Port Chalmers, Rochester Castle* and *Melbourne* entered Valetta harbour to great acclaim. The following day saw the still game *Brisbane Star* struggle to safety while the star of the show, the tanker *Ohio* and the precious cargo 10,000 tones of fuel, came in under tow to great acclaim by all those lining the walls of the Grand Harbour. The cost of getting these vital supplies to Malta included an aircraft carrier, two cruisers, a destroyer and nine merchant vessels while a further aircraft carrier, two cruisers and three merchant ships had been badly damaged. In return the Axis forces lost two submarines and at least forty aircraft.

While Pedestal had given Malta a period of relief the situation was still desperate, in fact, in November 1942, the possibility of surrender was discussed by the War Cabinet. However, it was decided to run more convoys to Malta. The first of these was Operation Stoneage which arrived almost unnoticed in November from Port Said while Operation Portcullis arrived in December completely unscathed. As a consequence this was the final run as the future of the island was now secure.

Keeping the attentions of Axis forces away from Malta were the landings in North Africa under the umbrella of Operation Torch which were undertaken in November 1942. This was possible because the war had turned in the favour of the Allies: the Russians had halted the German 6th Army at Stalingrad, the Afrika Corps was in retreat and the aerial war over Germany was being prosecuted by the RAF at night and the USAAF Mighty Eighth during the day. Operation Torch, originally named Operation Gymnast, was instigated by Stalin who pressured the Western Allies to open a second front in order to relieve the pressure on the Russian forces being exerted by the *Wehrmacht* even though the Germans were being fought to a bloody standstill at Stalingrad. It was the estimation of Stalin and the Politburo that the beleaguered Russian Army would collapse quite quickly should nothing be done to divert Hitler and his generals from further assaults upon the Russian homeland. Initially, the American commanders favoured opening the second front in Europe as Operation Sledgehammer however Churchill, at the behest of his General Staff, finally persuaded President Roosevelt that such a course of action at such an early stage in the war would be courting disaster as neither the British nor Americans were fully prepared for such a course of action. Therefore, the Allies switched their attentions to French held North Africa. While attacks on Europe might have forced the Germans to divert some resources away from the Russian front the benefits gained would have been short term. However, The attack on Africa not only tied up the Germans, but gave the Allies the chance finally to gain full control of the Mediterranean, thus neutralising the Italian fleet and the Vichy French fleet tied up at Toulon.

In mid October 1942 HMS *Furious* in company with HMS *Argus* departed British waters in company with the usual selection of support vessels and headed towards the Mediterranean where they would form the Central Naval Task Group. In charge of the entire Torch operation was General Dwight D Eisenhower based in Gibralter while the naval commander of the Allied expeditionary force was Admiral Sir Andrew Cunningham combining this role with that of commander of Force 'H'.

The assault fleets included the Western Task Force whose assigned target was Casablanca. This force was entirely comprised of American units that included the fleet carrier USS *Ranger* plus four escort carriers. The Eastern Task Force was charged with operations in Algiers and was a mixed British and American force. The Centre Task Force was aimed at Oran and was completely British in its make up. Although the American consul, Robert Murphy in Algiers, had undertaken the covert task of gauging the mood of the Vichy French forces it had been deemed advisable that the British forces wear American based Combined Task Force badges while the British aircraft involved would have their roundels replaced by the American star in all positions. The reasons for this were twofold: the first was to dissuade the Americans from shooting down their Allies, an unfortunate foible of that nation, while the other reason had to do with the British attacks on the French Fleet at Oran which might have left a sour taste in the mouths of some French officers. Although the task forces operated as three separate groups the air assets were divided in two, the first was under the command of Air Marshall Sir William Welsh and covered the area east of Cape Tenez in Algeria while the remainder covered the area to the west under the command of Major General Jimmy Dolittle. Operation Torch began on 8 November 1942 with the Centre Task Force which was charged with attacking and capturing three beaches: two west of Oran and one to the east. Covering the landings and providing both air patrols and ground attack support were the Seafires of Nos.880 NAS plus 801 and 807 NAS operating from *Argus* and *Furious*. The first mission for the *Furious* air wing was to attack the French airfield at La Senia. In the early hours of 8 November the Albacores of No. 828 NAS carrying 500 lb bombs took off to hit the aircraft based there. Fighter cover was the task of the Seafires while the escort carrier, HMS *Biter*, provided top cover with the Sea Hurricanes of No.800 NAS. Having completed the attack on La Senia the Seafires turned their attentions to the civil airport at Tafaroui; the home to Dewoitine 520 fighters. Further out to sea the fleet carriers *Formidable* and

Victorious were charged with general air protection of the fleet while the two battleships in the contingent were concerned with both providing shore bombardment if required and to act as a deterrent to the French battle fleet anchored in Toulon and their Italian counterparts tied up in Taranto. In the event the French sailors would scuttle their ships to prevent them falling into German hands while the Italian ships remained in harbour and out of the fighting. Although the British carriers would be in direct control of their own operations, the fleet also included a small liner converted to act as a command vessel with a full range of radio, radar and anti-aircraft guns and a complete command staff and was intended to manage the landings with the authority to divert aerial resources as needed.

The predicted weather for the day of the landings was clear over land while that over the sea was set to be cloudy. With the weather as predicted the first strike sorties were able to launch at sunrise fully briefed on the location of anti-aircraft guns along the coast and around the various strategic targets in the area. The despatch of the strike force at first light was intended to nullify the French aircraft as the light would be in the favour of the British especially as the French aircraft would be caught on the ground. As each carrier despatched its strike package they left with the final parting words to strike hard and strike sure. Eventually the attack group reached its target having been slowed by the sedate speed of the Albacores. The speed of the Fairey biplanes, or their lack of it, meant that the French airfields were alerted enough to launch some of their fighters against the approaching attackers. The escorting fighters took care of the French fighters while the Albacores attacked the airfield. The strike was successful although at least one Allied aircraft was shot down in flames. The Seafires from No.880 NAS would make amends by shooting down a Junkers Ju88. Although the central group landings were successful the post-landings debrief revealed a lot of ineffective management of aerial resources which resulted in crews and aircraft either hanging around fruitlessly waiting for employment or flying sortie after sortie without adequate rest. Fortunately these were the days where lessons were learned and acted upon as failure to do so could result in the loss of life.

The landings on the western beach were delayed slightly by the appearance of a French convoy which caused disruption in the minesweeping operations needed to clear the way to the beach. Unlike later amphibious landings Operation Torch suffered from inadequate pre-landing reconnaissance and consequently the landing craft found their way obstructed by uncharted sand bars which, coupled with a water depth shallower than originally thought, caused some vessels damage as they headed towards the beach. Having overcome the

'Put yer backs into it lads' as a group of naval armourers complete the loading of a torpedo underneath an Albacore based on Malta. (USAAF/NARA)

unmarked sea obstructions the troops were landed safely and established a beach head and captured the surrounding area with little resistance. The same cannot be said of a sub task, Operation Reservist, whose intention was to land at Oran and secure the harbour and prevent the French fleet from interfering with the landings. Unfortunately, the two destroyers carrying the troops were hit by shell fire forcing them to withdraw. This allowed the French fleet to depart the harbour and attempt to disrupt the landings. Thankfully this possibility had been designed into the Operation Torch plan and sufficient naval power was able to drive the fleet either to the bottom of the sea or back into harbour. Oran and its defenders also put up resistance during the first two days of the operation although this was soon broken when their positions were shelled by the heavy guns of the British battleships assigned to Torch. By 9 November the French forces in the Oran area surrendered and negotiations began aimed at integrating these forces into the Allied set-up. These ran into problems from the outset as General Henri Giraud, commander in chief of all French land forces in Africa, was deemed not to have the authority to assume control, also he had opted to remain in Gibralter instead of being in theatre to assume the mantle of leadership. Although not the preferred candidate, Admiral Francois Darlan was put forward as an alternative by Eisenhower as the only option and he was reluctantly supported by Churchill and Roosevelt. With Darlan in place and committed to the Allied cause the Vichy regime continued the use of German laws and concentration camps remained. This state of affairs caused great fury amongst the Free French forces with General Charles de Gaulle leading the opposition. Darlan was murdered in December 1942 and his place was taken by Giraud. In response to these moves Hitler ordered that the Vichy government in France be overseen by the Germans who occupied that section of the country while further reinforcements were diverted to North Africa to resist the Allies' invasion. Pressure was put on Giraud, who was seen as an ineffectual leader, to change the regime in North Africa which eventually led to the French Liberation movement being recognised as the legitimate government with de Gaulle at its head even though he was not too popular with the Allied leaders.

After the invasion the French forces in Tunisia, commanded by General Barre, pulled back to the Algerian border on 10 November leaving the country open to German occupation. For the next four days these forces stayed in camp determined not to take any part in hostilities but General Juin, the Commander, French Forces North Africa, still in Algiers after surrendering the city without fighting, ordered Barre and his men to attack the approaching Germans. Initially Barre remained in quarters but on 18 November he ordered his units to attack the *Wehrmacht* forces. Although equipped with outdated equipment the French Tunisian soldiery presented such a spirited fight that the British were quick to divert more modern weapons to their new Allies. Once the French territory had been secured the 1st Army under the command of Lieutenant General Anderson pushed on towards Tunisia until finally stopped by German forces under the command of General Walther Nehring. Further reinforcements for Nehring came from General Erwin Rommel and his Afrika Korps retreating westwards from Libya. While the 1st Army managed to contain the German forces General Bernard Montgomery was building up the 8th Army, also known as the Desert Rats, to take on these units. Operation Vulcan saw both the 1st and 8th Army begin a massive assault upon their German opponents. Once the air and naval support lines had been severed the overwhelming British assault plus the American forces reaching Bizerte on 6 May which forced the German forces to consider their position. On 13 May 1943 the Axis forces surrendered in their entirety.

The two other fleet carriers, *Formidable* and *Victorious* also deployed as part of Operation Torch. Aboard HMS *Formidable* was No.885 NAS with Seafires while two other squadrons, Nos.888 and 893 NAS, were equipped with Grumman Martlets and No.820 NAS with Fairey Albacores for attack purposes. HMS *Victorious* carried even more aircraft as part of its air wing consisting of No.809 NAS with Fulmars, No.882 NAS with Grumman Martlets, Nos.818 and 832 NAS with Albacores and No.884 NAS with Seafires. As both of these vessels were of a more modern build their access lifts were smaller than those of *Furious* and *Argus* therefore the Seafires had to be carried permanently on deck because these early versions did not have folding wings and so had to be parked on the flight deck outriggers. In addition to the flying examples each of these carriers carried a further half dozen aircraft in crated form which were off loaded at North Front, Gibralter, as the fleet passed through the straits. Further Seafires in crates were also carried aboard the escort carrier *Dasher*.

While the military and political repercussions continued to settle down it was the performance of these early Seafires that gave cause for concern. Just prior to taking part in Operation Torch, HMS *Furious* had undertaken the final Operation Train run which meant off loading some of her air wing which were replaced by 31 Spitfires VCs required to reinforce the Malta air defence forces. Having dispensed with its much needed load on the Grand Harbour dockside HMS *Furious* began the return journey to Gibralter. En route the carrier was attacked by a Junkers Ju88 whose arrival completely confused the standing fighter patrol as the

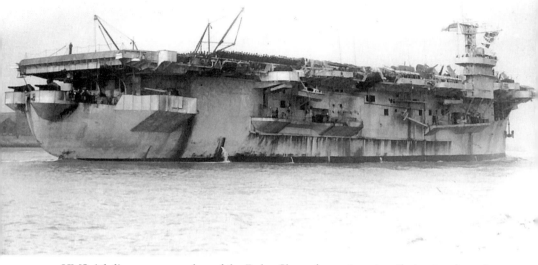

HMS *Atheling* was a member of the Ruler Class of escort carriers that entered service in October 1943 later being allocated to the BPF as a fleet training carrier. The vessel was returned to the USN in 1946 being sold on for conversion as a merchantman. (BBA Collection)

wing man had already landed aboard *Furious* while the patrol leader was in the landing circuit. After the Ju88 had dropped its bombs, which fortunately missed the carrier, the sole airborne aircraft gave chase. However, the 30 gallon ventral overload tank would not release and so, even with the throttle wide open, a top speed of only 310 mph could be achieved which was not quite enough to overtake the *Luftwaffe* attacker. Even so, the pilot opened fire causing some damage to the Junkers' fuselage. A further Ju88 attack took place later that day, yet again the defending Seafires failed to get within adequate range of the attacker.

Now established in North Africa the Allies turned their attention to what was called the soft underbelly of Europe: Italy. While the Italian military was the butt of much humour in reality their lack of enthusiasm for warlike adventures stemmed more from their leaders alliance with Hitler than from any lack of courage. It was against this background that the invasion of Sicily was planned. Given that the chosen target was an island it came as no surprise to find that the whole invasion was amphibious in nature. The British carriers assigned to this operation, Operation Husky, were HMS *Formidable* and *Indomitable* both part of

Force 'H'. Aboard *Formidable* was No.885 NAS flying Seafires while the remainder of the air wing comprised Nos.888 and 893 NAS with Grumman Martlets while the strike complement was provided by No.820 NAS with Fairey Albacores. In contrast to *Formidable* HMS *Indomitable* had a full complement of Seafires with Nos.807, 880 and 899 NAS while the strike side was covered by No.817 NAS with Albacores.

Operation Husky began on the night of 9-10 July 1943 in the face of a strong wind. The wind had both positive and negative effects. The negative was that many of the airborne troops landed in the wrong places, however the positive effect was that the attacks had an element of surprise which saw the British Forces landing almost unopposed throughout the entire campaign, even the Americans who met some resistance, achieved their goals with less trouble than expected. The entire campaign was completed by 17 August and was seen as an emphatic Allied victory. Although it was seen as a great success Operation Husky revealed that further training and co-operation was needed to ensure that all aspects of an Allied battle plan worked correctly as two failings were noted: the first was that the management of airborne drop operations needed better co-ordination to prevent misdrops of paratroops which increased casualties, and the second was the initial lack of air support that allowed the Axis forces to withdraw large amounts of men, vehicles and stores virtually unopposed.

The invasion of Salerno was another operation whose roots were set in disagreement amongst the Allies. The main proposer of this attack was Winston Churchill who was aware that the desired invasion of northern Europe initially pencilled in for 1943 was not a viable option as the Axis forces had not fragmented enough to weaken their grip on France. Churchill also wanted to build on the Sicily success and the growing dissatisfaction amongst the Italian people for the war in general and Mussolini in particular. Opposing Churchill was General George Marshall, the American commander, whose stance was to wait until the conditions were right to invade France and not to commit major forces on operations prior to that event. Eventually, Churchill would sway the Generals opinion pointing out successfully that invading Italy would force the Germans to reinforce that area using forces withdrawn from other fronts especially as their Italian Allies were proving less than enthusiastic about fighting the Allies. Churchill also pointed out that removing Italy from the Axis pack would negate the threat of the Italian navy and air force that in turn would allow convoys to move through the Mediterranean virtually unopposed. A further gain was that supply convoys could reach southern Russia thus cutting the number of dangerous Arctic convoys needed to supply the soviets.

The first move in this invasion was Operation Baytown was launched on 3 September and involved British 8th Army units which were shipped from the Port of Messina on Sicily directly across the Straits of Messina to Calabria on the toe of Italy. The entire landing was unopposed and had already been declared a waste of time by General Montgomery. Thus the 8th Army units were faced with making their way with greatest speed towards Salerno to aid the main invasion force. Alongside Baytown the US Army also launched Operation Giant II the intention of which was to drop the 82nd Airborne Division close to Rome. The first aircraft had already taken off when the operation was cancelled as received intelligence had revealed that the Germans had added two front-line regiments to the defence of Rome effectively replacing the previously incumbent Italian units.

The Salerno phase began on 9 September. By way of a diversion tactic a full blown attack upon Taranto, codenamed Operation Slapstick, was launched. However, although numerous troops and support units were deployed by both the British and Americans during the invasion of Salerno the opening phases of the attack were badly planned, the major omission being a full scale naval bombardment to soften up the Axis defences. Such a diversion from accepted tactics allowed the Germans, under the command of Admiral Kesselring, to place greater strength in areas where a possible invasion could take place. While the Italian surrender, which took place on 8 September, was seen as a bonus it would be some time before any of these units would be available for the Allied cause. Although the Germans put up a stout resistance, almost pushing the Allies back into the sea at one point, the determination of the Allies to succeed pushed back and secured the beachhead which in turn allowed the invasion of Italy to continue.

The seagoing part of the Salerno invasion was codenamed Operation Avalanche. Taking place between 9-12 September 1943 the operation involved two fleet carriers, *Illustrious* and *Formidable*, the aircraft support and repair vessel, *Unicorn*, plus the escort carriers *Attacker*, *Battler*, *Hunter* and *Stalker*. Aboard *Illustrious* was No.894 NAS plus Nos.878 and 890 NAS with Grumman Mallards and No.810 NAS with Barracudas while *Formidable* still carried its original air wing. Aboard HMS *Unicorn* were Nos 809, 887 and 897 NAS with Seafires plus No.818 Flight with Swordfish. Further aircraft came from *Formidable* which released some aircraft and crews from Nos.888 and 893 NAS with Martlets while *Illustrious* sent some Seafires from No.894 NAS. On board the escort vessels were Nos 879 and 886 NAS with Seafires flying from HMS *Attacker*, while *Battler* carried Nos 807 and 808 NAS equipped with Seafires. Nos 899 NAS plus 834 Fighter Flight and their Seafires were

Pictured flying over Britain is Grumman Martlet AL257 that was later assigned to No. 804 NAS based at RNAS Hatston in the Orkneys. (Will Blunt Collection)

aboard *Hunter* and No. 880 NAS with No. 833 Fighter Flight was aboard HMS *Stalker* also with Seafires. The carrier fleet was divided into two distinct groups, the fleet carriers were designated Force 'H' commanded by Rear Admiral C Moody, Rear Admiral Aircraft Carriers, while the remainder were designated Force 'V' the commander of which was Rear Admiral Sir Philip Vian KCB flying his flag aboard the anti-aircraft cruiser HMS *Euryalus.*

Having departed the Clyde the escort carriers, *Attacker, Battler, Hunter* and *Stalker* arrived off Gibralter on 9 August. Here their fighter complements were embarked after which they joined up with HMS *Unicorn* to conduct training exercises off Gibralter; the force sailing for Malta via Oran. It was during this period that doubts were raised about the standard of training given to pilots joining the rapidly expanding air arm especially as this transit voyage was the only time available for deck landing practice. While Force 'H' was charged with providing general air cover around the entire British part of the invasion fleet Force 'V' was tasked with providing close-in air support at both low and medium levels. When Forces 'H' and 'V' departed Malta on 8 September they made their own way towards Salerno. In transit Force 'H' was attacked by German torpedo bombers over the night of 8-9 September. During the extensive anti-aircraft defence the guns of HMS *Formidable* caused the accidental write off of one of No.885 NAS Seafires which was badly damaged by gun blast as it sat on an outrigger. This was the only damage sustained during this attack as the bombers missed their targets. The initial fighter patrols departed just before daybreak on 9 September, the last aircraft landing more than 13 hours later as dusk was falling. The first patrols had been launched by *Unicorn* and their task was to provide high level air patrols to compensate for the lack of land-based fighter cover. Further fighters were launched as the sun rose and their task was low level patrols in support of North American A-36A Avengers, the ground attack version of the P-51 Mustang, which, in turn, were tasked with attacking ground targets. The Mustangs were under the control of USS *Palomares* that was acting as the fighter-direction ship.

The primary airbases available to the Allies and able to provide the required air cover for Operation Avalanche were those on the newly captured island of Sicily although their use meant that the aircraft despatched to patrol the beachhead were forced to fly at least 200 miles in each direction which reduced their time on station. Such a transit time meant that the maximum number of aircraft available on station would number no more than 36 which also meant that the seaborne aircraft were vital for a successful conclusion to the assault. The location of the carrier groups no more than 30 miles offshore meant that the short range Seafires could provide at least one hour of patrol time each. Another factor that would improve the Allies chances of success was the reduction in Axis air strength as the losses sustained during the earlier Tunisian and Sicilian campaigns could not be replaced as every available aircraft and pilot was needed to combat the burgeoning Russian effort on the Eastern Front. Nevertheless, even with the lack of Italian air support the *Luftwaffe* would throw all their resources into repelling the invaders and Force 'H' experienced a torpedo attack on the night of 9 September and a further attack took place just after dawn. These attacks were unsuccessful as the handful of attacking Junkers Ju88s were intercepted by a Seafire patrol which forced the bombers to jettison their bombs without the fighters firing a shot. This would be one of the few attacks made by bombers as the greater number would be carried out by fighters such as the FW190 and Me109 acting as fighter bombers coming in fast and at low level. One of the larger fighter bomber raids would occur close to midday when at least a dozen aircraft were spotted travelling in from the north, but once again the Seafire patrols pounced and chased them away. While the fighters were managing to keep the Axis air forces at bay things were being complicated by the geography of the area. At the rear of the beaches and to the north was high ground that created extreme clutter on the fleets' radar screens thereby making the detection of enemy aircraft extremely difficult. The result of these difficulties was that the first indications of an attack was the aircraft breaking over the beaches. In an effort to counter this problem fighter patrols originally tasked for duty over Capri were diverted to act as airborne warning aircraft. At the end of a frantic day carrier Force 'V' had completed 265 sorties although the pilots were slightly disappointed in that having intercepted many enemy aircraft they had not managed to shoot down or damage any of them. During this first day of operations the Axis ground forces had put up a greater resistance than expected and thus one of the primary targets, Montecorinvo airfield, was still the scene of intensive fighting. As this was a key element for supporting the Allied ground forces the failure to capture it meant that the carrier fleet would be required for further air support missions instead of the single day originally planned. As the possibility of this had been foreseen extra supplies and stores had been carried for another day of intensive operations. To that end the carrier force was tasked with nearly 200 extra sorties. However, this proved be difficult as many of the Seafires had been damaged while landing aboard the smaller escort carriers thereby reducing the available aircraft. Even with this reduction the fighter force managed to launch 232 sorties on 10 September which was gratefully received by the area commanders as land-based fighter cover had been further reduced due to the lack of serviceable aircraft.

As the sun set on 10 September the airfield at Montecorinvo was in Allied hands although it was dangerous to use as artillery from both sides was roaring overhead. Even so two Seafires had made diversionary landings in between the barrages, these aircraft had been part of a group of four sent as replacements from Sicily and had not been able to find the carriers in the haze although the following pair did manage to reach the ships. Although Montecorinvo was still unusable a division of US Army engineers had managed to lay a 1,000 yard runway on a tomato growing estate near Paestum, although it would take until 12 September before it was ready for daytime use. Against this scenario Rear Admiral Vian conceded that the fighter force would have to remain in operation even though stores and ammunition were running low. Even more worrying was the lack of available Seafires as some were still being lost to landing accidents. While the engineers worked around the clock to repair as many aircraft as possible the credible fighter force was now at its workable minimum. In real numbers this meant that Force 'V' had 39 Seafires ready for the third day of operations against which they were scheduled to fly 130 missions: in the event the final total for the day was 160. During these sorties the fighters reported fewer encounters with German fighters although they did meet a new foe: Dornier Do217 bombers from KG100

The arrival of the Grumman Avenger gave the Fleet Air Arm a quantum leap in attack capability. Not only could the Avenger tote a good load of bombs, rockets or a torpedo, the aircraft also had a further role later in its career as an airborne early warning platform. (Will Blunt Collection)

equipped with radio guided bombs. The primary mission of these aircraft was to attack the gunfire support ships busily shelling the German positions. Dilution of their effect would mean that the single Panzer and two infantry divisions mounting a counter attack might manage to push the Allied forces back into the sea. As the Dorniers were flown by experienced crews they managed to evade the defending fighters long enough to launch their bombs which caused damage to some of the ships although not enough to divert them from their purpose, this was in total contrast to earlier that month when the same German unit had successfully sunk the Italian battleship *Roma* just after it had surrendered.

On 11 September, at dusk, Force 'H' was withdrawn from the war zone as their primary purpose had ended when the Italian fleet had surrendered, although they had exercised their secondary role of providing reinforcing air power to the smaller carriers. A total of 16 fighters were provided for support purposes and they flew patrols from dawn to dusk. Only one interception was made, by a patrol of Grumman Martlets, which successfully downed a Fiat RS.14 float plane. As concerns grew about the vulnerability of these large carriers to both U Boats and air attacks their departure from the area was seen as a necessity.

On 12 September operational flying resumed as soon as dawn started breaking, although patrol activity was limited to three sorties as the emergency strip at Paestum was declared ready for operations from mid-day. With all the patrolling aircraft safely back on their carriers the engineering parties worked hard to prepare as many aircraft as possible for use ashore because the air force fighters would not arrive from Sicily for a couple of days. A total of 26 Seafires was despatched to Paestum and all aircraft landed safely. The first operation carried out that day involved all the aircraft and was a tactical reconnaissance sweep for a reported German counter attack although the report proved to be false. On the following day a patrol launched at dawn consisted of 12 aircraft operating at medium altitude and supported by a further four flying as top cover. During these sortie the Seafires were bounced by a pair of USAAF A-36As one of which was promptly shot down before the other was identified as friendly. The next sortie was undertaken in the early afternoon and utilised twenty of the available Seafires. When they returned to Paestum they found the airstrip surrounds were overrun by nearly 100 Curtiss P-40 Warhawks. Obviously, operating in these conditions was impossible and, therefore, the Seafires decamped to Asa where they joined up with No.324 Wing RAF and gained vastly improved support as this wing was equipped with Spitfires. Only one further patrol was flown that day and involved eight aircraft as the others were receiving much needed attention from the RAF Servicing Commando of No.324 Wing. The naval contingent would fly only one sortie on 14 September and the eight aircraft involved took off at dawn. Upon returning to base the contingent was stood down for 24 hours as the RAF assumed responsibility for fighter patrols. On 15 September the Seafires departed to rejoin their respective carriers routeing via Falcone and Bizerta. During their sojourn on dry land the Seafires had flown 56 missions without loss to enemy action.

This was the last major invasion that would feature the fleet carriers as they were replaced by the smaller escort carriers and the bigger ships found themselves involved in operations off the Norwegian coast before decamping to the Indian Ocean finally ending up in the Far East as part of the British Pacific Fleet. In comparison to previous events this period was relatively quiet the naval forces being involved with convoy escort work. This was made possible as the French fleet had been scuppered, the Italian fleet, that which survived, was now operating as part of the Allied forces. The German forces had their own problems as the Allies were pushing them back up the Italian mainland and consequently no

German naval or air forces were available to interfere with the southern Russian convoys or those convoys running through to Gibralter and Malta.

The next major operation that would involve naval forces in the Mediterranean was Operation Dragoon, this was seen as a necessary adjunct to the success of Operation Cobra, the breakout from the Normandy beachhead. Also, the armies fighting through Italy had successfully captured Rome and were continuing their push northwards. Winston Churchill had originally argued against this course preferring to direct forces to the Balkans area in order to deprive the Germans of much needed oil supplies and to deter the Red Army from holding the area once the fighting had ceased. The Prime Minister was eventually persuaded that invading southern France was the better option as the 15th Army Air Force would take care of the Balkan oil supplies although this did not stop the Soviets from dominating the region after the war.

Operation Dragoon would utilise a mix of Free French troops and Americans drawn from the US 6th Army Group. The intended invasion area was intended to be Toulon, Marseille and St Tropez. Start date was set to be 15 August 1944 and involved the Royal Navy escort carriers HMS *Attacker* with No.879 NAS with Seafires, *Emperor* with No.800 NAS flying Hellcats, *Hunter* with No.807 NAS with Seafires, *Khedive* and its Seafires of No.899 NAS, *Pursuer* with No.881 NAS equipped with Grumman Wildcats, *Searcher* operating an enlarged No.882 NAS with Wildcats while the final ship was HMS *Stalker* flying the Seafires of No.809 NAS. All of these vessels were part of Task Force 88 under the command of Rear Admiral Thomas Troutbridge flying his flag aboard the command cruiser HMS *Royalist*. For the purposes of the invasion the force was split into two sections, TF.88.2 comprised *Hunter* and *Stalker* in company with the US Navy escort carriers *Tulagi* and *Kasaan Bay* while TF.88.1 comprised *Attacker, Khedive*, *Emperor*, *Pursuer* and *Searcher*. Operation Dragoon was an outstanding success as French Resistance fighters had already caused chaos in the occupying German forces that had been weakened by the diversion of troops to the Normandy battlefront. After the usual heavy naval bombardment the assault went ahead as planned. As the troops hit the beaches the Resistance fighters increased their attacks on the Germans and their lines of communication which allowed the invaders to cover 20 miles almost unopposed during the first 24 hours. By mid September the Operation Dragoon forces had met up with their Normandy compatriots and their continued success was helped by a mass uprising by the French Resistance in Paris.

At the conclusion of Operation Dragoon the escort carriers of Task Force 88 returned to Alexandria for re-storing and repairs arriving there

While the Avenger gave the Fleet Air Arm an attacking edge the Fairey Firefly presented the FAA with an excellent long-range fleet fighter that would see further service after the War. (Will Blunt Collection)

at the beginning of September 1944. Their next task, starting on 25 September, was to undertake offensive operations, codenamed Outing, Cablegram and Contempt, against the German garrisons in the Aegean Sea and the Dodecanese Islands. The premise behind these operations was that cutting off the supplies to these mainly island garrisons and softening them up with intensive air strikes would hasten their surrender. As before, the seven escort carriers undertook these operations with no losses reported. Once the strikes were well underway HMS *Attacker* in company with *Emperor* was detached on 13 October for Operation *Manna*: the occupation of Athens. At the conclusion of these operations the carrier force returned to Alexandria after flying over 1,500 fighter missions with minimal losses. As these operations had the desired effect it was decided that these carriers could be better employed elsewhere, consequently *Attacker* returned to the UK for modifications and on 7 December the carrier entered the docks in Taranto for a refit. Repaired and reconditioned *Attacker* departed from the Mediterranean theatre, transiting via the Suez canal, to join the East India Fleet at Trincomalee. HMS *Emperor* would proceed directly to the UK at the end of November 1944 for a much needed refit at Newport. The refurbished carrier departed Newport in March 1945 and sailed to join the East India Fleet (EIF). HMS *Hunter* also returned to Britain for a refit and sailed to join the EIF at the end of November 1944. HMS *Khedive* also joined the EIF in January 1945 having sailed to London in October 1944 for a refit. HMS *Pursuer,* having completed its work in the Mediterranean, returned to Britain to rejoin the Home Fleet receiving No.881 NAS and its Wildcats in the process. On 12 November the carrier took part in strikes on Narvik after which she returned to the Clyde for defect repairs. However, having escorted convoy UC.48B, the carrier later entered the dockyard at Norfolk ,Virginia, for repairs. On 31 March 1945 *Pursuer* embarked No.898 NAS and its Hellcats proceeding to join the EIF. HMS *Searcher* was delayed joining the EIF until the beginning of May 1945 because of a refit at Clyde in October 1944, having sailed via Gibralter and Belfast. This refit was completed in January 1945 and *Searcher* undertook a work-up with No.882 NAS aboard. After the work-up was complete the carrier joined the Home Fleet at Scapa Flow where No.746A NAS was embarked complete with its night fighter Fireflies. On 19 March *Searcher* undertook anti-shipping operations off the Norwegian coast which kept the carrier and its escorts employed until May 1945, having assisted in the relief of Copenhagen along the way. HMS *Stalker* would also return to Britain at the end of October 1944 calling in at Gibralter en route. After a month in Devonport the carrier departed again for Gibralter with No.809 NAS and its Seafires aboard entering the dock for refit. This was completed by the end of February 1945 and *Stalker* sailed to join the EIF via the Suez Canal.

Chapter 4

Prosecuting the War in India and the Far East

After Operation Avalanche had been completed attention turned towards the Far East. While the American forces were beginning their assault on the Japanese held territories the Royal Navy turned its attention towards the Indian Ocean where the Japanese were camped in Burma and had been threatening India with invasion. The first carrier to be allocated to No.1 Aircraft Carrier Squadron of the East India Fleet was HMS *Battler* which arrived in Bombay on 22 September 1943 with No.834 NAS flying a composite mix of Seafires, Swordfish and Wildcats. After working-up *Battler* spent from November 1943 to March 1944 escorting convoys in and out of Bombay. A refit in March 1944 in Durban was followed by a work-up period by both the ship and aircraft before joining convoy CM.53 in June, although for this voyage the fighters were left ashore and the only aircraft aboard were the Swordfish which were employed for anti-submarine duties. The return voyage was undertaken during the following month covering convoy KR.11. Then *Battler* carried out anti-submarine patrols in the Colombo area. This task kept the *Battler* fully employed until it was re-roled as a ferry carrier for the East Indies Fleet in November 1944. This task only lasted until the following month when it was ordered back to Britain, although this was via the scenic route calling at ports in Australia and the United States before reaching colder waters in March 1945. Allocated to Western Approaches Command *Battler* was used as a deck landing trainer in the Clyde until the end of January 1946 when the vessel was returned to American control.

The first fleet carrier to join the EIF was HMS *Illustrious* which arrived in Trincomalee, Ceylon, having departed the Clyde in January 1944. On board *Illustrious* were two squadrons of Barracudas, Nos.810 and 847 NAS, No.21 Torpedo Bomber Reconnaissance Wing and the Vought Corsairs of No.15 Naval Fighter Wing consisting of Nos.1830 and 1837 NAS which contrasted to the August 1943 air wing that had flown Martlets, Seafires and a lone Barracuda squadron. By the end of January *Illustrious* was working-up, both the ship and its air wing, for service in

With wheels and debris scattering everywhere this Seafire III heads for the barrier aboard HMS *Indefatigable*. Close observation reveals that the arrestor hook has failed to lower. (Rick Harding Collection)

the Far East. The work-up period ended in early March 1944 when *Illustrious* undertook her first mission: an intensive sea and air sweep on the look-out for Imperial Japanese Navy (IJN) cruisers that had been reported as operating the area. Returning to Trincomalee the carrier was replenished prior to setting out again, this time as part of a larger task force in company with the USN carrier USS *Saratoga* and 24 other vessels. The purpose of this sortie was to attack targets in Sabang, Sumatra. At the completion of this sweep *Illustrious* returned to Ceylon where the Barracudas were landed and replaced by the Grumman Avengers of Nos.832 and 851 NAS. Illustrious would meet up with *Saratoga* again on 17 May, both carriers attacking the oil refineries at Soerabaya, Java, followed by replenishment in Exmouth Gulf, Australia.

As the situation changed in the Atlantic and Mediterranean *Illustrious* was sent further company in the form of the escort carrier HMS *Atheling*. Aboard this ship were Nos.822 and 823 NAS flying Barracudas and Nos.1837 and 1838 NAS equipped with Vought Corsairs, although these units were actually in transit to HMS *Unicorn*. The carrier joined No.1 Aircraft Carrier Squadron(ACS) becoming part of convoy KMF.29A for the voyage. In March 1944 *Atheling* passed through the Suez Canal joining convoy AJ.2 which sailed from Aden to Colombo. Further convoys followed before the carrier returned to Colombo where the designated fighter wing, consisting of No.889 NAS with Seafires and No.890 NAS with Wildcats, was embarked. *Atheling's* aircraft were the first Seafire IIIs (taken from the first production batch) to serve outside Britain. The carrier was also blessed with pilots from No.834 Fighter Flight whose previous escort carrier experience made it easier for the entire pilot cadre to deal with the problems associated with operating off a small deck. The work-up was completed quickly and *Atheling* became available to take part in Operation Councillor in concert with the fleet carrier *Illustrious*. The object of this mission was to act as a diversion in the Indian Ocean in order to draw in the Japanese forces while the US forces attacked their positions in the Marianas. However, the Japanese were very aware of the Americans plans and therefore, although the British vessels created a nuisance of themselves 200 miles east of Sabang, they were completely ignored. *Atheling* would follow up this masquerade by providing combat air patrols over the Fleet Oilers and HMS *Illustrious* on 23 June. After refuelling *Illustrious* launched 51 aircraft for attacks on Port Blair in the Andaman Islands. It was during this operation that tragedy struck when the commander of the Seafire squadron, Lt Cdr F A J Pennington RNZVNR, collided with his wingman and both were killed. A further accident occurred six days later when a landing Seafire completely missed the arrestor wires ploughing into another aircraft killing two pilots and three of the deck party. With No.889 NAS reduced to six pilots and five aircraft, and *Atheling* being too slow to keep up with the main fleet, it was decided that the squadrons should be reassigned and the carrier was re-roled. Thus at the completion of this operation *Atheling* became a trade protection carrier which meant losing her fighters which were replaced by Swordfish from No.818 NAS. After trade protection duties *Atheling* was reassigned again as a fleet train ferry carrier operating in support of the British element of the American led Task Force 57.

To replace *Atheling* the Home Fleet released the fleet carrier HMS *Indefatigable* which was allocated to the British Pacific Fleet in November 1944. On 19 November the vessel departed Portsmouth en route to the Far East. On board were No.24 Fighter Wing comprising Nos.887 and 894 NAS equipped with Seafires while the strike element was provided by No1770 NAS with Fireflies and No.820 NAS with Avengers. The carrier arrived off Colombo on 10 December and became part of No.1 Aircraft Carrier Squadron, British Pacific Fleet. After acclimatisation training, the carrier was declared ready for service and her first mission was Operation Lentil. Operating in conjunction with HMS *Victorious* both air wings mounted strikes on the oil refineries at Pangkalan, Brandan and Sumatra. During strike operations combat air patrols were provided by the Seafires after which they also undertook early morning reconnaissance flights and fleet anti-submarine patrols. Originally this latter role had been the province of multi-seat aircraft, however, their ability to carry out strike duties meant that they were diverted away for this role while the low-level air patrols were better suited for the Seafires. Unfortunately for the Seafire patrols no submarines were ever spotted during these sorties and no attacks were ever made on British aircraft carriers by the IJN.

Whilst attacking the Japanese military forces captured the headlines it was the less obvious targets that the strategic planners had identified as crucial to defeating the enemy. Supply lines and their cargoes were top of the list for destruction, and fuel supplies even more so. Taking this phase of the war to Japan was the task assigned to the 1st ACS whose first sorties were launched on 24 January 1945 as part of Operation Meridian, aircraft being drawn from the carriers *Illustrious, Indefatigable, Indomitable* and *Victorious*, and the force was commanded by Rear Admiral Sir Philip Vian whose flag was aboard *Indomitable*. As the launch co-ordinates for these strikes was off the south-west coast of Sumatra the transit time was used for air defence exercises and general training. The Seafires acted as the fleet defence fighters but they also performed as attackers so that all aspects of fleet defence and attack were given a thorough workout. However, problems were experienced with the weather, especially the rain which managed to penetrate aircraft access panels and cause havoc with the delicate equipment within. The first Seafires were launched by *Indefatigable* at 06.30 hrs to provide standing air patrols and anti-submarine patrols around the fleet. No.24 NAW had a total of 48 Seafires available for this task and the entire force was used for seven hours to provide much needed cover. Given that the sea state was still rough and the carrier decks were pitching quite violently at times and the heavy swell also caused a slight corkscrewing effect which necessitated the air control batsman having to wave-off approach after approach it was gratifying to all involved that fighter losses on landing were kept to minimum. The targets for the strike aircraft were the refineries and storage depots at Pladjoe which dealt with aviation fuel and were designated valuable targets. The strike on the refinery resulted in its destruction and the depletion of the Japanese fuel supplies which in turn reduced their capability to provide air defence over much of the increasingly shaky empire.

Five days later the carrier group was in action again, this time the target was the refinery at Soengi Gerong: the second refinery complex in

Captured on film just as it hits the barrier this Seafire III of the 3rd Naval Fighter Wing has started to shred its propeller. The landing has been a hard one as the tail wheel has already sheared off and the arrestor hook forced back into its recess. (Ray Sturtivant)

the Palembang group. It had been intended to follow up the first strike against Pladjoe quickly, however the weather had deteriorated further and the heavy swells, sweeping rain and problems with replenishment equipment meant that the fleet was unable to launch their attacks as soon as planned. Just after a very early breakfast aboard *Indefatigable* the first Seafires were launched to provide patrol coverage, the carrier having adequate aircraft available for the period of the operation. Having successfully destroyed one Japanese refinery and storage complex with little opposition it came as no surprise when counter attacks were launched by the Imperial Japanese Air Force(IJAF). Having detected the British carrier force by aerial reconnaissance, further sorties were despatched to shadow the carriers and assist in the co-ordination of the aerial reprisal. *Indefatigable's* radar had first detected an incoming intruder at 07.40 hours although the vectored aircraft had failed to engage. Having completed their patrol the first group of fighters landed on *Indefatigable* at 08.25 hours having been replaced for the next round by a similar number of aircraft. At 09.13 hours an incoming contact was reported travelling fast. The sector was patrolled by No.887 NAS and they were vectored to the area but failed to make contact. However, thirty minutes later the

This Seafire III of No.807 Sqdn noses over amidst a pile of spinning debris aboard the escort carrier HMS *Hunter*. The pilot is still sitting stunned in his cockpit awaiting rescue. (Rick Harding Collection)

same section spotted a Ki 46 Dinah travelling fast over the fleet at 15,000 ft undertaking reconnaissance. Under normal circumstances the Seafire would struggle to catch an aircraft such as the Ki 46 but the Japanese pilot made a slight error of judgement by making a shallow turn just as the Seafires reached altitude. Sub Lt Kernahan was quick to appraise the situation and let loose a long burst from his guns and the Dinah went spiralling down in flames a few minutes later. Having scored the first success for No.24 NAW the patrol returned to *Indefatigable* passing their replacements on the way. As activity by the IJAF was increasing, the third patrol of the day was larger, consisting of ten aircraft. For most of their patrol this flight spent much of its time chasing detected targets but most of these turned out to be aircraft of the strike force returning to their respective carriers. These fruitless diversions meant that this patrol was running out of fuel near the end of their airborne time. Realising this, and the increased vulnerability of the carriers during aircraft recovery, a further four Seafires were launched as reinforcement. However the airborne strength of 17 aircraft was misleading as six were desperately short of fuel while two others were experiencing radio problems. Into this situation at 11.47 hours flew a mixed force of Ki21 'Sally' and Ki48 'Lily' bombers en route to the fleet. These seven aircraft were later discovered to be suicide aircraft. The No.887 NAS flight was the first to attack the incoming bombers and managed to shoot down a Ki 21 although return fire from the Japanese bomber caused severe damage to the attacking Seafire and left the pilot with no option but to abandon it. By the time the rest of the flight began their attacks the Japanese force had entered the Gun Defence Zone which meant that the Seafire pilots were chasing their targets through a hail of anti-aircraft fire. Either the British pilots were lucky or the air defence was not as tight as expected, because one of the defending Hellcats managed to shoot down another bomber while the remainder were followed by the Seafires. Overall this was a most successful day for No.24 NAW as everything had gone according to plan. Two further strikes had been planned on other targets in the Netherlands East Indies, however because of the lack of ships' fuel and the lack of oilers in the vicinity the oil refineries were left alone for the time being. The fleet headed for Freemantle in Western Australia for replenishment before continuing to Sydney to prepare for operations with Task Force 57 in the Pacific.

While the fleet carriers were in Australian waters preparing for the main strikes against Japan another carrier force was preparing to carry the war to Japan in the Indian Ocean. The vessels chosen for this task force were HMSs *Attacker, Emperor, Empress, Hunter, Khedive* and *Stalker*, all six vessels were allocated to No.21 ACS of the East Indian Fleet. HMS *Attacker* had completed its refit at Taranto in December 1944 and sailed to Trincomalee on 1 April 1945 with No.879 NAS with Seafires aboard. Departing slightly earlier from Britain was *Emperor* which arrived off Ceylon at the end of March 1945 with No.800 NAS flying Hellcats assigned to long range escort duties. HMS *Empress* was another Hellcat carrier, these being No.888 NAS flying the reconnaissance version of the Hellcat with a fighter flight from No.804 NAS for escort duties. Completing the carrier's complement was No.845 NAS with Avengers. The carrier arrived off Ceylon in February 1945. HMS *Hunter* was the second carrier that carried Seafires (No.807 NAS). *Hunter* had been refitted in Malta in December 1944 arriving at Trincomalee in February 1945. HMS *Khedive* was the first carrier to arrive for No.21 ACS at the beginning of February 1945 carrying the Hellcats of No.808 NAS. Not long after *Khedive* arrived off Ceylon HMS *Stalker* turned up with No.809 NAS flying Seafires.

The first combat operation for the carriers of No.21 ACS was Operation Sunfish the allocated carriers being *Emperor* and *Khedive*. The purpose of the mission was to undertake photo reconnaissance of Port Swettenham then carry out a strike on Emmahaven. The aircraft allocated for the mission were the Hellcats of Nos.800 and 808 NAS plus the Avengers of No.845 NAS. Operation Sunfish was carried out on 4 April and quickly followed by Operation Dracula which involved strikes on Rangoon and the Tenasserim coast. The entire force was commanded by Rear Admiral A W La T. Bisset whose flag was aboard the command cruiser HMS *Royalist*. As much of the flying was to be done over water a Supermarine Walrus amphibian from No.1770 NAS was supplied for search and rescue duties. The fleet departed from Akyah on 21 April in company with the assault convoys, the plan being that the attack would take place nine days later. The total aerial strength aboard the carriers consisted of 44 Hellcats and 54 Seafires.

In the early hours of the following morning Operation Dracula began. Poised to strike a decisive blow against the Japanese the carrier force pilots were slightly disheartened to find the defensive resistance around Rangoon was almost negligible as the Japanese forces were in the process of pulling out. For the strike pilots this meant unopposed bomb runs against the remaining anti-aircraft batteries and the coastal defence batteries near Thakutpin. All eight bombs dropped hit their targets. Supporting the four fighter-bomber attacks were 36 air patrols and tactical reconnaissance sorties which drew no enemy fighters while the reconnaissance revealed nothing of interest.

The monsoon conditions returned in force the following day which kept all the aircraft aboard their carriers. A short clearance in the weather the following day allowed a few missions to be flown, however the monsoon weather returned later that day. As the forecast for the next few days was more of the same the decision was made to withdraw No.21 ACS, especially as the carrier group had completed its tasks on the first day. So that the carriers could be better utilised they redeployed off the coast of Tenasserim looking for better weather and targets. Arriving off the coast during the morning of 5 May the carriers soon had combat air patrols in operation while a flight of six Seafires was launched with the brief of looking for inshore shipping targets. Once the *Stalker* aircraft had completed their sweep they returned to the fleet passing a dozen Seafires from *Hunter* also engaged in the same task. The *Hunter* strike force was obviously more confident in finding trade as each aircraft carried a bomb on the centreline. Having swept the area and finding nothing to attack the Seafires were left with no option but to jettison their bombs before returning to the carrier. There was a small sign of resistance as one Seafire

With the escort carrier HMS *Stalker* in the background HMS *Hunter* prepares to anchor off Singapore. The leading aircraft belongs to Lt Cdr Baldwin and has had its camouflage scheme removed. Replacing it was a silver finish with black SEAC bands and anti dazzle panel. The aircraft is NN300. (Rick Harding Collection)

from No.807 NAS suffered slight shell damage from anti-aircraft fire while passing over the coast. On 6 May the carrier group once again launched strike aircraft and escorting fighters. The bomb carriers were Grumman Hellcats and the Seafires provided fighter cover. Unlike the previous day's sweeps this sortie had a definite target: Port Victoria. While the Hellcats dropped their bombs on the port facilities and sank a barge the Seafire pilots strafed any targets in the area. While *Stalker* provided the roving strike flight HMS *Hunter* provided the combat air patrol over the carriers, although they were diverted later in the day to search for the Japanese cruiser *Haguro* which was reported to be en route to the Andaman Islands to assist in evacuating the garrison there. Having completed their designated missions and having missed the *Haguro* the fleet returned to base arriving off the harbour on 9 May for repair and re-storing.

With Rangoon in the hands of the Allies and the campaign across

The Fairey Firefly was an important part of the BPF strike force, not only could it carry out ground attacks once the external weapons had been used the type could revert to its other role that of being a long range fighter. (Rick Harding Collection)

Burma starting to take off the Japanese High Command decided that withdrawal from the Andaman Islands was in their best interests as the long-range flying boats used for reconnaissance duties normally based there had either been destroyed or damaged beyond repair. As the garrison on the islands would be much better employed in defending other parts of the Empire further efforts were made to recover them. On 9 May 1945 the Royal Navy launched Operation Dukedom in response to the original sighting of the Japanese Navy heavy cruiser *Haguro* which, in company with the destroyer *Kamikaze,* had departed Singapore bound for Port Blair. Spotted by the reconnaissance submarines *Statesman* and *Subtle* on 10 May in the Malacca Strait the Japanese force's course and direction was passed to the C-in-C East Indies Force. The force assembled, under the command of Vice Admiral Sir Arthur Power, was a large one which included the battleships HMS *Queen Elizabeth*, the French *Richelieu*, the carriers *Hunter, Khedive, Emperor* and *Shah*, the heavy cruiser *Cumberland* and the control cruiser *Royalist* plus a small group of destroyers acting as the anti-submarine screen. HMS *Hunter* was carrying No.807 NAS with Seafires plus a single Westland Walrus from No.1700 NAS. *Emperor* and *Khedive* carried the Hellcats of Nos. 800 and 808 NAS plus a Walrus. HMS *Shah* had the greater variety of aircraft with the Seafires of No.809 NAS and No.851 NAS with Avengers plus a flight of Hellcats from No.804 NAS. Designated Task Force 61 this fleet had put to sea as soon as the *Haguro* had been sighted on 10 May setting course for the Malacca Strait. Fortunately for the Japanese force their reconnaissance aircraft were still available thus, on 11 May, the British Task Force was spotted heading towards the cruiser and its escorts which promptly returned to Singapore. On 14 May *Haguro* flying the flag of Vice Admiral Hashimoto again departed Singapore for Port Blair. Task Force 61 had remained in the area and began to send reconnaissance sorties from HMS *Shah* drawn from the Seafires of No.809 NAS as soon as dawn had broken. By mid morning these flights had succeeded in discovering the small Japanese naval force and a strike package was assembled to attack the ships. The first Avengers were launched from *Shah* but once they were airborne the catapult on the carrier went unserviceable which meant that the remainder of the Avengers had to be flown across to the carrier *Emperor*. As this carrier was unable to support strike aircraft, being configured as a fighter carrier, the Grumman aircraft would only be able to undertake one mission should the first one fail to have an impact. Although little Japanese air force activity was expected groups of Hellcats were sent along as escorts while the Seafires undertook fleet protection. The Avengers of No.851 NAS attacked the cruiser and its escorts causing some damage to the *Haguro* although one aircraft was lost. Although the IJN force had suffered little in the air attack the ships were still being shadowed and thus it was that the 26th Destroyer Flotilla was able to plot an intercept course towards the enemy ships. By midnight of 16 May the range had dropped to less than a mile and the 26th Destroyer Flotilla, fully aware of the position of the cruiser, had formed a semicircular formation that the Japanese sailed straight into. By the time the Japanese became aware of the British ships they were in the centre of the semicircle, they promptly increased speed and started to zig zag however the range was rapidly dropping and at 6,000 yards the destroyers opened fire. Although the smaller ships were outgunned they did get close enough to launch torpedoes which hit the cruiser. While the Japanese ships managed to escape the encircling British the *Haguro* had been damaged enough to cause a list of 30 degrees. In the early hours of 17 May the cruiser sank by the bow while the *Kamakazi* escaped to Penang although she would return a few hours later to rescue 320 men from the cruiser's crew.

The Japanese reacted to the loss of the *Haguro* by immediately despatching reconnaissance aircraft to shadow the British fleet, although a low cloud base prevented the patrol aircraft from intercepting the

Japanese aircraft as they flew into the cloud when approached. While the cloud reached up to 20,000 ft a combat patrol from No.807 NAS was vectored onto a large radar blip which turned out to be four Ki 43 Oscars travelling at high speed towards the fleet at an altitude of 15,000 ft some 500 feet below. In the event the eagerness of the Seafire pilots saw them open fire too early as the fighters did not have the required speed to catch up with the bombers once they were alerted. Even so the fighters did manage to damage two of the bombers and the attackers were driven off. A further pair of Oscars was spotted by the next patrol and all four fighters dived into the attack. Damage was caused to one of the Japanese bombers before both undertook violent manoeuvres which resulted in their escape. These were the only two air engagements between the fighters of No.4 Naval Fighter Wing and the Japanese Air Force in the Bay of Bengal region. While en route to Trincomalee the fleet still kept up its anti-shipping patrols although no enemy vessels were spotted. On 19 May HMS *Khedive* and *Shah* arrived in port and were followed by *Hunter* and *Emperor* two days later.

While the carriers made for harbour the aircraft of No.4 Fighter Wing flew ashore to Trincomalee. The Seafire squadrons were kept ashore because enough Hellcats were available to provide fighter cover for continuing operations. No.809 NAS went aboard HMS *Stalker* on 18 June 1945 to take part in Operation Balsam in company with HMSs *Ameer* and *Khedive*. The purpose of this sortie was to undertake a photographic reconnaissance of the airfields in southern Malaya after which the airfields on Sumatra would be attacked. The reconnaissance sorties were completed on 20 June and were followed by the fighter bomber attacks. While the Hellcats attacked Medan and Bindjai airfields the Seafires of No.809 NAS attacked Lhokseumawe airfield. During the attack a Ki 43 was destroyed, a Ki 21 was damaged and the airfield buildings were given a pasting. While on the return trip at least one train was successfully destroyed and another was severely damaged.

Upon returning to Ceylon *Stalker* joined in exercises with *Emperor*, *Hunter* and *Khedive* all taking place within sight of Trincomalee. The purpose of all this training was Operation Zipper: the reoccupation of Malaya and Singapore. This operation began on 10 September although it proceeded without air cover from the RAF and bombardment support from the Royal Navy as the support deception mission codenamed Operation Slippery was cancelled. The selected targets for this invasion were either Port Dickson or Port Swettenham both located on the west coast of the Malay Peninsula. The fleet despatched to the area consisted of the four original carriers plus *Archer, Pursuer and Trumpeter*. The other vessels involved were the battleships *Nelson* and *Richelieu* and the

Seen from underneath this Firefly has everything out and down prior to landing. It would appear that only four of its high explosive rockets have been used on its last sortie. (Rick Harding Collection)

With explosions in the background from previous attacks this Grumman Avenger of the BPF turns toward its target. The Avenger was a popular aircraft with both the RN and the USN as it was a typical solidly built Bethpage machine. (FAAM Yeovilton)

Although slow and ungainly the Supermarine Walrus was a welcome sight to downed aircrew as the alternative was the sharks or the Japanese. (Ray Thomas Collection)

cruisers *Nigeria, Cleopatra, Royalist* and *Ceylon* plus 15 destroyers that supplied the anti-submarine and escort support. Commanded by Vice Admiral Walker the complete force would split into two with the carriers *Hunter* and *Stalker* plus escorts departing to form Task Force 65; their purpose was to supply cover for two of the beach landings. During this period No.807 NAS flew four sorties on 8 September followed by a further 29 missions on the following day. However, as the majority of the Japanese were more interested in surrendering there was no aerial activity therefore further flying was cancelled at lunchtime. Over 100,000 troops were landed at various points along the coast, fortunately resistance to the invasion was light as the landings were later described as chaotic. The troops deployed during this operation not only took over Malaya and Singapore but were also tasked with recovering various other territories once occupied by the Japanese including Hong Kong and the former Dutch territories. Once the Indonesians became aware that the islands were to be handed over to the Dutch they raised a revolt against their erstwhile liberators. To redress the balance the limited British units had to turn to their prisoners to provide extra fighters. Eventually the situation was calmed although Indonesia would eventually gain independence. At the completion of Zipper the fleet entered Singapore harbour in triumph on 11 September to accept the official surrender of the Japanese High Command.

While the other carriers were preparing for Operation Zipper HMS *Attacker* was preparing for another mission: Operation Jurist for which No.879 NAS and its Seafires were embarked. On 17 August 1945 *Attacker* and *Hunter* plus escorts sailed for Penang arriving there on 28 August. Both ships remained offshore until 3 September although calls for their services were limited as the Royal Marines landed without opposition. *Attacker* remained on station while *Hunter* sailed to join Operation Zipper, *Attacker* eventually joined the rest of the fleet in Singapore Roads on 11 September. After the surrender of the Japanese forces in the Malaysian area the operational service of No.21 Aircraft Carrier Squadron and No.4 Naval Air Wing came to an end and the various carriers and other vessels started the long journey home. By the end of 1945 all the escort carriers had returned to Britain and were paid off and de-stored. Eventually the ships were returned to the US Navy for disposal; most were transformed to merchant vessels.

When the British Pacific Fleet was assembled for the assault on Japan it was the largest gathering of British Warships since the Grand Fleet of WWI. The reason for such a gathering had been precipitated by the desire of the Japanese to spread their empire further across the Pacific. Having successfully defeated the Russian Navy earlier in the century the Empire of the Rising Sun bent all its industrial muscle and military prowess in developing weapons to expand its influence in the Pacific. The culmination of all this effort plus the humiliation of having their battleship tonnage restricted under the terms of the Washington Treaty gave the Japanese further impetus to begin their expansion. The most dramatic display of this intent was the attack on the American Fleet at Pearl Harbor on 7 December 1941. Amid the tragedy of sinking and destroyed battleships one important part of the fleet survived, the small force of American aircraft carriers. In response the Americans turned their massive industrial might into rebuilding their fleet and adding more aircraft carriers. The Japanese moved down the Pacific Islands pushing the Americans and British all the way. Malaya, Burma and other territories fell to the Japanese although they fell short of actually reaching their final goal, Australia. The cause of the disturbance in the Japanese plans was America which had not only built a new fleet of fast carriers but battleships to support them in the anti-aircraft role. Modern heavily armed aircraft were designed and built for operation aboard the new carriers and this new fleet plus the massive mobilisation of manpower began to unravel the new Japanese empire.

Although Britain would like to have retaken the parts of the

Commonwealth captured by the Japanese events in the Atlantic and the Mediterranean were keeping the Royal Navy fully occupied and it would be much later in the war before Britain could look to the east. The first operations in that direction were undertaken in the Indian ocean before the fleet carriers split off and headed for Australia much to the chagrin of the American commanders in the region. Having battled through Midway, Guadalcanal and Leyte Gulf the American Pacific Fleet, the mightiest fleet on earth, felt they were more than capable of defeating the Japanese on their own. It was pressure put on President Roosevelt by Winston Churchill that forced the US Navy to accept the presence of the Royal Navy.

The first statement of intent to supply ships of the Royal Navy for the Pacific war was initially put forward at the Sextant Conference held in Cairo in November 1943. Originally the Americans were much against this interference, however the promise of a modern fleet in place by mid 1944 swayed their decision. With the Americans close to accepting the British presence the next task was to put the support in place to back up the operating part of the fleet. The major but unseen part of this operation was the all important fleet train. The US Navy quite rightly raised this point as their experience of operations in the Pacific had seen their fleet support train grow to massive proportions and they were concerned that the Royal Navy would have to depend on the US Navy at some point. The Royal Navy exerted great pressure on the Ministry of War Transport to provide enough shipping for this purpose, however pressure on other fronts meant that not enough oilers, ferry carriers and supply ships were ever available. While the mobile part of the plan was being hastened further work was needed to create a fixed base from which the fleet could operate. To that end a fully operational harbour needed to be prepared in Australia almost from scratch, a major undertaking even with the help of the Australians and the US Navy. The chosen location for the main base was Sydney, although completion of the work took longer than expected. Plans were also laid to create intermediate bases along the projected attack path, however, this work was never undertaken as American generosity allowed the Royal Navy to share their base at Manus. Part of the problem was that Britain did not have the organisation to develop bases in such a compressed period of time and the intermediate base was not ready before October 1945. In contrast the United States had the 'SeeBee' divisions which could take a desolate island and transform it into a fully operational base within weeks.

The circumstances that controlled the deployment of the Royal Navy in the Pacific all centred around the Battle of the Philippine Sea which

Even in calmer waters aircraft could suffer accidents on landing. Here a Grumman Hellcat has ended up hanging over the deck of its escort carrier home having skidded on touchdown. (Rick Harding Collection)

took place in June 1944. Although the Japanese would throw the majority of their fleet and aircraft into this battle the overwhelming American might would smash this force with little effort. Japan would pull back the remainder of its forces to protect the home islands and the bases in Malaya in order to protect their access to vital oil supplies. Initially, the Americans had planned to fight their way up to the Philippines, however, the commander of the Fast Carrier Force, Admiral Halsey, changed the plans at the last moment. Massive air strikes were undertaken against the airbases on Formosa, Okinawa and minor bases in between. Not only was massive damage and destruction caused to these facilities but 50,000 tons of enemy shipping was sunk. Allied losses were minimal as the 12 strong carrier force was surrounded by battleships and cruisers all of which formed a tightly honed anti-aircraft umbrella which attacking aircraft found almost impossible to break through. During mid October the Fast Carrier Force continued to strike against targets at sea and on land, the major strike was a heavy attack against the Japanese bases at Luzon in the Philippines. This was the moment the Americans had been waiting for: a massive assault began on the Philippines, land, sea and air forces piled into the attack. The Japanese forces were caught completely off guard and although the land

As the crew scramble clear of their stricken Swordfish, it begins to sink underneath them. The crew were picked up slightly dampened. The Swordfish was not widely used by the BPF, however this example looks to have been involved in clandestine operations. (Rick Harding Collection)

forces fought back to the best of their ability the lack of effective air power meant that the American fleet was virtually untouchable. To give themselves some sort of edge the Japanese turned to a weapon of desperation, the kamikaze or Divine Wind. Initially drawn from volunteers who believed in dying for their Emperor the whole programme was eventually the province of draftees. While an alien concept to western minds the kamikaze was initially a successful option as the cruiser HMAS *Australia* found out when one such hit the ship's bridge and killed all personnel stationed there. Such was the extent of the damage the vessel was forced to withdraw to Manus for repairs.

The British Pacific Fleet, under the command of Admiral Somerville, sailed into this potential maelstrom. Formed from the most modern ships available to the East Indies Fleet in 1944 the first appearance of the British ships in concert with the American Task Force took place in early 1944 when the battleships *Queen Elizabeth* and *Valiant* plus the fleet carrier *Illustrious* and the required screen of modern cruisers and destroyers under the command of Admiral Sir Arthur Power who, as second in command of the BPF, was flying his flag aboard the battlecruiser *Renown*. Aboard *Illustrious* the air wing consisted of No.21 Naval Fighter Wing made up of of Nos 1830, 1833 and 1837 NAS equipped with Vought F4U Corsairs and the Fairey Barracudas of No.21 TBR wing. Although this was a small force the fleet carriers *Formidable, Indefatigable, Indomitable* and *Victorious* were scheduled to join the fleet within weeks and the repair carrier *Unicorn* plus the escort carriers *Begum* and *Shah* also arrived to become part of the supply train The roles of *Unicorn, Begum* and *Shah* were to ferry replacement aircraft to the front line and act as spare flight decks when required and because of the nature of these roles these three vessels had no assigned units. The first attack undertaken by this small force was mounted on 16 April 1944 in company with the US Navy carrier USS *Saratoga* against targets at Sabang, Sumatra. The fleet involved in this attack numbered 26 vessels which included extra reinforcements in the shape of the French battleship *Richelieu* and the Dutch cruiser *Tromp*. In the early hours of 19 April, while the fleet was 100 miles south west of Sabang, the first sorties were flown off. The aerial armada consisted of 46 bombers, mainly Avengers, and 40 escort fighters. During this attack the refinery was extensively damaged, two merchantmen were sunk and damage was caused to the harbour and airfield facilities. In return the force lost one US Navy fighter, although the pilot was rescued by an escort submarine. This was the last operation in which the Barracudas were involved as they were soon replaced by the Grumman Avengers of Nos. 832 and 851 NAS. After refuelling at sea from oilers in Exmouth Gulf, Australia, another attack was undertaken on 17 May against the oil refineries located at Soerabaya, Java. Again the *Saratoga* was involved in this operation which improved the chances of success. The carriers reached the launch position, 180 miles south of Java, on 17 May. A similar strike force was launched in the early hours of the morning and the result was the same as at Sabang with the only Japanese gain being an aircraft lost to anti-aircraft fire. After this strike the *Saratoga* and the usual selection of support vessels returned to American control. Even though the British force had been reduced in size one more strike had been planned by Admiral Somerville's operations staff. The chosen target was Port Blair in the Andaman Islands. As it was intended to launch the strike closer to the target the Avengers were landed and the Barracudas reloaded. *Illustrious* was carrying 57 aircraft on this mission and of these 51 were airborne during this operation. While little damage was achieved due to the lack of suitable targets the attack raised further doubts in the minds of the Japanese High Command who now had to contend with the might of the Americans advancing through the Pacific Islands and the British applying their pin pricks to various targets on the other flank. At the end of this mission the carrier group withdrew to Ceylon for rest and replenishment.

Reinforcements in the shape of the carriers *Indomitable* and *Victorious* arrived at the beginning of July. As both ships' crews were inexperienced both vessels, in company with the remainder of the fleet, undertook an extensive work-up period which quickly bedded them in. The first strike, which utilised *Victorious* and *Illustrious,* was undertaken on 25 July 1944 and was codenamed Operation Crimson. Their role was to provide air cover for the battleships who were engaged in bombarding Sabang as part of the softening up and demoralising process that was aimed at the Japanese forces in the area. The fleet consisted of the two carriers plus the battleships *Queen Elizabeth* and *Valiant,* the battlecruiser *Renown*, six anti-aircraft cruisers and ten destroyers for screen purposes. The airstrike, launched in the early morning, comprised 80 Corsairs and nine Barracudas. The Corsairs were given clearly defined roles, eight acted as bombardment fleet spotters, a further dozen acted in the combat air patrol role while the remainder were briefed to attack the airfield at Koetaradja. There was a slight delay in the assault as the weather was against the attackers, however, there were enough clear patches to allow those aircraft briefed to attack the airfield to do so. The surface units moved in under the thunder of the battleships' guns to attack targets on shore and in the harbour. The only loss was a single aircraft whose pilot was picked up by the cruiser *Nigeria.* At the completion of Crimson HMS *Illustrious* departed to Durban in South Africa for a much needed refit. Also leaving the scene was Admiral Somerville who departed to take up a post in the United States and he was replaced by Admiral Sir Bruce Fraser. Fraser was regarded within the Royal Navy as a fighting Admiral being responsible for the destruction of the German battlecruiser *Scharnhorst* in December 1943.

While the veteran *Illustrious* was away it would fall to the other two carriers to carry the fight to the enemy. Their first showing was on 29 August 1944 against Emmehaven and Indaroeng where air strikes were undertaken against targets in the area. Operation Light followed on 18 October with attacks against the Nicobar Islands. Commanded by the second in command, Admiral Power, the fleet departed Ceylon on 15 October intending to act as a diversion for American attacks taking place elsewhere in the region. Although these minor attacks were an annoyance to the Japanese their main attention was focused on the US Task Force. While few targets of note were available for attacking by

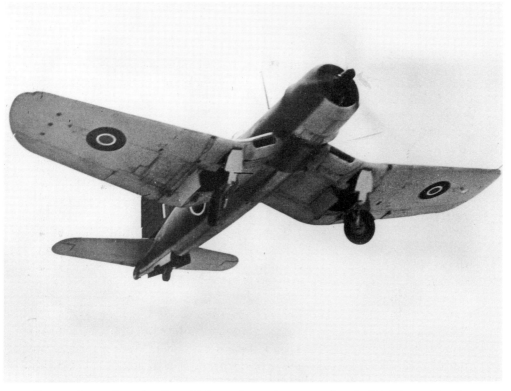

Captured just after takeoff , with its undercarriage retracting, is this Chance Vought F4U Corsair which wears the temperate northern finish. Later aircraft destined for the BPF wore a gloss blue scheme overall. (Rick Harding Collection)

either air or sea the operation itself reinforced the British dominance of both arenas.

This would be the parting of the ways for Fraser and Powers as the former would depart to take command of the British Pacific Fleet while the latter would assume command of the East Indies Fleet. Joining Admiral Fraser would be Admiral Sir Phillip Vian who would assume command of the 1st Aircraft Carrier Squadron. Moving into the support role for the BPF was Vice Admiral Charles Daniel whose post would be Vice Admiral Administration BPF. This was a fairly innocuous title for a very important job which entailed more than paper shuffling as its roles included logistics throughout the length of the Pacific, the allocation of manpower and the planning of every support operation for the attack fleet. While Admiral Fraser was in command of the BPF its proposed secondment to the United States control meant that such a senior officer could not in reality be in command at sea. To avoid any embarrassments the sea commander was Vice Admiral Sir Bernard Rawlings; this meant

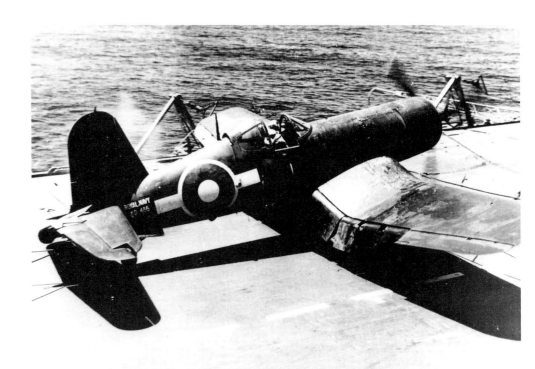

A C-V Corsair IV, KD264 takes the wire successfully as it slows down aboard the fleet carrier HMS *Colossus*. The aircraft was assigned to No.1846 NAS, a wartime only unit. (Rick Harding Collection)

that Admiral Fraser was initially based in Australia but he later moved his headquarters northwards as the war progressed towards Japan.

Prior to taking the carrier force to the BPF Admiral Vian set off to undertake Operation Outflank. In company with *Illustrious* and *Indefatigable* were three anti-aircraft cruisers and five destroyers. Departing port on 17 December the fleet arrived at its launch point in the Malacca Strait on 20 December. The original target was Pangkalan Brandan however bad weather completely obscured this target thus the secondary target at Belewan Deli was attacked instead. As before, the strike was launched in the early morning and the oil refineries and harbour were severely damaged. No aerial resistance was encountered and no aircraft were lost to the light anti-aircraft fire put up as resistance. On 1 January 1945 the carriers were officially assigned to the 1st ACS of the BPF, on the same date Admiral Fraser flew via Australia to Pearl Harbour where he met up with Admiral Nimitz. These meetings were fruitful as both Admirals Nimitz and Spruance, alternate commanders of the US Navy carrier force, were more than pleased to add the British Pacific Fleet to their arsenal. While the commander of the BPF was meeting his American counterparts Admiral Vian took the fleet to sea on 4 January to undertake a strike, codenamed Operation Lentil, against the oil facilities at Pangkalan Brandan. Such was the accuracy and strength of this assault from the air that the refinery and its storage facilities were completely wrecked. The result of this destruction was a massive and permanent reduction in oil supplies to the Japanese which, in turn, reduced their ability to fight. On 16 January the 1st ACS in company with its escorts sailed for Australia to undertake their part in the final assault on the Japanese.

The first mission for the 1st ACS was undertaken on 24 January 1945 when all four available carriers: *Indomitable, Illustrious, Indefatigable* and *Victorious* were assigned to the strike as Task Force 63. Of this group *Indefatigable* was the only carrier equipped with Seafires. The target was Pladjoe refinery and the bombers were 43 Avengers carrying 172 500lb bombs, 12 Fairey Fireflies plus 50 fighters drawn from all four carriers. While the American fighters escorted the Avengers and Fireflies the Seafires from *Indefatigable* performed the much needed air patrol duties above the fleet. This was a most successful mission. Five days later the same carrier group struck at the Soengi Gerong refinery, this time 16 aircraft from the carriers were shot down, however, 30 Japanese defending fighters were shot down and a further 38 were destroyed on the ground. This group of refineries had originally been operated by Standard Oil and Royal Dutch Shell and processed at least 50 per cent of all the oil used by Japan and even more importantly 75 per cent of the aviation fuel used throughout Japan. This strike, which caused massive amounts of damage, reduced permanently the Japanese capability to prosecute the war against the Allies. Also, the Japanese were facing a loss of oil tankers, which were torpedoed by US Navy submarines, at an alarming rate, which also had a deleterious effect on Japans ability to fight. Having withdrawn from the area the British vessels refuelled en route to Freemantle arriving on 4 February. Six days later the Fleet arrived at Sydney, the BPF's permanent base in Australia. The first ship to arrive was the *King George V* class battleship HMS *Howe* which had been designated the BPF flagship and was followed soon after by the remainder. Soon after arriving HMS *Illustrious* required docking to investigate problems with the centre propeller shaft which had been thrown slightly out of alignment during a bomb attack in January 1941. As the facilitates or the time for the repair of such a major item was not available the only answer was to remove the shaft. Although this reduced the carriers top speed to 24 knots it did mean that the vessel was still available to No.1 ACS.

Although the BPF front line element was now in place the equally essential Fleet Train was not so complete. Obviously, for a naval strike force to withdraw back to its main base after every attack was impractical and, therefore, the BPF shared the US Navy facilities at Manus. Forward of this base was an area of ocean designated the Operating Area which was located close to the proposed target but far enough away to keep the vulnerable tankers and stores vessels safe from attack. Between these locations would operate the ships of the Fleet Train. Within this organisation were oilers, tankers, supply and ammunition ships all of which required their own escort vessels. In the Operating Area the refuel was intended to take place around dawn. To that end the oilers and other vessels were strung out in a line each having its own defensive destroyer while frigates acted as an outside anti-submarine screen. The task force would arrive in the operating area to find their respective oiler steaming in the same direction, each assigned combat ship would come alongside its designated oiler, refuel and move to make way for another. After the refuel ships requiring stores or ammunition would move alongside the relevant vessel. As the BPF fleet train had been assembled in a hurry some of methods of re-storing were very basic, a complete contrast to the US Navy whose train consisted of specially designed ships all of which were outfitted with the best handling equipment available. Also included in the fleet train were the escort carriers whose role in this theatre was to supply replacement aircraft to the carriers and take back those repairable machines for transit to the BPF repair facilities. In the beginning refuelling and replenishment of the Task Force after each strike took at least three days however slicker handling procedures and the use of the battleships and fleet carriers to refuel the smaller ships reduced the entire process to two days. The entire force and the fleet train would remain at sea for up to four weeks, the only changes being those enforced by damage or major mechanical defects. While the US Navy maintained four equally large task forces and their equally large fleet train, the BPF was a single entity thus the withdrawal of their fleet train meant that there would be no British presence in theatre for days at a time. Fortunately, Rear Admiral Fisher was the man for the job and the disparate collection of ships at his disposal managed to keep the BPF supplied with its needs at all time.

While the Allies had successfully disabled or driven the Japanese out of their peripheral captured territories it was quickly realised that a decisive attack on a Japanese main base would accelerate the end of the war. To that end Operation Iceberg was planned: a massive assault on Okinawa. The task of the BPF was to apply control to the area around the Sakishima Gunto islands. Placing the BPF in this area would provide a block on the potential flow of aircraft and supplies from either the

Seen aboard the flight deck of a fleet carrier this clutch of Corsairs will soon be airborne for another sortie against the Japanese forces. (Rick Harding Collection)

Japanese main islands or Formosa. Designated Task Force 57, the American TF57 being rested, and operating in conjunction with the US Navy Task Force 58, the BPF put to sea but felt lost in the massive 1,200 strong armada heading towards Okinawa. The American fleet began its operations on 14 March striking airfields in the south of the Japanese Islands. A counter attack by the Japanese resulted in damage to the carriers USS *Intrepid* and *Enterprise* on 18 March. Given the size of Task Force 58 the damage to these carriers did not lessen the force's strike power. Five days later the Americans retaliated against Okinawa which was followed by an extensive minesweep of the sea around the island so that the battleships could close in and deliver the heaviest weight of explosives ever delivered by naval vessels. The bombardment commenced on 24 March, two days later the neighbouring island of Kerama Retto was captured from the fleeing Japanese forces. The capture of this piece of real estate allowed the Americans to establish a repair facility and jumping off point for their forces.

On 14 March Task Force 57 departed from Manus, the fleet consisting of the 1st Battle Squadron, the 1st ACS, the 4th Cruiser Squadron plus the 4th, 25th and 27th Destroyer Flotillas. By the following day the Fleet Train, designated Task Force 112, was also on the move. The task force was divided into task units the first being TU112/2/1 consisting of the escort carrier HMS *Stalker* with three escorts, the second was designated TU 112/2/5 consisting of three oilers, the carrier *Speaker* acting as a ferry

Unless the carrier was tied up alongside the pier that contained the repair-depot ship any replacement aircraft had to be moved to the ship by lighter and craned aboard which is the fate that awaits this Corsair. (Rick Harding Collection)

and air defence vessel plus two escorts. Task Force 57 commanded by Admiral Rawlings was the largest British naval force ever gathered since the days of the Grand Fleet at Jutland in 1916 and consisted of the battleships *King George V* and *Howe* plus the fleet carriers *Indomitable*, the flagship of Admiral Vian, *Illustrious*, *Indefatigable* and *Victorious*, all escorted by five light cruisers and eleven destroyers. The air components of each carrier were *Indomitable*: 29 Hellcats and 15 Avengers, *Indefatigable*: 40 Seafires and 20 Avengers, *Illustrious*: 36 Corsairs and 16 Avengers and *Victorious*: 37 Corsairs, 14 Avengers and two Supermarine Walrus for air sea rescue duties. The intention was that the American built aircraft would act as the strike component while the Seafires, hampered by limited range, would carry out combat air patrols above and around the fleet. During the transit voyage all the vessels were refuelled after which anti-aircraft exercises were carried out using a Martin B-26 Marauder unit towing target drogues. In the early hours of

26 March command of the fleet was transferred to Admiral Vian as the policy was that in action the aircraft carriers and their operations were the controlling influence. The first fighter sweeps were launched when the carriers were 100 miles due south of Miyako Jima, their targets being the airfields at Ishigaki and Miyako. Each airfield was heavily defended by anti-aircraft weaponry which made the task of keeping the Japanese aircraft on the ground very difficult. The first sweep produced only one loss, an aircraft which ditched in the Tarima Shima and the pilot was rescued by one of the Walrus amphibians. The second attack of these airfields saw a full strike package despatched from all four carriers complete with heavy fighter escort. This attack saw the runways heavily cratered and a few aircraft destroyed on the ground. Obviously prepared for such an eventuality the Japanese defenders quickly repaired the runways which made the Task Force's mission more difficult.

The next phase of the attack was an intended bombardment of the airfields, however, an incoming typhoon was menacing the refuelling area, this, coupled with the fact that some vessels were running low on fuel meant that the bombardment was cancelled. As the assault on Okinawa was scheduled to begin on 31 March it was more important that all vessels be ready to undertake airstrikes on the BPF's targets during the period 31 March to 2 April. In the refuelling area, designated Midge, all the ships were refuelled and defective aircraft were replaced which kept the BPF ships fully occupied from 28 to 30 March. In the early hours of 31 March Task Force 57 was back in position and launched its first air reconnaissance. Again the airfields on Ishigaki and Miyako were the targets and again losses were light; just one Avenger lost and the crew was successfully rescued by a US Navy submarine on lifeguard duties.

At 06.00 hours on 1 April the American land forces stormed ashore on Okinawa and quickly established a wide beachhead. However, the Japanese defenders had survived a massive bombardment and were well prepared. As well as well placed defences the kamikazes came out in force. On that day the BPF fighter patrols were flown off as usual and were quickly diverted to intercept incoming unidentified aircraft that turned out to be Japanese. Further BPF fighters were scrambled to reinforce the fleet defences but even so a handful of aircraft managed to break through after four of their number had been shot down. The incoming aircraft strafed *Indomitable* and *King George V* and this diversion allowed a kamikaze aircraft to hit the carrier *Indefatigable* at the base of the island and 14 were killed and 16 injured. The damage and injured would have been greater had not avoiding action been taken, the kamikaze had also been severely shot up by the Bofors gun crews. Unfortunately for one of *Indefatigable*'s pilots the hail of shells put up in defence of the carriers also took his life. This was a hazard of air operations in such dangerous areas. Unlike their American counterparts the British carriers were fitted with armoured flight decks, the American carriers were fitted with wooden decks which burnt easily. On the same day the American Task Force 58 was attacked by 700 aircraft of which fifty per cent were deemed to be kamikaze. Although the Americans destroyed over 300 aircraft they did lose a picket ship. On 7 March the US Navy got their revenge for Pearl Harbor. The super battleship *Yamato*, complete with its 18 inch guns, and travelling on fuel oil scavenged from the rest of the Japanese fleet and with the cruiser *Yahagi* and eight destroyers in attendance was spotted travelling at speed towards the transport fleet off Okinawa. Having been detected by an American air patrol the Japanese ships increased speed towards their target, however, they were greeted by 380 torpedo and dive bombers that completely overwhelmed the massed Japanese anti-aircraft fire. By mid afternoon this last expression of the battleship had been sunk as had the cruiser and four destroyers while the others limped away damaged.

On 8 April the Americans requested that the BPF divert their attention away from their current targets and refocus on the airfields on Formosa. The reason for this change of emphasis was based on the deduction that the pilots flying from Formosa were experienced combat pilots unlike those facing the British who were no more than glorified trainees. Although the crews of the US Navy and the USAAF were trying their best to control these attacks it was felt by the US commanders that more experienced pilots would be more than welcome. Accordingly Admiral Rawlings signalled the BPF to alter course towards Sakishima which they did on 10 April. Two days later Task Force 57 was in position some 30 miles off Yonakumi Shima where preparations were begun to start a sequence of strikes on Matsuyama airfield. As before, the first launches were scheduled for dawn, however, they were hurriedly brought forward as incoming aircraft were detected by the radar pickets. The patrolling Seafires quickly dived into the fray shooting down one out of four Zekes and damaging another. While this fracas was taking place the planned strike packages and escorting fighters departed to Shinchiku and Matsuyama airfields but the weather was extremely bad over the latter therefore this group changed course to attack Kiran harbour and targets which included the adjacent chemical plant, shipping, a railway station, a factory and a bridge. Further incoming enemy aircraft were intercepted by a pair of Fairey Fireflies over Yonakumi Shima. They had finished acting in the bomber role and had become long range fighters, this was unfortunate for five Japanese 'Sonias' of which four were shot down and the other damaged. After these moments of excitement over enemy territory the aircraft returned to the carriers for refuelling and rearming. Fortunately this had been completed by mid afternoon as a large Japanese air group was detected heading towards the carriers. All four ships launched their guard fighters while others were quickly brought to readiness and launched. The BPF pilots tore into the attackers downing eight Japanese aircraft before the attack fizzled out, the BPF suffered a single loss when a Hellcat crashed on landing killing the pilot.

The next day started as usual with dawn attacks on the fleet and, as before, the fleet's fighters rose to the occasion while the strike packages departed amidst this chaos to attack their designated targets. This time the weather was clear and both airfields were attacked with vigour, the bombers hit the infrastructure while the fighters strafed the aircraft on the ground. All aircraft returned safely to the carriers which then withdrew to the south to take up their night positions. A further move to the Operations Area took place on 14 April so that refuelling could take place. Upon arrival in the area the fleet found *Formidable* waiting to replace *Illustrious* which departed to Leyte in company with a pair of destroyers so that serious defects could be rectified. On 15 April the fleet started the return voyage to the combat area with flags at half mast as a mark of respect for the late President Roosevelt. By 16 April the BPF was back on station ready to resume operations. Strike packages with their escorting fighters were launched against the airfield at Ishigaki and Miyako and the radar station at the latter. By this time the carriers were running short of fighters, not only for escort duties but for combat air patrols over the fleet and accordingly Admiral Vian informed Admiral Rawlings that it would be better to withdraw. Although Admiral Rawlings was aware of the situation the American commander requested one more attack before the task force was withdrawn. On the morning of 17 April a strike package was despatched to attack Miyako which left the airfield devastated. An Avenger was forced to ditch just off the coast but the Walrus rescue aircraft undertook a daring rescue to pick up the crew. At the close of operations for the day the fleet withdrew to Operation Area Mosquito for refuelling and replenishing. The next day saw the fleet back on station undertaking further strikes on the airfields on Ishigaki and Myako Islands. At the completion of this day's combat the Task Force departed the area finally arriving in San Pedro Roads , Leyte, on 23 April.

The BPF stayed in port until 1 May when Task Force 57 departed once more to engage the enemy entrenched on Okinawa. While the British Fleet was anchored at Leyte the Japanese had increased their attacks on the American fleet causing damage to many vessels. Also, the land war had stalled until on 11 May the American forces pushed forward in strength to fight from bunker to bunker in an effort to clear the enemy out. This was the hardest part of the war as the Japanese showed no inclination to surrender while the kamikaze raids increased in strength. Even at this stage in the assault on Okinawa the American High Command wanted the BPF diverted away to tackle Borneo but Admiral Nimitz persuaded them otherwise, preferring them to attack Sakishima Gunto beginning on 1 May. This time the task force consisted of the battleships *King George V* and *Howe*, the carriers *Formidable, Indefatigable, Indomitable* and *Victorious* plus four cruisers and fourteen destroyers. The other carrier assigned to the BPF, *Illustrious*, departed Leyte for the naval base at Sydney as the Leyte repair crews did not have the facilities to repair the ship properly. By 3 May the BPF had reached Operation Area Mosquito where refuelling was carried out and the fleet arrived on 4 May ready to begin operations against the bases on Sakishima. Drawing on previous experience the defensive fighter patrols were launched just before dawn and were quickly called into action to attack a small incoming raid. The fighters shot down one aircraft and dispersed the others. While the fighters were covering the fleet the strike packages had departed to attack the airfields at Ishigaki and Miyako, one thing noted during this attack was that the anti-aircraft fire had increased.

The use of high flying reconnaissance aircraft by the Japanese was a continual worry to the fleet as the patrolling fighters were unable to reach these altitudes and the use of the battleships' heavy guns were unable to disrupt their over flights. In order to end this menace Admiral Rawlings took the battleships and a destroyer escort towards the Islands in order to undertake a naval bombardment. With the battleships and their extensive anti-aircraft armament away Admiral Vian redeployed the escort vessels around the carriers in order to spread the anti-aircraft fire around the fleet. The high flying reconnaissance aircraft had obviously reported the departure of the battleships as four incoming raids were reported heading towards the carriers. One group angled south of the carriers drawing the fighters away while the others dropped off the radar and popped up later to catch the fleet unawares and the Japanese aircraft began their dives to bomb the carriers. With the main defending warships away the available anti-aircraft fire was not as heavy as normal. *Formidable* was the chosen target and the carrier undertook a series of violent manoeuvres to throw the attackers off balance. However, one attacking aircraft managed to reach the carrier and dropped its bomb load just by the island before crashing into the flight deck. The resultant conflagration set fire to many of the aircraft in the deck park, tore a large hole in the armoured deck, killed eight crew, wounded 47 others and rendered most of the radar equipment useless. While the damage control parties struggled to bring the fires under control HMS *Indomitable* became

HMS *Indefatigable* enters Portsmouth in 1946 after war service in the Far East. During its time with the BPF the carrier was badly damaged during a Kamikaze attack although further damage was contained by the armoured deck. The carrier would enter long term reserve before being scrapped. (BBA Collection)

the next target for a pair of attackers. One was shot down just short of the ship while the second aimed for the starboard bow. Fortunately, *Indomitable* was turning away and thus the attacking aircraft, riddled with cannon shells, hit the flight deck at a shallow angle, skidded across the deck and fell into the sea. Other incoming attackers were shot down by the air patrols before they even reached the fleet. Eventually the fires aboard *Formidable* were quenched, the deck was repaired and the carrier declared ready for operations which allowed the waiting aircraft to land.

The battleships meanwhile began their bombardment of the airfields and other installations with the spotting provided by the escorting fighters. The firing lasted nearly an hour and the shells proved most effective as the spotting aircraft later revealed. Each of the battleships' big gun turrets cratered every part of the runways and other parts of each airfield guided by the spotters. At the completion of this shelling the battleships and escorts departed to rejoin the carriers. With the bigger warships now back in the fold the co-ordinated anti-aircraft defence was fully restored. Further air attacks began soon afterwards and some of the

Japanese attackers were shot down by *Indefatigables* fighters. At the completion of this mission the BPF withdrew to Operating Area Cootie. Here all the vessels were refuelled and replacement aircraft transhipped. While in the Operation Zone news was received concerning the surrender of Germany plus the deaths of Hitler and most of his close entourage. The fleet returned to the combat area on 8 May but increasingly bad weather forced the cancellation of all attacks. Fortunately, the weather cleared the next day and the carriers resumed their attacks. The chosen target was Hirara airfield which the reconnaissance flights had reported as fully usable again. Four strike packages were launched against the airfield rendering it unserviceable. The Avengers and their escorts returned without casualties passing the Seafires which had spent much of the day chasing away Japanese reconnaissance aircraft.

Formidable would be the next carrier that would receive the attention of a kamikaze. Although the carrier and the defending warships sent up a veritable barrage of steel, the battered attacker continued to head towards the carrier and finally ploughed into a deck park full of aircraft. The explosion destroyed seven aircraft on deck although the armoured deck was not penetrated. To assist the fire crews in fighting the conflagration the carrier reduced speed. As the crews continued to fight the fires, leaking fuel from the damaged aircraft seeped into the hanger below and started a second fire. Fortunately, the fire suppression system and dividing doors kept the destruction to 18 aircraft only. Given the strength and design of this type of carrier the fires were quickly suppressed which allowed *Formidable* to resume limited operations very quickly. In order to replenish and repair the damage the Task Force departed to Operating Area Cootie just as night was falling. The refuelling zone was reached on 10 May where all the ships were quickly refuelled, replacement aircraft transhipped and vital repairs carried out. During this lull both the damaged carriers were inspected and cleared for further service although the damage to one of the aircraft lifts on *Victorious* gave cause for concern. Even with this misgiving the BPF resumed operations on 12 May preparing to attack Ishigaki and Miyako. Casualties were light and no kamikazes approached the fleet and they withdrew for the evening. Operations continued over the next few days finally ending on 25 May when the fleet departed for their base. After 62 days at sea undertaking Operation Iceberg the BPF staged via Manus on their way to Australia where they would prepare for the next series of operations.

The American forces had, by now, overwhelmed the Japanese forces on Okinawa and other areas such as Borneo, this time under the command of Admiral Halsey, but the BPF was despatched all over the globe so that the ships could undergo much needed refits. The four British carriers, as to be expected, received the greatest attention, however *Indomitable* was found to be in a far worse condition than previously thought. Fortunately *Implacable* with attendant cruisers and destroyers had arrived to replace the disappointed *Indomitable* crew. While *Implacable* had used the time in transit to train both air and ships crews fully they had no recent combat experience therefore they were tasked to attack the Japanese base at Truk. Once the main Japanese base in the area a massive strike by the US Navy in 1943 had rendered it almost useless, most of the remaining Japanese aircraft and ships had been dispersed to the Philippines and Malaya. The BPF ships for this attack were designated Task Force 111/2 under the command of Rear Admiral E J P Baird whose units consisted of Task Unit 1 which comprised the carrier *Implacable,* whose air wing consisted of 21 Avengers of No.828 NAS and 48 Seafires of No.38 Naval Fighter Wing, Task Unit 2 consisted of the escort carrier *Ruler* with No.885 NAS, this being a composite equipped with Avengers and Hellcats plus two escorts, two further Task Units, 5 and 15 comprised cruisers and destroyers. On 16 June 1945 Truk was attacked by the Avengers and Seafires and the whole area's facilities were given a thorough pasting before the whole ensemble returned to Manus unscathed.

On 16 July the BPF, now redesignated Task Force 37, joined the American naval force. The ships in this fleet were the carriers *Formidable*, Admiral Vians flagship, *Implacable* and *Victorious* plus the battleship *King George V*, six cruisers and 15 destroyers. The battleship *Howe* was still on refit in Durban while the carrier *Indefatigable* was stuck at Manus where the ship's defective air compressors were being repaired. The command ship of the US 3rd Fleet was the 'Mighty Mo', USS *Missouri*, where Admiral Halsey was in command, when Admiral Nimitz was in command the designation changed to the 5th Fleet. Admiral Rawlings went aboard Mighty Mo to consult with Admiral Halsey about the role of Task Force 37. The given options were that TF37 could be part of the 3rd Fleet and be fully integrated into the American attacks, that it could operate semi independently separated from the Americans or that it could be a loner hitting the softer Japanese targets. Admiral Rawlings decided that the first option was best for TF37, a decision much admired by Admiral Halsey. On 17 July 1945 the final assault on the Japanese homeland islands began. Already being pounded heavily by USAAF Boeing B-29 Superfortresses the Japanese hierarchy was already aware that the war was lost and that an invasion was coming. The first target area hit by TF37 was the Tokyo Plain. All three carriers despatched strike

HMS *Implacable* seen from above, of note is the extensive anti aircraft fitment fitted to this class of carrier of which *Indefatigable* was one. (BBA Collection)

aircraft and fighters against airfields, factories and other targets of interest. Due to periods of bad weather only eight days of flying were possible in these first 25 days of operations during which 1,000 sorties were flown.

Operations scheduled for 3 August in the Hiroshima area were abruptly cancelled by a signal the previous evening, the fleet were ordered to withdraw from the Japanese coastal areas. Further operations were undertaken on 9 August against shipping anchored in Onagawa Wan. During this attack Lt RH Gray DSC RNVR of No.1841 Sqdn was awarded a posthumous Victoria Cross for attacking a Japanese destroyer whose anti-aircraft fire was threatening the lives of his comrades.

On 6 August a B-29 Superfortress of the 509th Composite Group departed Tinian en route to Japan piloted by Colonel Paul Tibbets. The *Enola Gay* droned on towards its target, Hiroshima and over the city the bomb doors were opened and the bomb 'Little Boy' was dropped. The devastation was almost complete; much of the city and its inhabitants were destroyed. While much debate has been generated about the use of the atomic bomb the reasons at the time were that the invasion of the Japanese home islands, known as Operation Olympic, would have generated immense casualties on both sides. Although the Hiroshima attack had inflicted a great wound on Japan the combined fleets and the American bombers continued their attacks. On 9 August heavy strikes were launched by TF37 against airfields and other targets in the vicinity of Honshu that resulted in much damage and the destruction of 250 aircraft destroyed on the ground without loss.

The effects of the atomic bomb drop on Hiroshima were slow to be appreciated and so on 9 August another 509th Composite Group B-29, *Bockscar*, commanded by Major Charles W Sweeney departed Tinian and headed for Kokura. Upon arriving over the primary target it was completely obscured by cloud cover. As the bomb drop had to be undertaken in clear conditions the secondary target was chosen and thus Nagasaki felt the violent heat of 'Fat Boy'. The following day, realising that the war was all but over, the Japanese negotiators began talks to end the fighting although one stumbling point was that the Emperor was to remain enthroned, a condition to which the Americans were much opposed. In order to reinforce Japan's defeat Admiral Halsey proposed further heavy attacks against the remaining military and industrial targets. By this time TF37 was running short of almost everything and the deficiencies of the British Fleet Train had come to the fore. In order to retain some British naval presence TF38/5 was formed consisting of the carrier *Indefatigable*, the battleship *King George V* plus two cruisers and nine destroyers. The remainder of the fleet was forced to return to Manus for refuelling and much needed repairs.

Although two atomic bombs had been dropped on Japan and the High Command was trying to negotiate a surrender the Japanese continued to fight. The major weapon was again the kamikaze, however the British and American fleets were well aware of how to deal with them and, consequently, few attackers penetrated the defensive fire. The final mission for *Indefatigable* was undertaken on 15 August when a force of Avengers and Seafires was attacked by a dozen Zeros. During the ensuing melee eight Japanese fighters were shot down for the loss of one Seafire. At 07.00 hours the following day Admiral Nimitz signalled that all offensive operations were on hold until future notice. It would appear that the Japanese had not read this order as at least one aircraft managed to get close to the *Indefatigable* and drop two bombs alongside before being shot down by the orbiting Seafires. Except for some minor skirmishes with stubborn Japanese troops this was the end of the road for this most modern part of the Royal Navy. Having fought across two oceans and faced great dangers it is a great shame that the efforts of this force are still largely ignored, no wonder they refer to themselves as the Forgotten Fleet.

Chapter 5

Korea: the Seafire Interlude

While the events in Europe towards the end of 1945 captured much of the headlines other events in the Far East were unfolding that would have longer lasting consequences. On 6 August 1945 the Boeing B-29 Superfortress *Enola Gay* of the 509th Composite Group departed Tinian and proceeded to drop the atom bomb *Little Boy* over the Japanese city of Hiroshima. This attack and the one that followed upon Nagasaki finally forced the Japanese High Command to undertake surrender talks as both sides realised that the planned invasion of the Japanese Home Islands by the Americans would cause horrendous casualties on both sides. Having spread their tentacles over much of the Far East the removal of the Japanese interest from their former forced colonies resulted in a massive power vacuum. One of the most affected countries was Korea which had originally been annexed by the Chinese early in its history, although by 1884 Japan had assumed

Roaring down the flight deck of HMS *Triumph* is Seafire FR.47 VP458 using the RATOG packs mounted on the wing roots. Having joined No.800 NAS in July 1949 the aircraft was lost in a crash in December after an engine failure. (FAAM Yeovilton)

The classic landing pose captured as a Seafire FR.47 VP493 of No.800 NAS complete with Korean striping and with everything out and down prepares to land on HMS *Triumph*. (FAAM Yeovilton)

Wearing Korean War stripes and RATOG units for a boosted take off this Seafire FR.47 VP479 of No.800 NAS departs HMS *Triumph*. The aircraft would be badly damaged during landing in April 1950. (FAAM Yeovilton)

Seafire FR.47 VP431 is pictured on the lift of HMS *Ocean*. After service aboard *Ocean* the Seafire was transferred to *Triumph* where it was damaged during a landing. Transit home aboard HMS *Unicorn* ended with a visit to Eastleigh for repairs although the aircraft never re-entered service being scrapped in July 1951. (Rick Harding Collection)

control and had forced the Chinese-based dynasties out of power. Having taken over the country Seoul became a point of competition between Russia and Japan although the former would see its influence decline after the Russian defeat by the Japanese at the Battle of Tsushima. It was this campaign that finally proved to the Japanese that they had a navy capable of matching any other on the planet. With the Russian Imperial Forces removed from the scene Korea was declared a Japanese protectorate in 1905 and it was completely annexed in 1910. Although not directly involved in the events between 1939 and 1945 units of the Imperial Japanese Army were retained in Korea to protect the area and keep the quarrelsome populace under control. With the fall of Japan in 1945 the forces in Korea were ordered to lay down their arms although even this was not a straightforward process. Disarming the remaining Japanese troops in 1945 was divided between the forces of the Soviet Union above the 38th Parallel and below this point the United States forces were responsible for the same duties. As this was the start of the burgeoning Soviet global expansion it came as no surprise to find the

Seafire XVII SX194 was on the strength of No.1832 NAS based at Culham when this portrait was taken. These aircraft were the prime equipment for the reserve units as the FR.47's were needed for the 'Police Action' in Korea. (Rick Harding Collection)

Russians uncooperative over reunification of the country. In reply the United States formed a government in the south to match that of the north, the border being the aforementioned 38th Parallel. All this was in strong contrast to the Cairo Declaration of 1943 and the following Potsdam Declaration of 1945 which stated that Korea would become a free and independent state at the end of the war. The Russian involvement in Korea was the result of a canny political move by the Politburo which declared war on Japan a few days before the surrender having concentrated purely on Europe and the repulsion of the Germans before that.

During the period 1945 to 1948 the emergent United Nations made numerous attempts to persuade the Soviet Union to remove its personnel from North Korea, but all attempts were repulsed by a very awkward Russia which was fully aware that much of the west had no stomach for yet another global conflict. In response the United Nations would create South Korea below the 38th Parallel and as the country was to be a democracy elections for a president were held. The Republic of South Korea was recognised in 1948 as was its first ruler President Syngman Rhee, the only opposition being that of Russia and its in-thrall satellites. It was Russia that sponsored pseudo elections in North Korea that resulted in the formation of the Korean Peoples Democratic Republic which then laid claim to the whole of Korea. In December 1948 the Soviet Union withdrew its armed forces with the Americans doing likewise in July 1949 although a handful were to remain at the request of the South Korean administration. Except for this handful of advisors the South Koreans were entirely responsible for their own border security, the only help being weaponry and training. While this was taking place another abortive attempt was made by a UN Commission to reunite the country which again failed

Initially any military action was kept to mere border squabbles although the Korean forces on both sides were heavily supported by their respective Cold War supporters. The forces of the north received massive quantities of weaponry from Russia which led eventually to the army consisting of 90,000 troops supported by 180 tanks and 175 combat-capable aircraft. In contrast South Korea sported a similar number of troops but they were sadly lacking in armour, artillery and any type of combat aircraft. This period of relative calm was shattered on 25 June 1950 when the Soviet Union goaded the North Korean government to attack the south. In the early hours of that Sunday morning, after an intensive artillery and mortar barrage, the North Korean forces stormed across the 38th Parallel heading towards Seoul, the South Korean capital. Seoul is only 30 miles from the border and, therefore, the city was the centre of attention for at least 100 tanks and 100 aircraft from North

All marks of Seafire were prone to undercarriage problems and Seafire XV PR494 is no exception as the starboard main leg has failed while moving across the deck of the aircraft carrier. (Rick Harding Collection)

Seafire FR47 VP482 banks towards the camera. After service with No.800 Sqdn aboard HMS *Triumph* the aircraft was transferred to No.1833 NAS, a reserve unit, at Bramcote being withdrawn in September 1953. (FAAM Yeovilton)

Korea. Also attacked by this force was the town of Chunchon in the centre of the country while a third army column, supported by armour and more aircraft, proceeded down the east coast defeating quite easily the minor resistance encountered en route. Lacking in any form of heavy support the South Korean forces were continuously forced backwards for the next four days. Eventually the government set up home 100 miles further south at Taejon.

Such was the speed and ferocity of the North Korean advance that they must have thought that the war was over after a few days. While the navies of both sides were fairly evenly matched, Korea being a peninsula it was susceptible to the influence of any major sea power. This would be the starting point from which the United Nations General Secretary, Mr Trygve Lie, and the organisation would start their negotiations, planning and eventual voting. A special general meeting of the Security Council was held during the afternoon of Sunday 25 June during which those members present voted 9-0 to take action to drive the North Korean forces from the south. The only abstention from this vote was Yugoslavia. The Soviet representative did not attend the meeting as the UN had refused to recognise Communist China. Four days later the Soviet Foreign Minister, Mr Gromyko, sent an official note to Washington in which he claimed that the conflict had been started by the south invading the north. (Ah, the good old days of the Cold War !)

Having passed a resolution condemning the invasion the UN then passed a second that requested those nations, that were able, to provide forces to aid the South Koreans in ridding their country of the unwanted invaders. Three days after the resolution was passed 32 states out of a possible 52 had pledged support including Australia, Canada and New Zealand while Britain pledged ground and naval forces. It would be the United States who would lead the way deploying the largest air, ground and naval forces to the region. President Truman immediately began consultations with the Chief of the Joint Chiefs, General Omar Bradley, concerning which forces to deploy immediately and those that could follow later. The first recommendation was that the 7th Fleet deploy ships between Korea and the Chinese mainland thus cutting off that supply route early in the conflict. The responsibility of patrolling the Pacific shore was passed to Admiral Radford , Commander in Chief (C-in-C) US Pacific Fleet, based in Hawaii. Overall control of the forces in the area was placed in the hands of General of the Army Douglas MacArthur who was based in Tokyo, Japan.

The British response is recorded as being unequivocal, the government of Mr Clement Attlee recording that it was their duty to act

Prototype PS944 was the first folding wing Seafire F.47. From the outset the aircraft was fitted with a Griffon 87 engine and contra rotating propeller and was engaged in clearing the type for flight. (FAAM Yeovilton)

in concert with other UN members to repel the northern invaders. This was followed on 7 July by the establishment of a Unified Command in Japan which was put under the control of General MacArthur.

On that fateful day the British aircraft carrier HMS *Triumph*, commanded by Captain AD Torlesse DSO, was engaged in a cruise off Japan in company with other ships of the Far East Fleet. The intention of the cruise and some of the less exciting anchorage's was part of a plan by the C-in-C Far East Station, Admiral Sir Patrick Brind, to keep his vessels clear of the summer heat in Singapore and Hong Kong. On 8 June the carrier and its attendant vessels were anchored off Ominato in northern Japan then an unprepossessing fishing village. It had been the intention that during the following week HMS *Triumph* would undertake sea going exercises with her supporting ships and the onboard air wing. At the completion of these exercises the carrier was scheduled to return to Chatham by 13 November for a refit. However, the carrier's new duties meant that an immediate return to sea that June. Immediately, No.800 NAS, commanded by Lt Cdr I M Maclachlan, with its Seafire FR.47s started practice Rocket Assisted Take Offs, (RATOGs), while the other unit aboard, No.827 NAS, commanded by Lt Cdr B C Lyons, exercised

Having proved itself in the Pacific War the Fairey Firefly would be drafted to undertake missions during the Korean conflict, here a crew climbs out of their aircraft after completing another sortie. (FAAM Yeovilton)

Assigned to No.825 NAS Fairey Firefly AS.5 WB259 288-J undertakes a practise training sortie before the carrier HMS *Theseus* departs for Korean War service. (Rick Harding Collection)

their Fairey Fireflies. No.800 NAS's complement of aircraft included VP492, VP430 to VP432, VP442, VP450, VP453, VP455, VP460, VP462, VP471, VP473, VP477, VP482, VP485 and VP495 while No.827 NAS was equipped with PP420, PP429, PP432, PP433, PP434, PP459, PP464, PP468, PP469, PP473 plus PP478 to PP481. During these exercises two Seafires were written off early in the week due to severe skin wrinkling caused by overstressing of the tail-fuselage joint on landing while a further two were badly damaged later in the week, these including VP430, VP432 and VP450.

At the completion of the exercises HMS *Triumph,* in company with the destroyer HMS *Cossack,* departed its position off the coast of Japan on Saturday 24 June setting course for Hong Kong intending to pass south through the Sea of Japan between the Japanese Home Islands and the Korean coast. While the carrier was heading south towards its destination the Flag Officer 2 I/C Far East Fleet, Rear Admiral W G Andrewes, was aboard the cruiser HMS *Belfast* heading from north Japan to Yososuka when the news of the Korean invasion was received by signal. Upon receipt of the signal aboard the cruiser orders recalling HMS *Triumph* were immediately issued: the carrier was ordered to join *Belfast*

Fairey Firefly AS.6 WB438 274-A was assigned to No.826 NAS which spent much of its time aboard either the carriers *Ocean* or *Theseus* undertaking the support training task in the Mediterranean Sea. (Rick Harding Collection)

off south Japan. Once the recall had been issued the carrier immediately placed a pair of fully armed Seafires on deck standby while the Fireflies carried out deck landing practice. By mid week the carrier and its escort had refuelled at Kure before joining up with the cruiser HMS *Jamaica* and the escort vessels HMS *Consort* and HMAS *Shoalhaven*. Also in this task force was the tanker RFA (Royal Fleet Auxiliary) *Wave*. After refuelling, the aircraft carrier disembarked its damaged aircraft thus easing the load on the carrier engineering teams. Once these preparations had been completed the task force was placed at the disposal of US Naval Commander for Korean Operations, Vice Admiral C T Joy.

On 29 June HMS *Triumph* and escorts departed Kure and sailed to join Admiral Andrewes aboard *Belfast*. En route anti-submarine patrols were flown by the carrier's Firefly squadron. While in transit the latest intelligence arrived stating that enemy aircraft had been encountered and that the first American troops had landed in Korea. By 2 July the carrier and its escorts joined up with the United States 7th Fleet commanded by Vice Admiral Struble flying his flag aboard the cruiser USS *Rochester*. The US Navy vessels were designated TF 77 while the British contingent was designated TF 77.5. Soon after arrival the Fireflies of No.827 NAS began to undertake anti-submarine patrols around the British vessels while a further Firefly and a Seafire flew around the American ships to familiarise them with the British aircraft in an effort to reduce accidental shoot downs. On 3 July *Triumph* launched its first strike against enemy positions which consisted of 12 Seafires escorting nine Fireflies. The selected target was the airfield at Kaishu which was some 120 miles from the fleet. As with all such attacks the plan was to run in from low level, however, the weather was not privy to that script thus the strike force had to climb over the encroaching cloud. Fortunately, the weather cleared again and the aircraft were able to drop down to a lower level. Initially the Seafires attacked followed by the Fireflies then the final flight of Seafires. The entire attack was unopposed and, although many of the installations were badly damaged, it was decided that pre-strike reconnaissance was a requirement as many of the targets were attacked without a definite plan. The following day saw *Triumph* launch 12 Fireflies and seven Seafires, there being a lack of serviceable machines, with a wide ranging brief to attack targets in the vicinity of Haeju, Ongjin and Yonan. During this weapons-free patrol army positions were strafed, bridges attacked plus various vehicles were destroyed.

Having completed these initial attacks the British Fleet turned south, the *Belfast* and the two destroyers finally arriving at Sasebo while the remainder anchored at Okinawa; all required refuelling and re-storing. The carrier remained in port for six days for refit and it was during this period that the familiar black and white striping was applied, initially the Seafires were the priority as the Americans reckoned that it closely resembled the Soviet built Yak 9. It was at this point that some support questions were raised that mainly centred around aircraft repair and resupply. At Sasebo facilities were limited for the anchoring of an aircraft carrier therefore it was proposed that HMS *Unicorn* be sent to the region to improve support. *Unicorn* had been built as an aircraft support ship and would act as the base for the *Illustrious* class of carriers. Unlike a conventional carrier *Unicorn* was fitted with transport rails and winches in both hangars for the transfer of major components while the aft end of the upper hanger could be opened for engine runs. The flight deck was longer aft than normal, the overhang being used to house the self-propelled aircraft lighter hanging from davits. This layout allowed a serviceable aircraft to be moved from the upper hanger onto the lighter for transfer to another carrier. As well as the mechanical engineering side the *Unicorn* was fully equipped with workshops that could deal with airframe, avionics, electrical and engine components. As there was little requirement to hold large quantities of aviation fuel and armament more space was available for an extensive spares holding that could cater for all the frontline aircraft currently in service. During the invasion of South Korea the vessel had been in Singapore de-storing prior to returning to Britain. As the ship's services were needed in a hurry it was hastily prepared for sea departing for Japan in late June 1950. By 20 July *Unicorn* had arrived at Sasebo where the workshops were landed while the vessel concerned itself with shuttling aircraft, spares and stores between Hong Kong and Sasebo: on one voyage the vessel carried 300 barrels of vital rum. During its time supporting the *Triumph* operations *Unicorn* embarked the Middlesex Regiment and the Argyll and Sutherland Highlanders on 25 August. The troops disembarked on 29 August and were the first British troops to land on the Korean peninsula. Having completed this task *Unicorn* departed Korean waters for Hong Kong where it arrived in early September for a refit. Once this was completed *Unicorn* departed from Hong Kong carrying a full load of aircraft, stores and ammunition arriving off Sasebo in mid October.

On 17 July *Triumph* in company with the remainder of the fleet departed Okinawa to undertake support operations off the Korean coast. On 18 July the 1st Cavalry Division was landed near Pohang by ships of the US Navy to establish a beachhead. Completely unopposed, 10,000 troops plus vehicles and stores were landed and thus began the fight back against the North Korean forces. While there was little air opposition to these landings the pressure on ground positions continued. Most of the supporting air strike missions were flown by aircraft for the US carrier USS *Valley Forge*. This left the *Triumph* air wing with the tasks of flying air defence and anti-submarine patrols around the fleet during which some 140 flying hours were completed. HMS *Triumph* would leave the area of operations earlier than expected as a stern gland on one of the propeller shafts had been showing signs of failure. Not wishing to cause further damage the vessel left for Sasebo on 21 July where repairs were undertaken. While in Sasebo harbour the opportunity was taken to replenish the stocks of aircraft from those held aboard *Unicorn*. Quickly made ready for sea *Triumph* departed Sasebo on 25 July heading for a position just off Quelpart Island. During the transit to join TF 77 deck training for the air wing was undertaken during which a further two Seafires were written off. Due to a lack of trade it was decided to move *Triumph* and its escorts to the east coast of Korea. The carrier arrived at its new station on 26 July. While waiting for targets to present themselves both the Seafire and Firefly squadrons undertook combat air patrols over the fleet, the latter combining these with anti-submarine patrols. Two days later during a reported incoming bogie report resulted in a Seafire FR.47, VP473, from *Triumph* being shot down by a USAF B-29 Superfortress which had mistaken it for a Yak 9. Fortunately the pilot, Commissioned Pilot D R

WD887 was a Fairey Firefly AS.6 was assigned to No.814 NAS when photographed. The squadron was embarked aboard HMS *Vengeance* at the time. When that carrier retired the Firefly was transferred to the Australian Navy for Korean War service. (Rick Harding Collection)

White, was rescued by the destroyer USS *Eversole* and returned to his ship. HMS *Triumph* departed from the combat zone on 31 July returning to Kure for a refit. During this break a further change over of aircraft was undertaken and completed by 8 August; all unserviceable machines were replaced by serviceable aircraft. The following day the carrier and escorts departed Kure for Sasebo where they picked up Admiral Andrewes and his staff and they sailed for the west coast and the maze of islands in the area. The air wing's task was to carry out aerial reconnaissance over this zone in an effort to intercept the small vessels that were able to navigate through the various channels. Further reconnaissance sorties were flown over the north Korean harbour of Chinnampo where three ships were discovered at the mouth of the Taedong estuary. Both Seafires and Fireflies undertook attacks on these ships, hits being noted on all three.

By 18 August the *Triumph* and escorts were operating off the west coast of Korea in the area of Inchon-Kunsan. During the next three days the aircraft of No.827 NAS went hunting for surface targets sinking at least one gunboat although at least one Firefly was employed in anti-submarine patrol duties. While the Fireflies were chasing ships the Seafires of No.800 NAS were undertaking photo reconnaissance sorties, their air patrols for that period being covered by aircraft from the US 7th Fleet. Led by Lt Cdr Maclachlan, the Commanding Officer of No.800 NAS, the Seafires ranged north as far as the North Korean capital, Pyongyang. Very little was seen although all the factories were noted as working hard and were well defended by anti-aircraft guns. As a result

While the majority of Fleet Air Arm squadrons were equipped with single engined fighters some attempts were made to introduce heavier types into the service's inventory. The first of these was the de Havilland Sea Mosquito TR.33 however few reached front line units. (BBA Collection)

of these operations the Seafire strength was reduced to nine flyable machines, the other three awaiting repair. This reduction in strength meant that there were only 16 Seafires left in theatre, the other seven being aboard HMS *Unicorn*. After the completion of these missions *Triumph* returned to Sasebo where the carrier joined up with the other two carriers USS *Valley Forge* and the *Philippine Sea* on 23 August.

After three days of refitting and restoring HMS *Triumph*, with the usual selection of escorting ships, departed Sasebo and headed for the west coast of Korea again. As the Task Force approached the coast the Seafires resumed a more intensive air patrol as a result of an earlier air attack upon the USS *Comus*. This left the Fireflies free to concentrate upon armed reconnaissance sorties. These missions took place over the ports of Inchon, Chinnampo, Kunsan and Mokpo and revealed little activity, however, a couple of motor boats carrying supplies were attacked and sunk. During this period of active service tragedy struck on 29 August 1950 when a Firefly FR.1, PP433, landed without a working arrester hook which resulted in the propeller striking the carrier's deck. After impact one of the blades flew through a window of the flying control position killing Lt Cdr Maclachlan who was in the carrier's Operations Room. This gallant pilot was buried at sea that night with full military honours. The following day the carrier and its escorts returned to Sasebo where *Unicorn* took on the last 14 aircraft available comprising six Seafires and eight Fireflies.

During these operations HMS *Triumph* had provided much needed support to the carriers of the US Navy whose primary task had been the support of the American forces holding the Pusan Perimeter. In concert with USAF bombers the Navy aircraft kept the inexperienced ground forces protected and supplied until such time as they were able to start the push back.

HMS *Triumph* resumed its service on 3 September arriving off the west coast the following day damaging a Seafire early on when the belly-mounted fuel tank came adrift on take-off, fortunately the Seafire returned to the deck safely. However the damage was such that the aircraft was struck off charge. While the Seafires were having adventures the Fireflies were undertaking spotting assignments for the cruisers *Jamaica* and *Charity*. The following day the Seafires undertook the same task, targets at Kunsan being bombarded by the cruisers. The following day *Triumph* departed to the east coast of Korea to replace the 7th Fleet Carriers which had been withdrawn for re-storing, recuperation and maintenance. By 8 September the carrier group was some 100 miles north of the 38th parallel from where sorties were launched against Wonsan, the primary port on that coast. The strike force consisted of six each of Seafires and Fireflies attacking the communications network with both rockets and cannon fire. Once the strike aircraft had returned to *Triumph* they were quickly refuelled and rearmed for the afternoon missions. This involved six Seafires and four Fireflies, the main target being the goods yard at Kowon and that at Yonghung; both places were subjected to rocket and cannon fire. The return to the carrier was not without incident as three machines were badly damaged on landing namely two Seafires, VP430 plus VP431 and a Firefly, PP549. The following day saw a handful of sorties launched despite the inclement weather, however, yet again the returning aircraft suffered damage, this time four Seafires were badly damaged. As this reduced No.800 NAS ability to act as a cohesive unit it was decided that *Triumph* would return to Sasebo and it duly arrived there on 10 September.

After two days of refitting, during which the Sasebo engineers worked miracles repairing damaged Seafires, HMS *Triumph* departed from Sasebo, as part of CTF 91, to take up blockade and covering duties along the west coast. On the two days prior to the proposed landings at Inchon the *Triumph* provided air cover over the south-west corner of Korea until after the landing when the carrier and its escorts formed the anti-submarine screen for the vessels of the US Navy 7th Fleet. As the air wing aboard *Triumph* was severely limited each sortie had to be carefully considered; thus a combat patrol was on standby, two aircraft were on spotter bombardment duties while two others were on reconnaissance and blockade missions. While the Royal Navy was providing support and cover the carriers of the US Navy were launching wave after wave of air strikes against targets in the vicinity of the Inchon and Seoul area destroying as much enemy hardware and their facilities as possible.

Known as Operation Chromite the assigned role of the *Triumph* air wing was to provide air cover for the primary attack on Wolmi do, the main North Korean defence command post while the supporting ships would bombard Inchon, not only to destroy any targets in the zone but to also act as a decoy. In the early hours of 13 September the US Navy began a massive assault up the Salee River using destroyers and rocket ships to attack the strongholds along the banks. While the Americans were letting loose in all directions HMS *Triumph* was launching a pair of Fireflies complete with overload tanks so that they could cover spotter duties for the cruisers HMS *Jamaica* and *Kenya*. During this bombardment one of the cruisers hit a hidden ammunition store which resulted in one of the most spectacular explosions of the attack. During these missions another Seafire was badly damaged on landing reducing the carriers aircraft complement even further. Another Seafire, VP495, was lost because it was unable to lower its arrester hook or clear its belly fuel tank. As the aircraft was unable to land on the carrier the pilot, Lt Berry, was left with no option but to bale out and he was rescued by the USS *Bataan*. The suddenness and strength of the attack had surprised the North Koreans although they were warned about the build-up of Allied forces by signals from Inchon. Almost unopposed the Americans had landed 13,000 troops plus their weapons, stores and equipment.

Although *Triumph* had a reduced aircraft complement its crews were still used to provide combat patrols and they were preferred for bombardment spotting because they used accurate and clear spoken English. On 17 September the only North Korean air attack was undertaken. In the early hours of the morning a Yak-3 and an IL-10 Stormovik surprised the American fleet. During this attack the USS *Rochester* was slightly damaged by bombing and HMS *Jamaica* was raked with gunfire. The intruders did not have it all their own way as the *Jamaica* opened fire with the full panoply of anti-aircraft weapons successfully downing the Stormovik. In retaliation for these attacks the cruisers *Jamaica* and *Kenya* shelled targets in the Inchon area before withdrawing further from the coast.

The *Triumph* air wing had a quiet day on 18 September, only a section of Seafires were airborne and they attacked a pair of barges in the region of Heaju. A similar exercise was flown by the Seafires the following day, again shipping in the area was subject to attack. Later that day a further attack was carried out on a pair of junks but they were not the ones originally reported, these having disappeared. While the Seafires were giving the local shipping a pasting the Fireflies were undertaking their usual round of anti-submarine duties although they did engage in some spotting duties for the cruiser HMS *Ceylon*. Shipping attacks were the order of the day for the Seafires and all aircraft returned safely. This was considered a bonus as No.800 NAS only had three flyable aircraft left. No.827 NAS was in slightly better shape with eight machines still available for duty. Although *Triumph* could still perform a limited series of duties it was decided by Admiral Andrewes to return the carrier to Britain as its replacement, HMS *Theseus*, was due on station within the week.

While HMS *Triumph* was leading a relatively quiet life at sea the American land forces were capturing their assigned targets, the US Marines successfully capturing Kimpo airfield: quickly basing their own aircraft there to provide closer local air support. Further pushes by ground forces with extensive air support saw the Communist forces being pushed back from the Pusan perimeter: first evidence of this being noted on 23 September. Four days later units of the US Army and Marine Corps met up at Osan. A further push saw Yongdung-po and Seoul being recaptured after much bitter fighting on 28 September, the South Korean president returning to the capital the following day. While this could be seen as General MacArthur's final triumph it was also the point where a more violent phase of the war would begin. The General, having proved that his instinct to land at Inchon was correct, had the exclusive ear of President Truman who was content to authorise the General to conduct operations over the 38th Parallel. What the UN forces were unaware of was that Communist China had stated that such move would bring that country into the war.

When the Supermarine Walrus was finally retired it was replaced by the slightly more advanced Sea Otter. In perilous circumstances in enemy or shark infested seas either type was a welcome sight. (FAAM Yeovilton)

Seen operating off the Korean coast HMS *Theseus* sports a full range of Sea Furies on the forward flight deck, all of which sport Korean identification stripes. (Rick Harding Collection)

HMS *Triumph* entered Sasebo harbour so that minor repairs to the propeller gland could be undertaken prior to the long voyage home. Repairs complete, the carrier arrived in Hong Kong harbour on 29 September to find the replacement carrier, HMS *Theseus*, waiting to depart for Korea. *Triumph* finally arrived at Portsmouth in November where, after a much needed refit, the carrier was converted for troopship duties. In this new role *Triumph* would sail between Britain and the Far East until the end of 1951. In early 1952 HMS *Triumph* undertook an important series of trials that saw an angled deck painted onto the normal fore and aft deck. Although numerous types of aircraft carried out controlled approaches, they did not land as the arrestor wires were still in the original positions. It would be joint trials by the RN/USN aboard the USS *Antietam* with a proper angled deck and arrestor cables moved to accommodate it. The flight deck trials were the last time that *Triumph* was actively involved in aircraft movements. Laid up at Portsmouth from 1957 to mid 1962 the carrier was later converted to a heavy repair ship for use in the Far East. From the beginning of 1965 *Triumph* operated in Far East waters before returning to Chatham in early 1972. Although refitted for further service the carrier remained in reserve until placed on the disposal list in 1981 finally departing to Spain to be broken up in December.

Chapter 6

Korea: the Sea Fury Years

The carrier that replaced *Triumph*, HMS *Theseus*, had been completed for service in February 1946 and had initially been allocated to the Far East Fleet with No.804 NAS and its Seafires plus No.812 NAS and its Fireflies aboard. After a refit in Rosyth Dockyard during 1947 the air wing was re-equipped with Sea Furies and Fireflies of Nos 807 and 813 NAS. After working-up the carrier departed for Sasebo on 8 October 1950 in company with the cruiser HMS *Kenya* plus *Constance, Sioux* and *Cayuga*. En route to Sasebo extensive and concentrated flying training was carried out to ensure that the pilots could land their aircraft safely thus reducing the workload overall on the maintenance teams, who would be fully stretched keeping the aircraft rearmed and maintained during operations, without having to repair damaged airframes. The deck parties also worked hard to ensure that their duties were performed without mistakes and, in particular, the deck landing officers studied each approaching aircraft and would wave it off if there was any doubt.

Having missed the arrester wires aboard HMS *Vengeance* this Sea Fury F.10 of No.802 NAS is heading straight into the barrier. At this time the Sea Fury was still undergoing testing and accidents involving a new type were not unexpected. (Trevor Jones Collection)

Seen overflying the soon to be decommissioned aircraft carrier HMS *Formidable* is the Sea Fury F.10 during flight testing. While the carrier would go to the breakers in 1953 this first version of the Sea Fury would remain in use until 1959. (FAAM Yeovilton)

Having arrived in Hong Kong on 29 September the carrier would depart for Sasebo on 2 October, the air wing arriving back on board after having been ashore at Kai Tak from 24 September. The journey was slowed slightly as there was a typhoon warning in force and the aircraft were secured for this eventuality and the carrier and escorts slowed down to reduce the possibility of damage to the smaller ships. The delay meant that the ships did not arrive until 4 October. Once secured in Sasebo *Theseus* received extra aircraft from HMS *Warrior* which had replaced *Unicorn* as the carrier support vessel. Unlike *Unicorn* HMS *Warrior* had been built as fully functional aircraft carrier before assuming its new role in June 1950. With its full inventory of aircraft aboard the ground crews applied black and white striping to all the aircraft for recognition purposes. With a full complement of vessels available

Admiral Andrewes decided to reorganise the ships so that Task Element TE 95.11 comprised *Theseus* plus escorts, TE 95.12 was for surface patrol and blockade, TE 95.13 was the screen element while another handful of small ships and aircraft covered minesweeping and general tasking. On 9 October *Theseus* undertook its first operational patrol off the Korean coast, combat cover was provided by the Sea Furies while the Firefly squadron carried out anti-submarine patrols. By this time the Firefly had been fitted with a radar pod in place of one of the under-wing fuel tanks; it detracted little from the aircraft's performance and its addition gave the aircraft better capabilities. The main patrol area for *Theseus* was the Yellow Sea close by the Shantung Peninsula. While the carrier was fitted with a very good air warning radar it was decided that the standing air patrols would be maintained during daylight hours for increased security. During these patrols the Sea Fury pilots felt themselves to be most unlucky not to engage in any air to air combat although they did manage to intercept various Neptunes, Sunderlands and B-29 Superfortress bombers heading to bomb the bridges on the Yula River.

Sea Fury FB.11 VR940 100-Q survived this nose over aboard HMS *Vengeance* in August 1948. After repair the aircraft would transfer to No.807 NAS aboard the carrier *Theseus* being lost on operations on 26 January 1951, the pilot being killed (FAAM Yeovilton)

This Hawker Sea Fury FB.11, VX642, is surrounded by and carries the full range of fuel tanks and weaponry cleared for this type. Much of this clearance was originally carried out using the F.10. (FAAM Yeovilton)

This view shows both versions of Sea Furies as operated by No.802 NAS. The nearest machine is an FB.11 while the remainder are the earlier F.10 model. (Trevor Jones Collection)

Missions selected for *Theseus* included the usual selection of standing air patrols and anti-submarine patrols to which were added armed reconnaissance and air strikes, the latter being handed down by the Joint Operations Centre, initially located in Seoul and later in Taegu. Prior to departure on patrol the carrier was provided with all the intelligence and target data current at that time, any updates concerning new targets and bombing missions would be sent by immediate signal. To improve targeting the aerial operational areas were marked out on special maps that broke the country up into designated squares which were also marked with roads that were allocated colours and numbers. As soon as a target was spotted within any area it could be quickly identified on the armed reconnaissance map and aircraft assigned to attack. This method of attacking available targets soon drove the North Koreans to find another way of using the roads. By night it was far easier while in daylight extremely good camouflage was needed, even so as aircrews became familiar with their assigned territories any unusual changes were quickly spotted and these potential targets could be dealt with. In order to protect the aircraft and crews it was recommended that general area over flights be carried out at 1,500 ft while over zones with a greater concentration of defences the recommended height was 5,000 ft. Ground strikes in support of ground forces was normally managed using the British method of strike management. This consisted of an aerial controller flying in an NAA T.6 Harvard in contact by radio with spotters on the ground. Using this method of control allowed fast moving aircraft to come close to their targets as they sprayed the area with bombs, rockets and cannon fire. Obviously this lack of accuracy meant that the targets suffered only minor damage so the Americans developed and deployed napalm bombs while the Fleet Air Arm concentrated upon improving their accuracy which in turn caused greater casualties amongst the enemy. The crews of both Fireflies and Sea Furies also had to contend with the fact that their area of operations was highly mountainous, to their credit not a single aircraft was lost to terrain collision accidents. As the flights from the aircraft carriers were over nearly 80 miles of sea it was common practice to have a destroyer placed approximately at the mid flight point between the carrier operating point and Inchon this being known as 'Bird Dog'.

When *Theseus* arrived in theatre its air wing complement consisted of 23 Sea Furies of No.807 NAS commanded by Lt Cdr A J Thomson DSC and No.813 NAS commanded by Lt Cdr L W A Barrington with 12 Fireflies plus a Sea/Air Rescue (SAR) component consisting of either a Sea Otter amphibian or a helicopter. The vessel's captain was Captain A S Bolt DSO, DSC. When the air wing was tasked with sorties the single-seater fighters were fitted with 45 gallon external fuel tanks while the two-seaters had 55 gallon tanks installed. These were needed because the sortie lengths were timed at two and a half hours. Added to the extra fuel load was the internal and external weapons loads which required that either the catapult be used for launching or, if that was out of action, each aircraft had to be boosted by RATOG packs. Initially the Sea Furies were launched with a weapons load of two 500 lb bombs, although this was later changed to the lighter 60 lb rockets as the required over-deck speed of 28 knots was not achievable by *Theseus* as the carriers hull required scraping and was therefore only capable of 22 knots. Changing the bomb loads to the Fireflies meant that the carrier needed only to achieve a top speed of 21 knots. As the handling crews became more experienced the launch and recovery rates improved; when operating with the US 7th Fleet carriers they were well able to match the launch rate of the Americans even though *Theseus* only had the one catapult. During the carrier's deployment it was found that the best launch rate was 50 sorties per day however this could be pushed to 66 per day should the need arise. The first strike launched by *Theseus* on 9 October consisted of six Sea Furies carrying eight 60 lb warhead rockets and four Fireflies armed with a pair of 500 lb bombs each, the strike leader being Lt Cdr Stovin-Bradford DSC, the air wing commander. The assigned targets were Paengyong-do and the Fireflies concentrated upon the more hardened targets while the fighters strafed and rocketed everything that moved and much that did not. All aircraft returned to *Theseus* without damage after two hours airborne. The afternoon saw the next strike launched this time only five Sea Furies were sent although the Firefly complement remained the same. The target was the harbour area at Chinnampo. As before the Fireflies attacked the more hardened targets with better success than the morning raid while yet again the fighters attacked the slightly softer targets. During both sorties very little anti-aircraft fire was encountered and was restricted to some rifle fire.

The following day the air wing resumed the more mundane duties of anti-submarine patrols which were coupled with searching for mines. During one of these flights an 810 NAS Firefly crew reported the possible existence of a minefield to the north of the carrier group. Although not an immediate threat efforts were promptly made to remove it. While the rolling patrols were being undertaken *Theseus* launched four Fireflies escorted by a pair of Sea Furies tasked with attacking the railway bridge at Chang-you and two spans were successfully downed. Once the Fireflies had finished, one being slightly damaged by blast from its own bombs, the Sea Furies attacked rail and road vehicles in the vicinity of the railway station. While one strike force was demolishing a bridge and

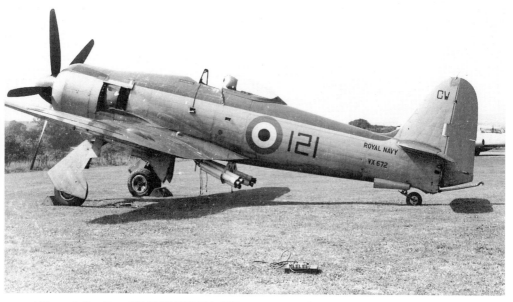

Although Sea Fury FB.11 VX672 121-CW was assigned to No.736 NAS amongst other second line fighter units it is seen here sporting a complete RATOG setup. It is obviously on trials work as careful observation shows a remote initiator to the foreground. The aircraft obviously survived this operation as its fuselage was later sold back to Hawkers. (FAAM Yeovilton)

giving the locals a hard time a further four Sea Furies led by the air wing commander attacked other buildings and positions around the area. During these attacks a Sea Fury, VW628, flown by Lieutenant Leonard was damaged causing the engine to fail. The pilot managed to retain control long enough to crash land in a local paddy field. In an effort to protect the pilot who had remained trapped in his wrecked aircraft a pair of his companions in Sea Furies circled the area until fuel ran short at which point another Sea Fury took over. While providing support for their downed compatriot a request had been made for a rescue helicopter from Kimpo. Within the hour the helicopter touched down to be met by gunfire from a nearby building. As the onboard doctor helped the seriously injured airman from his cockpit the helicopter pilot laid down covering fire from his aircraft while urging the doctor to hurry. Eventually Lt Leonard was extracted from his aircraft and both the patient and doctor returned to the helicopter which took off safely. While the USAF helicopter was performing its rescue, support was given by an USMC Grumman F7F Tigercat which destroyed the Sea Fury as the final act of this drama.

While the RATOG units were great for boosting aircraft into the air they occasionally went wrong. In this view Sea Fury FB.11 VX623 103-R from HMS *Glory* uses RATOG to launch the aircraft into the air. Just after this the aircraft rolled off its flight path and crashed into the Hal Far, Malta, airfield. Fortunately the pilot escaped successfully. (FAAM Yeovilton)

The afternoon sorties went ahead as planned comprising four Fireflies and six Sea Furies armed with bombs and rockets respectively. While the Fireflies caused some damage to their target the Sea Furies, operating in pairs, attacked lesser targets of opportunity. All aircraft would later return to *Theseus* safely. Of the strikes planned for 11 October only the morning sorties were launched in an effort to catch the North Koreans still in the open. Unfortunately, they quickly disappeared as the fighters came near but even so some targets were found and attacked with some success. A further mission was launched later that morning against the islands off the west coast but this was the last attack possible before the weather deteriorated below flying minima. As no further flying was possible that day *Theseus* moved off to the replenishment area near Inchon to refuel the destroyer escort before returning to its station the next morning. No sorties were flown on the morning of 12 October, the plan being to launch a major attack against targets in the vicinity of Chang-yong. Although the attempt to take out the bridge failed, strafing and rocket attacks against troop trenches, ammunition dumps and anti-aircraft emplacements were more successful, at least one dump blowing up most satisfactorily. These continued harassing attacks seemed to be driving enemy forces out of the Haeju-Ongjin area, however, Admiral Andrewes decided that *Theseus* would continue operations in the area as the harbour at Haeju was a useful port and that the enemy could still have his communications harassed in the Chinnampo area. The following day was a relatively quiet one for the *Theseus* air wing, the Fireflies carried out their assigned patrols while the Sea Furies strafed some junks suspected of being mine layers. A further sortie launched that afternoon saw the Sea Furies attacking various small vessels suspected of being employed by the enemy; during these attacks both rockets and cannons were utilised garnering some success.

The original mission planned for 14 October was against targets in the Sariwon area but the alternative at Chinnampo was selected. The Firefly contingent bombed buildings with some success while the fighters used their rockets and cannons to attack targets of opportunity. On their way home from the harbour the Sea Furies attacked some junks and troop trenches. As some of the junks had escaped from the fighters attention it was decided to refuel and rearm them quickly so that they could return

Currently preserved Sea Fury FB.11 VX653 was mainly used by the second line training units to prepare pilots for service over Korea although it served for a short period with the RCN aboard HMCS *Warrior*. (FAAM Yeovilton)

A situation not unknown to many pilots of the Sea Fury operating over Korea, the damage to the airframe caused by making an emergency landing; these being frequently caused by engine or hydraulic failures. (Rick Harding Collection)

Carrying both underwing fuel tanks plus rocket rails is this Sea Fury FB.11 WG603 138-CW which spent much of its time being used in the weapons training role. (Rick Harding Collection)

to finish the job. The attack was successful and the junks destroyed. Having dealt with the shipping the fighters went onto harass troops positions in the area surrounding Chinnampo harbour while the Fireflies concentrated upon the docks. The weather on the following day played a part in curtailing the aerial operations from *Theseus* although one attack was made again on the bridge at Sariwon although it survived the attentions of the Fireflies. One of the Fireflies would just manage to return to the carrier as its engine was close to failing. A similar fate befell the air wing commander whose engine failed just after touchdown. Once the strike force had landed it was the turn of the combat patrol to make the attempt, by that time visibility had reduced drastically although both did manage to touch down safely. Both the damaged aircraft were struck down into the hanger where engine changes were carried out bringing them both up to a serviceable status. On 16 October the Sea Furies were launched in late morning to attack some minelaying junks proceeding up the coast which blew up dramatically after being hit by fire from all aircraft. Following this spectacular part of the mission the fighters attacked warehouses at Chinnampo destroying them with their remaining rockets. Once the fighters were safely recovered HMS *Theseus* departed for Inchon for refuelling from the tankers RFA *Green Ranger* and *Wave Premier*. During this phase of the deployment serviceability amongst the aircraft was at least 99 per cent, a credit to the ships engineering staff.

Around breakfast time on 18 October HMS *Theseus* departed from Inchon and the first flights were launched soon afterwards, as normal the Firefly squadron put up an anti-submarine and mine patrol while the Sea Furies provided air cover. While *Theseus* had been in port the ground forces had pushed the North Koreans hard and the designated bomb line, the movable point on the tactical map above which weapons could be used without restriction, was moving northwards rapidly. This meant that targets were few and far between. As there was little trade for the aircraft the Fireflies over flew the frontlines while the Sea Furies took a look at the harbours along the coast, while little was to be seen one Sea Fury experienced anti-aircraft fire which damaged the engine, fortunately the pilot was able to make an emergency landing on the carrier. With so little to do in their assigned area the *Theseus* Task Force moved further north taking up a position which enabled the air group to fly comfortably in the Sinanju-Chongju-Sonchon zone, arriving on 19 October. The first operations were launched the next morning, their targets being in the vicinity of Chongju. The Fireflies attacked buildings used for storage while the Sea Furies attacked various warehouses and the infrastructure of the local railway. As the town had been severely

Pictured on the lift of HMS *Glory* is Sea Fury FB.11 VW546 110-R complete with Korean identification striping. Once clear of the lift the aircraft would be prepared for its next mission. (FAAM Yeovilton)

bombed by the USAF B-29 force there was very little of significance left to attack. While further sorties were launched in the afternoon and the following morning not enough targets remained in the area to justify *Theseus* remaining on station, therefore, the Task Force was ordered back to port at Sasebo. The return to Sasebo was well timed as the reeving of the catapult was found to be worn through while the arrester cables were also in need of an overhaul.

Such was the need for *Theseus* to resume patrol duties that the carrier was ordered back to sea earlier than expected. Prior to leaving Sasebo on 27 October three damaged Sea Furies were returned ashore and six Fireflies would fly off for Iwakuni as *Theseus* had no catapult available. In return a US Navy helicopter would land aboard the carrier for the task acting in concert with the minesweepers to clear the approaches of Chinnampo harbour. With a reduced number of Fireflies aboard their task was restricted purely to anti-submarine and mine spotting. In contrast the Sea Furies undertook armed reconnaissance duties throughout their assigned patrol area. As there were weight restrictions due to the lack of a catapult the fighters had to fly without external fuel tanks, rockets or bombs which left the 20 mm cannon as their only offensive capability. Having taken off under their own power for their first patrol it was decided for the next day's flying that due to the lack of a decent headwind that RATOG would be used to get the patrol airborne. The first three departed in accordance with the pilots notes however the fourth suffered a possible misfire and flipped over on its back just after take-off. Fortunately quick reactions by the pilot saved it from crashing into the sea and the patrol continued after the RATOG had been jettisoned. As there was little work for the carrier to do it was decided to return the vessel to Sasebo. En route to port the six missing Fireflies were flown on, a further three would be transhipped from HMS *Unicorn* in port. While en route the ships engineering department replaced the acceleration and retardation ropes for the catapult which was a feat in itself as it was normally a task reserved for a well equipped dockyard. This practice would later become the norm for this class of aircraft carrier. On 8 November *Theseus*, in company with HMS *Sioux*, departed for Hong Kong. During the passage to Hong Kong the ships were warned that the remnants of Typhoon Clare was headed their way. While the carrier rode out the storm quite well the smaller ship suffered some damage but, even so, both vessels arrived safely on 11 November.

After completing re-storing *Theseus* put to sea for catapult trials which were successfully carried out. With the carrier fully serviceable the air wing was put through its paces and while some incidents occurred, both squadrons passed muster, the final aircraft arriving from Kai Tak on the evening of 30 November. On 1 December HMS *Theseus* departed from Hong Kong arriving in Sasebo some three days later. The continued presence of a carrier in the far east was fortuitous as it had been intended to reduce the Royal Navy contingent in the war zone as the United Nations forces appeared to be winning, however the tone of the war was soon to change. On 25 October the UN forces had reached the Yula river and were in the process of consolidating their positions when they were subject to heavy attacks by units of the Chinese Red Army. Further incursions saw the UN frontline reversing course rapidly finally reaching the Chongchon river where a new front line was established. In support of the ground forces the US 7th Fleet launched every aircraft to attack the advancing Chinese forces with further attacks being mounted by the USAF units in theatre. In order not to lose too many troops it was decided to lift off an many as possible by sea. Evacuation was already underway from Wonsan with the rescued troops being deposited further south where they could be redeployed.

With fuel tanks and rockets under the wings this Sea Fury aboard HMS *Glory* prepares to launch. In the background further aircraft prepare for launching. (Rick Harding Collection)

HMS *Theseus* with Admiral Andrewes aboard departed from Sasebo on 4 December as part of Carrier Task Group 95.1 with three escorts. Their role was to provide air cover for the amphibious rescue effort. To that end a constant stream of Fireflies and Sea Furies began operations on 5 December attacking targets in the area on Chinnampo. The railways in that area, so vital for moving supplies, were heavily hit. Flying throughout that day was hampered by the first fingers of winter as snow showers were hampering either launches or recoveries. The following day was similar but, even so, targets along the coast were attacked with rockets. With all aircraft safely returned the carrier departed to Inchon as one of the propeller glands was exhibiting signs of overheating and needed repacking. Fortunately this was quickly carried out and *Theseus* was back on station in the early hours of the following day. Over the following two days the Sea Furies and the Fireflies attacked various enemy targets along the coast and around the outskirts of Chinnampo. The following day the weather worsened resulting in the aircraft from *Theseus* landing at Kimpo.

Strikes resumed on 11 December and were particularly successful as a pair of rail bridges were attacked while the Sea Furies totally wrecked a moving train. Pyongyang was the focus for the air wing the following day with a dam and two bridges attacked. While in the area the aircraft also took the opportunity to destroy buildings once occupied by the UN and to destroy any stores remaining in the area. The following day a similar range of targets were treated to some destruction as were some truck convoys and small shipping off the coast. After four days on station Theseus returned to Sasebo. The time in port was short as *Theseus* departed the next day complete with its usual selection of escorts. The carrier's arrival on station was a bit premature because the weather deteriorated rapidly which meant that although flying was possible it was delayed as the aircraft needed de-icing and the flight deck required clearing of snow. However, the usual range of patrols was launched as was a small Sea Fury strike group. While the patrols had an uneventful time the strike mission enjoyed the freedom to attack trucks trapped by the weather near the Chongchon river. Once the Sea Furies had returned the patrols were quickly recalled as the weather was worsening. On 19 December the Sea Furies had a field day in Hangju-Sariwon area where they successfully destroyed a large amount of trucks and some tanks. The Fireflies also undertook bombing raids along the roads although they had to do it through gaps in the clouds.

The following day also saw further strikes being launched with Sea Furies attacking buildings in the area of Chinnampo and Sariwon after which they strafed a bulldozer, hit two petrol, oil and lubricant (POL) dumps and some lorries. Over the next two days similar sorties were undertaken although all were interrupted occasionally by the snow. Even so bridges, trucks and buildings were given close attention by the roving aircraft. On 22 December the carrier had a rest day for refuelling with flying resuming the following day. This time the sorties by the Fireflies were unproductive and some aircraft jettisoned their rockets before landing. However, the Sea Furies had more joy attacking a troop concentration near Pyongyang and trucks and buildings with good results. While most of the world was looking forward to Christmas the *Theseus* air wing was again in action on Christmas Eve successfully attacking a column of troops en route to Sariwon after which Sariwon itself was subject to attack. On Christmas Day two strike sorties were launched against Sariwon again where, once more, troops, vehicles and buildings were hit. The follow-up mission and the standing patrols were halted when fuel checks revealed that the fuel in some of the aircraft was contaminated by water. Once all available aircraft had been checked those confirmed as clear were launched to provide the standing patrols which remained airborne until the strike sortie had returned. Once all aircraft had landed-on, the carrier plus escorts set course for Sasebo. When in Sasebo on 26 December the carrier picked up a new group of pilots before departing for Kure. Arriving in port the carrier moored alongside *Unicorn* where damaged aircraft were replaced by serviceable machines. It would be New Year's Eve when *Theseus* finally celebrated Christmas, a good time being had by all.

While *Theseus* was enjoying a belated Christmas the UN forces had established a defensive line from Munsan-ni and partly along the 38th parallel towards Yangyang on the east coast. Again this line across Korea would be shattered when large Chinese forces started assaulting the whole front, massively outnumbered, the UN forces withdrew south in good order. The 8th Army and the Republic of Korea forces had to pull back further, by 3 January 1951 Seoul had been abandoned again and the President and the government were resettled in Pusan. Further advances by the Chinese saw the defensive line stretching from Pyongtack in the west to Wonju in the east. On 5 January *Theseus* departed from Kure arriving off the Korean coast on 7 January. Flying operations started immediately, the task being to carry out armed patrols up towards Chinnampo and to destroy any enemy shipping and other targets found in their area. As the harbours and various inlets were frozen there was little activity at sea therefore Admiral Andrewes contacted the Joint Operations Centre and offered his fighters for close support work. On 8 January the Sea Furies from *Theseus* provided support for the US 25th Division operating under the control of the USAF forward air controllers flying modified North American T-6A Texans known as Mosquitoes.

While the air wing was engaged with attacking targets on behalf of UN commanders they were also undertaking patrols along the coast and over the airfields at Chinnampo, Haeju and Ongjin which, although abandoned, were still capable of usage by the North Korean air force. As *Theseus* was stationed quite a distance away from its area of operations the decision was taken to place a rescue ship halfway between each point which greatly reassured the air crew. An alteration in operations began on 15 January when the airfields at Suwon and Kimpo were recaptured as was the port at Inchon. During the run-up to these recaptures many of missions were interrupted by bad weather as snow showers were frequent and heavy. Even so the air wing was able to give air support to the US 25th Army Division at a crucial time in its operations. Over the following few days the Sea Furies were heavily engaged in attacking ground positions in support of the US Army always under the control of a Mosquito Forward Air Controller (FAC). Given the accuracy of their supporting fire the FAC pilots preferred the Sea Fury in support in preference to other forces. Occasionally when the FAC had to return to base for a refuel he was able to designate specific areas as weapons free. On 14 January the Sea Furies were given such an order and operating in severely cloudy conditions they rocketed and strafed the airfield at Suwon blowing up two supply dumps in the process. Also attacked were obvious groups of troops plus lorries, bridges and a haystack that blew up with a large bang.

The weather also played a part in delaying operations on 15 January as the over-deck wind speed was too low to launch aircraft, however, some juggling of the deck park and the use of RATOG allowed the patrols and strike sorties to get airborne. As *Theseus* had moved closer to the area of operations the sortie lengths were reduced and the air wing was able to generate 58 sorties that day. By this time the UN forces were pushing back successfully and the fleeing enemy forces were easier to spot and extensive casualties resulted amongst these troops. The following day saw the sortie rate increase to 60 during which vehicles, oil tanks and sampans were destroyed. Having completed this phase of operations *Theseus* returned to Sasebo being replaced by USS *Bataan*, a light carrier. *Bataan*'s escorts took over the responsibility of patrolling the area and became CTE 95.11 in the process. This addition to his forces allowed

Sea Fury FB.11 WF611 undertook combat operations from both the *Glory* and *Ocean*. It is pictured here aboard the latter vessel coded 106-O for No.802 Sqdn, the aircraft would be forced to ditch alongside the carrier after suffering flak damage, the pilot being rescued successfully. (FAAM Yeovilton)

Admiral Andrewes to create an 18 days operational cycle for each vessel which meant that up to nine days were available for operations, one was allocated to sea replenishment, two were required for transit and six days were in port for rest, recuperation and repair.

By 24 January the Chinese had been halted on a line from Pyongtaek to Wonju. Further advances by UN forces resulted in Seoul being recaptured again on 14 March. This situation would change on 22 April when the Communist forces began their Spring Offensive on the left flank. Although the UN forces were pushed back to the Han river the capital was still held by Allied forces. It was during this offensive that the Gloucestershire Regiment suffered grievous losses with only 169 men left out of the original 850 men. Although these losses were grievous the Allied counter attack was successful and pushed the enemy back further. It was during this period that General MacArthur was replaced as Supreme Commander by General Ridgway with General Van Fleet replacing Ridgway as Commander of the 8th Army. A further Communist offensive was launched in mid May against the right flank although this was quickly countered by the UN forces. The resulting defensive line would remain virtually unchanged for the remainder of the war although there were some vicious battles along the way over such real estate as Pork Chop hill and Heartbreak Ridge.

On 25 January HMS *Theseus* departed from Sasebo with four destroyers as escorts, this allowed the USS *Bataan* to return to port for its harbour rest period. The operating zone for the air wing was around Suwon and both the Fireflies and Sea Furies were carrying increased weapon loads with the former adding rockets to the normal bomb load. Both types were attacking targets under the control of FAC Mosquitoes and villages, vehicles and shipping along the coast were attacked with some success. It was during these operations that the *Theseus* lost an aircraft when a combat patrol Sea Fury, VR940, piloted by Lt A C Beavan was seen to spin into the sea the and the pilot was lost. The following day a similar pattern of operations was undertaken with the Fireflies coming to the fore as buildings, troop emplacements and villages suspected of containing enemy troops were attacked. Until 31 January flying operations continued as before, the carrier then taking its rest and replenishment day. *Theseus* resumed operations on 1 February, although flying was restricted by weather conditions. Some sorties were undertaken in the afternoon, support being given to beleaguered US forces in the Kumnojong area. Similar sorties were undertaken the following day although one of the returning Sea Furies was damaged on landing when the carrier pitched at the wrong moment causing damage to the undercarriage and its mountings. The following day saw both of the air wing's squadrons undertake even more sorties in support of the Allies, the Fireflies successfully attacked troop positions in the vicinity of Suwon while the Sea Furies patrolled the coastal areas destroying vehicles and some warehouses at Wonum. At the completion of that day's flying HMS *Theseus* departed for Kure handing over the duty to the USS *Bataan*. Once anchored in Kure *Theseus* took replacement aircraft from *Unicorn* and returned its damaged machines in return.

At the completion of its period of rest *Theseus* departed Kure on 12 February to resume its station and activities. While the carrier had been in port UN forces had recaptured the Inchon peninsula with Inchon and Kimpo falling on 10 February. While in transit the *Theseus* pilots undertook deck landing training to introduce the new pilots to the carrier and its deck practices. Operations began the next day when the Fireflies undertook sorties against enemy forces near Seoul and the Sea Furies concentrated on the area between Seoul and Pyongyang with over-flights of Haejin and Ongjin airfield also being undertaken. Sorties undertaken later that day saw the Sea Furies hitting troop concentrations that had been marked by smoke, the fighters were praised for their accuracy as the UN forces were only yards away. Over the next four days the squadrons undertook a range of attacks against enemy forces and conducted armed reconnaissance although bad weather did see some of the missions cancelled or curtailed. On 19 February the carrier had its rest and refuel day returning to its operations zone the following day. As before, weather hampered operations although sorties were flown in support of UN forces as well as their normal duties during which they destroyed the usual range of trucks, vehicles and troop concentrations. On 23 February HMS *Theseus* was replaced on station by USS *Bataan* setting course for Sasebo.

On 4 March HMS *Theseus* departed from Sasebo on its penultimate patrol arriving on station so that flying could start in the morning. The Sea Furies were tasked with over-flying the airfields of Ongjin and Haeju while the Fireflies concentrated upon the bridges at Chaeryong, successfully damaging them both. The afternoon sortie consisted of two Sea Furies and three Fireflies, although one of the escorting fighters had to return to the carrier with engine trouble. As the Fireflies were acting in the bombing role they were carrying 1,000 lb bombs. As these bombs were of a higher weight than normal the 20 mm cannon ammunition was removed. The bombs from the Fireflies hit the tunnel at Haeju which blocked the line and the Sea Fury undertook pre and post strike photo reconnaissance. On the following day flying was restricted due to bad weather, however they air wing made up for it the next day by successfully controlling bombardments from HMS *Kenya* on targets in the Chinnampo area.

Bedecked with very neat identification stripes the Sea Furies prepare to depart from the carrier HMS *Theseus* for another sortie over Korea. (Rick Harding Collection)

On 8 March the Sea Furies were tasked with reconnaissance duties in the Seoul, Kaesong and Sinmak area. During these sorties railway installations were successfully attacked as were troop concentrations and artillery positions. Although one Firefly was badly damaged on landing all the aircraft landed safely and the carrier was able to pull out for replenishment on 9 March. Once again flying was cancelled the following day due to weather although it resumed as normal on 11 March. During this mission railway installations were again attacked successfully by both the Sea Furies and Fireflies. Having caused chaos amongst the railway services the Sea Furies then turned their attention to troop concentrations in the area of Sariwon while the Fireflies again turned their attention to bridges in the area. The next day saw the Sea Furies attacking the airfields at Ongjin and Changyon where they encountered heavy anti-aircraft fire in the process. Even so the hangars at Ongjin were successfully damaged by rockets while two ammunition dumps were set alight. The afternoon sorties were dedicated to attacking troop positions under the control of a Mosquito FAC. The final active day of the patrol found the Sea Furies attacking targets in the Chinnampo area and they successfully bombed various buildings and workshops and also destroyed a junk on the way home to *Theseus*. The afternoon was another Mosquito FAC occasion although a Firefly was lost after being hit by anti-aircraft fire. The crew Lt G H Cooles and Flt Lt D W Guy RAF perished. After this sad end the carrier departed for Sasebo arriving on 14 March, on this day the UN forces recaptured Seoul again.

HMS *Theseus* departed from Sasebo on 22 March in company with its usual flotilla of escorts. Upon arrival in the operational area the Sea Furies were despatched to carry out a full reconnaissance of their assigned operational area to find out if any significant changes had occurred. Once the photos had been studied and tied into the intelligence the next batch of sorties were planned. The first sorties involved the Fireflies attacking troop concentrations in the region of the ridge near Kaesong while the afternoon sorties again involved the Fireflies with 1,000 lb bombs against the bridge at Kingyong-ni while the escorting Sea Furies attacked anything that moved in the area. No flying took place the following day due to poor weather. The following day the Sea Furies attacked concentrations of vehicles in the region of Chosan-ni and Nanchonjon successfully destroying quite a few in the process. It was during this sortie that Lt Cdr Gordon-Smiths aircraft was hit in the fuselage fuel tank by an armour piercing shell, although the pilot managed to make a successful landing at Suwon. However the aircraft was written off in the process. The afternoon's missions were under the control of the Mosquito FAC during which the Fireflies successfully bombed their assigned targets. Bad weather prevented any flying the following day but missions resumed on 26 March. As before targets in the usual area of operations were attacked while the afternoon sorties were under the control of a Mosquito FAC. Another mission saw three Fireflies with 1,000 lb bombs with a pair of Sea Furies in attendance attack villages near Haeju after which the railway and its bridges near Kaesong came in for some attention. The weather on the following day was poor which curtailed flying and so the carrier departed the area for a replenishment session. *Theseus* arrived off the Korean coast on 29 March and resumed its usual range of sorties around Pyongyang. As before, railway installations and troop concentrations were given close attention. Shipping was the order of the day on 30 March with six large vessels being badly damaged in Haeju harbour by the Sea Furies while the Fireflies turned their attention to a bridge near Sariwon which was damaged.

The final day of the patrol on 1 April saw the sorties delayed due to low cloud over the target area. However, it cleared enough to allow a Mosquito FAC sortie to be flown against designated targets around the Sariwon area after which *Theseus* returned to harbour at Sasebo for rest, recuperation and repair. *Theseus* returned to operational duty on 8 April although this time the location was the Sea of Japan as the fleet carriers had been transferred to Formosa as some indication had been given that Communist China might invade that island. Although this did not happen it meant that the sea going air support was purely in the hands of *Theseus* and USS *Bataan*. Although this removed the carrier support from the west coast of Korea this was compensated for by flying long range missions from the carriers. On 9 April two Sea Furies of No.807 NAS were undertaking a reconnaissance in the area of Wonsan when they were attacked by a pair of Vought F4U Corsairs whose aircraft recognition was as always decidedly suspect. Noticing the American fighters heading their way the Sea Furies decided to turn and break. That of Lt Leece was hit by cannon fire which damaged the engine and set fire to the starboard wing fuel tank. The other Sea Fury piloted by Lt Lavender managed to take evasive action both aircraft returning to *Theseus*. The badly damaged Sea Fury was found to have 21 bullet holes in it while the bottom skin of the integral tank had burned away letting the remaining fuel vent away completely, the other aircraft suffered a single-round strike. Two other Sea Furies were also lost that day, one was lost to a 37 mm flak round which resulted in the pilot having to make a forced landing. Unfortunately, the pilot was captured on touchdown. The other fighter was also hit by anti-aircraft fire which forced the pilot to make a high speed landing at Kangmung at the end of which the Sea Fury flipped over, although the pilot escaped suffering just shock.

These losses notwithstanding the *Theseus* resumed operations the next day and the Fireflies bombed the bridges at Hungnam with great success although one aircraft had to be abandoned over the sea after the engine was damaged by ground fire. After a few minutes in the sea the crew was picked up by a rescue helicopter. Refuelling and rest occupied much of 13 April. Flying resumed on 14 April with the Fireflies hitting bridges in the Hungmam area while the Sea Furies concentrated upon the rail yards at Chinnampo. It was during this attack that an aircraft, VW658, of Lt Bowman was hit by ground fire which caused him to make a forced landing after which a rescue helicopter collected him, the aircraft was destroyed by the circling fighters. *Theseus* continued to provide air support until 19 April when TF 95.11 departed from Korean waters for the last time arriving at Sasebo the next day to hand over the duty to HMS *Glory*. On the morning of 25 April HMS *Theseus* departed for Hong Kong en route to Portsmouth. The carrier arrived home on 25 April and

While the Fleet Air Arm frequently used amphibians to recover downed aircraft the USAF preferred to utilise the helicopter for this purpose. Eventually this concept would be adopted throughout most carrier fleets. (USAF/NARA)

was presented with the Boyd Trophy by the First Sea Lord, Admiral of the Fleet, Lord Fraser.

HMS *Glory* took over officially from HMS *Theseus* on 23 April 1951. In command was Captain K S Colquhoun DSO. The air wing, 14th CAG, commanded by Lt Cdr S J Hall consisted of No.804 NAS with Hawker Sea Furies commanded by Lt Cdr J S Bailey and No.812 NAS operating Fairey Fireflies commanded by Lt Cdr F A Swanton. Fortunately for the troops on the ground the carrier's arrival coincided with the Chinese spring offensive. Lt Cdr Hall was most unfortunate as he was shot down whilst flying VW545 in September after the aircraft was hit by flak, the Sea Fury crashed near Choppeki Point and Cdr Hall was picked up by the ship's helicopter. Unlike the previous offensives intelligence gathering had shown that the enemy had built up even greater forces than ever before. The offensive kicked off over the night of 22/23 April against the 8th Army along the line from Kaesong to Chorwon to Kumhwa. The initial point of attack was Kapyong but that was repulsed by ground forces. This attack was followed by a similar push against Kaesong which saw the Chinese crossing the river at Imjin. The

HMS *Perseus* was built from the outset as an aircraft repair carrier. Although it was fully equipped for repair duties the vessel's only role was to transport stores and spares to the Korean War zone. This view shows the secret trials that were conducted with the steam catapult which in this case utilised de Havilland Sea Hornets. (FAAM Yeovilton)

Gloucester Regiment managed to hold off the attack for three days losing many men in the process. Even this gallant effort was not enough to completely hold back the Chinese forces which continued to push hard against the 8th Army which had to fall back to Kimpo putting Seoul in danger.

In the face of this HMS *Glory* departed Sasebo on 26 April arriving on station only to find that the weather on 27 April cancelled flying. The following day saw a Sea Fury combat patrol being launched while a single Firefly was used for the anti-submarine patrol. Other aircraft from *Glory* carried on from where *Theseus* left off attacking targets in the Haeju region. It was during one of the Sea Fury attacks that Lt E Stephenson became detached from the rest of the flight and apparently crashed into the sea. On 29 April the carrier launched a Sea Fury mission at the request of the Mosquito FAC against targets near Yanju and Chidong-ni with rockets and cannon. The last day of the month was fairly easy for the *Glory* air wing as their allotted targets were any ships near the coast. Over the first week in May the Sea Furies and Fireflies attacked junks, sampans and ground targets all over their allotted area. During one of these runs Lt Barlow had his Sea Fury, VX610, badly damaged by enemy fire but, although the aircraft was destroyed, the pilot was safely collected by a USAF rescue helicopter. HMS *Glory* returned to Sasebo on 7 May for rest and recuperation.

Four days later HMS *Glory* was back on station and resumed attacks on junks and sampans moving up the coast after which the Sea Furies and Fireflies turned their attention to vehicles travelling along the road towards Haeju. On 12 May the Fireflies attacked the bridges at Wontan and Yonan. The Firefly crews were most surprised to find that the bridges had been rebuilt overnight; this was a fact of life when fighting the Chinese. The Sea Furies attacked tunnels with 60 lb rockets starting their attacks in a shallow dive and successfully exploding stores and equipment hidden there. Replenishment took place the following day and the carrier resumed station on 15 May sending four Sea Furies out to attack targets along the coast and further inland. During one of the attack runs the Sea Fury,VW669, piloted by Lt Winterbotham was hit by anti-aircraft fire, the damage was severe enough to cause the pilot to ditch in the sea. Although the aircraft was lost the pilot was rescued by an American vessel after the pilot had swum to a sampan which took him to a nearby island. The following day saw a similar series of attacks carried out against enemy targets before the carrier departed for Sasebo, however, the vessel could only manage 19 knots as one of the propeller glands was overheating. *Glory* finally arrived in harbour late on 20 May entering the dry dock for repairs the following morning. Five days later the carrier was swinging at its buoy.

HMS *Glory* finally left Sasebo on 3 June to relieve USS *Bataan* with operational flying restarting the next day. Shipping and railway vehicles plus troops concentrations were given close attention although the air wing would lose another aircraft when Lt Watson was forced to ditch and, thankfully, he was rescued very quickly. Over the following few days the Sea Furies and Fireflies continued attacking the usual range of targets although the maintenance crews were being overworked as the Sea Furies were coming back with little holes in the skinning. Investigation revealed that some were caused by anti-aircraft fire, light weapons and shrapnel from their own rockets. On 9 June *Glory* underwent its replenishment day returning to station the following day. The first strike was against the village of Osan-ni with both the Fireflies and Sea Furies hit the village with full loads of bombs and rockets and left the target with the village burning fiercely. Chinnampo was also visited by the Sea Furies where warehouses were destroyed. Further operations were curtailed when the aviation fuel aboard *Glory* was found to be contaminated by water. The next day's missions were limited to what the aircraft could manage with the fuel left in the aircrafts' tanks and consequently they were limited to a quick attack against Osan-ni. With this completed the carrier departed for Kure and cleaned the tanks en route. Upon arrival in harbour *Glory* was moored to a quay shared with *Unicorn*. Using the dockside crane defective aircraft were swapped for serviceable machines.

HMS *Glory* sailed from Kure on 21 June with the destroyer HMS *Cockade* for company. The carrier was in position ready to begin flying operations on 23 June. The first sortie involved the Sea Furies which were requested by the Joint Operations Centre to attack Taegu while the Fireflies were engaged on a bombing mission against a bridge near Sariwon and a stores depot at Chinnampo. The following day both the Sea Furies and the Fireflies carried out similar attacks against targets from the previous day the latter successful in blowing up the railway bridge at Hwasan-ni causing extensive damage. Over the next four days the *Glory* air wing undertook similar missions blowing up junks and ox carts and communications routes. On 30 June the Sea Fury detail was launching when the aircraft of Sub-Lt Howard suffered a cold launch into the sea, although the aircraft was lost the pilot was safely recovered. Unfortunately the launch trolley badly damaged the catapult putting it out of action. As the remainder of the strike sortie was still on the flight deck RATOG units were quickly attached which allowed the mission to continue. The following day required all missions to be launched using RATOG, overall 29 Sea Furies and 18 Fireflies were despatched in this manner. The gap between each set of mission was around two hours during which the flight deck crew had to recover the returning aircraft, prepare them for relaunching while launching those already waiting. After striking their usual range of targets the aircraft returned to the carrier which in turn departed for Sasebo and much needed repairs.

Two days later, on 3 July, HMS *Glory* reached Sasebo having battled through the ferocious remnants of Typhoon *Kate*. Once secured in dock dockyard parties set about repairing the catapult while the aircraft were replaced where required and fuel, stores and ammunition were taken aboard. On 8 July *Glory* departed Sasebo and arrived at its operating position the following day. The first mission for the carrier was a strange one as it involved the recovery of a MiG 15 lost in shallow water and which the Americans required recovering for study. While this recovery was being planned the first round of Peace Talks had begun on 15 July 1951 at Kaesong. The recovery plan finally began on 19 July using a Sea Fury flight to pick out a safe channel as the maps of the area were inaccurate. Eventually, the small fleet of recovery vessels reached the correct position managing to recover much of it before the tide turned. *Glory* returned to Kure for rest and replenishment arriving on 22 July. Time in port was curtailed as the carrier was needed to reinforce the presence of USS *Sicily* as the ceasefire talks were in difficulty. Such was the haste of departure that six aircraft and some aircrew were left behind. HMS *Glory* arrived on station on 26 July although the sorties planned for the following day were cancelled due to bad weather. A similar situation existed on the following day although a few sorties were flown against those few targets visible. On 29 July the weather had improved and allowed the Sea Furies to operate in the Yonan area throughout the day. The next day the weather worsened again; not only was there extensive cloud but rough seas and high winds added to the misery. A similar situation arose the following day and was also forecast for 1 August therefore the decision was taken to undertake the replenishment that day. Returning to the operations zone the following day *Glory* found that the weather was suitable for flying therefore Sea Furies were launched with explicit orders to hunt down junks and rafts known to be operating along the coast with supplies for the North Korean and Chinese forces. Intermittent bad weather seemed destined to plague this period at sea as the sorties for 3 August were reduced although the Sea Furies did manage to strafe and rocket a large body of troops with great success. A similar situation occurred on 4 August although again some troops were spotted with similar results to the previous day's exploits. As the weather was forecast to worsen it was decided that *Glory* should return to Sasebo arriving there the following day.

Fortunately for *Glory* HMS *Warrior,* acting as an aircraft support vessel was nearly at Sasebo finally arriving on 7 August with much needed spare aircraft. A newly replenished *Glory* departed on 10 August sailing via Iwakuni to collect more replacement aircraft before arriving at the assigned patrol area on 13 August. Flying resumed on 15 August. The Sea Furies attacked junks and sampans between Hanchon and Chinnampo damaging and destroying three in the process. The Sea Furies also tried a new idea: that of dropping full fuel tanks on a village suspected of harbouring enemy troops. As the tanks hit the ground the Sea Furies strafed them setting them well alight. While the Sea Furies were attacking shipping the Fireflies concentrated on troops and communications links

As crash and rescue crews cluster around this badly damaged Sea Fury the pilot prepares to depart his aircraft. WG621 would be repaired and later return to undertake flying duties from HMS *Glory*. (Rick Harding Collection)

in the Yonan area with some success. Further anti-shipping sorties occupied the Sea Furies the following day while the Fireflies concentrated on shore based targets. A hasty move south that evening was needed as Typhoon Marge was reported heading in that direction. Waiting for the typhoon to blow itself out kept the carrier out of theatre for the next two days. As there was little opportunity to continue attacking targets in Korea *Glory* set out for Kure sailing via Okinawa and arrived at Kure on 25 August. Post storm inspection of the aircraft lashed on deck revealed that some had suffered surface finish damage and all would require extensive cleaning.

With its aircraft problems fixed HMS *Glory* was ready to return to the fray, which duly took place on 2 September. Flying started soon after arrival with both squadrons attacking light shipping and railway infrastructure. It was during one of these attacks that the Sea Fury of Lt Howard was struck by anti-aircraft fire which badly damaged the engine. The pilot was left with little option but to make an emergency landing on the beach at Paengyong although the aircraft did turn over leaving the pilot to dig himself out of the sand. Over the following three days the Sea Furies continued to attack shipping while the Fireflies continued to bomb buildings and bridges. A replenishment day followed on 6 September although this was completed earlier than expected. Given this extra time it was intended to launch a range of missions, however, after two of the

Sea Furies had been catapulted away it was noticed that it was not functioning correctly. Investigations revealed that the catapult would need repairing and so all aircraft launches would need RATOG packs. Further work by the ship's engineers overnight cleared the catapult for further use, therefore any aircraft with RATOG fitted had them removed. The final patrol day, 9 September, saw *Glory* launch 84 sorties which was a record and was a credit to the engineers and deck handlers. After the aircraft had returned to the carrier *Glory* started the journey to Kure arriving there on 11 September.

HMS *Glory* departed Kure on 15 September resuming operations on 18 September. Both squadrons launched aircraft on that day and concentrated on enemy positions in the Wonsan area. Flying was delayed the following day due to inclement weather. As soon as conditions had cleared the catapult decided to fail again which meant that all launches again required the use of RATOG. The Sea Furies were tasked with attacking buildings after which they spotted for the destroyers bombarding targets on shore. Having been forced to use most of their RATOG equipment *Glory* made a quick trip back to Sasebo to collect more plus extra fuel. Returning to the fray the carrier launched a limited range of sorties on 22 September. During one of these launches a Firefly failed to get airborne correctly and crashed into the sea, the pilot was rescued but the observer was lost. The ship's engineers redoubled their efforts to repair the catapult and the efforts finally bore fruit much to the relief of the aircrews. With the catapult back in action it was time for the Sea Furies to attack the increased sea traffic in the Chinnampo area as well an increase in rail traffic. Once airborne the Sea Furies set about destroying these targets with gusto while the Fireflies attacked buildings and troop concentrations. The following two days saw a similar pattern of attacks undertaken during which one of the attacked junks exploded dramatically. On 25 September HMS *Glory* undertook her final set of missions. As before the Sea Furies attacked vessels with cannon and rockets while the Fireflies concentrated on harder targets. When the final aircraft returned to the carrier it turned away to begin its voyage to Kure. Berthing at Kure the *Glory* found that the replacement carrier, HMAS *Sydney*, berthed against the other face of the jetty. As *Sydney* was mainly equipped with Sea Furies it was decided to increase the vessels effectiveness by transferring the *Glory* Fireflies and spares to the Australian vessel. On 1 October HMS *Glory* sailed for Hong Kong calling there en route to Australia where a refit, repair and reconditioning was carried out.

HMAS *Sydney* would be the active carrier in Korean waters from 30 September 1951 to 27 January 1952 the assigned air squadrons being Nos 805, 808 and 817 NAS.

Chapter 7

Sea Furies in Korean Skies

HMS *Glory* returned to Hong Kong from Australia where it had restored and acquired aircraft and equipment from HMAS *Sydney*. From Hong Kong *Glory* set sail for Sasebo with No.804 NAS with its Sea Furies and No.812 NAS and its Fireflies aboard. She arrived on 5 February 1952. The following day *Glory* was back on station as part of TF.95.11 after five months away. The primary task for the carrier and its air group was to provide protection for the Allied held islands off the west coast which included Chodo and Paengyong-do codenamed 'Bromide Baker'. As these islands would be useful to the Communists they made repeated efforts to recapture them, therefore the Sea Furies would provide a roving combat patrol over the islands armed with both cannons and rockets although they were warned to be aware of the extensive anti-aircraft protection installed along the coast. The first sorties were launched on 7 February over a snow covered country which made navigation difficult. Even so the Sea Furies found enough targets to keep them happy. Their task was made easier by the Communists who had removed extraneous persons from the coastal zones, therefore any movement was of enemy forces.

While the Sea Furies were strafing and rocketing any moving targets the Fireflies were hitting fixed targets. Their first target was the tunnel mouths at Changyon into which they skip bombed 500 lb bombs with short timer fuses which caused a landslide and damaged the rails. Having blown up the rail tunnels the Fireflies turned their remaining bombs to a bridge at Haeju. Further bombing raids on the railway tunnels at Haeju were carried out by the Fireflies on 9 February and the entrances were destroyed. The Sea Furies on the other hand had a quieter day acting as spotter aircraft for the cruisers *Porterfield* and *Ceylon*. On 10 February the Sea Furies again acted as spotters with the target being a series of blister buildings near Wongol which was well defended by anti-aircraft guns. Unfortunately the target remained almost unblemished after the efforts of the cruisers. The following day the carrier and escorts was spent on refuelling and replenishing stores operations. The Sea Furies undertook armed reconnaissance of the Yonan area which saw the destruction of buildings and other positions this being followed by a

Pictured while on the strength of No. 738 NAS is Sea Fury FB.11 VX652 133-CW based at Culdrose. This aircraft sports a full load of rockets under the wing. This squadron acted as a weapons training unit for pilots destined for service in Korea. (Rick Harding Collection)

strafing run along the beach at Paengyong-do where a large body of troops were foraging and training, at least 20 casualties were reported by the pilots. It was during this attack that the Sea Fury, WE804, of Lt Knight was hit by small arms fire which hit the engine causing an oil leak, the pilot made a successful landing near Paengyong-do although he missed the emergency airfield and ended up on a mud flat where the aircraft was wrecked. As before, the Fireflies attacked buildings and troop concentrations scoring some success. The Sea Furies had quite a successful day on 13 February when they attacked some warehouses near the Koho-ri peninsula, although their greatest success was an accidental strike on a wooden building which exploded spectacularly. A further attack on the blister area at Pungchon followed during which the Sea Fury, WE688, piloted by Lt Overton was hit in the engine. The only option for the pilot was to ditch in the sea although he was quickly picked up by a rescue craft. Meanwhile the Fireflies were attacking positions near Ongjin where another violent explosion occurred courtesy of a direct hit on an ammunition dump. Flying was restricted the following day as the weather was inclement but even so the Sea Furies found plenty of trade along the coast and destroyed vessels secreted at various points along the coast. Further inland the Fireflies attacked

Sporting a partial set of Korean War stripes is this Sea Fury blasting of the deck of HMS *Ocean* courtesy of RATOG. The aircraft appears to be off on a bombing mission as the underwing pylons are home to a pair of 500 lbs bombs. (FAAM Yeovilton)

suspected buildings in Punchon destroying at least two. Once all the aircraft had returned to the carrier *Glory* set course for Sasebo arriving on 15 February.

Once anchored in Sasebo replacement aircraft were transferred from HMS *Unicorn*, mainly Sea Furies. HMS *Glory* departed Sasebo on 24 February to relieve her US Navy counterpart USS *Bairoko* and restarted flying operations on 25 February. The first missions for that day involved the Sea Furies of No.804 NAS who attacked troop concentrations near Sogang-ni near Chinnampo with rockets. No.812 NAS and its Fireflies again concentrated upon buildings in Chanyon. The weather would play a part in this drama as a rapid decline in visibility meant that the last handful of aircraft required a carrier controlled approach. All touched down without incident, a great achievement as the weather continued to worsen.

Overnight the weather cleared which allowed *Glory* to resume operations quickly. It was the Sea Furies that started the ball rolling by destroying ox carts suspected of carrying supplies in the Koho-ri region.

This was followed by the Fireflies attacking and successfully damaging railway infrastructure at Charyon. On 27 and 28 February both squadrons had very little trade. The first day of March was afflicted by bad weather which delayed the start of operations although the air wing soon made up for this delay. The Fireflies bombed Changyon then strafed villages and troop concentrations in the Chinnampo area while the Sea Furies roamed along the various roads and rail links looking for traffic of which there was little. It was during these operations that a converted fuel tank fitted with reconnaissance cameras was fitted under the wing of a Sea Fury of Lt Cdr Bailey which could be used for pre and post strike analysis. No.804 NAS lost another Sea Fury ,WE691, when that of Lt Fraser suffered an engine failure on approach to HMS *Glory*. The pilot was back on deck within a minute. Operations resumed as normal the following day with the Fireflies attacking rail related targets and fixed positions in the vicinity of Changyon while the Sea Furies joined in the fun by hitting the marshalling yards at Sinchon and the locomotive sheds at Haeju with great success. On 4 March the catapult on *Glory* started to suffer from leaks which meant that any launches had to be RATOG powered. Unfortunately, this equipment was in short supply and, therefore, only four aircraft could be launched, two on combat patrol over the carrier and another two were launched on long range armed patrol. While these aircraft were airborne the ships engineers worked flat out to get the catapult working again, in this they were successful and further aircraft launches used the catapult. With normal flying operations possible the Fireflies were successfully able to attack rail infrastructure in the region of Ongjin while the Sea Furies concentrated upon looking for shipping along the coast. At the completion of that day's missions HMS *Glory* handed over patrol responsibility to USS *Bairoko* after which the carrier and its escorts departed to Kure for rest, recuperation and restoring. It was during this combat patrol that the HMS *Glory* pilots completed 5,000 deck landings while eight would celebrate the completion of their 100th sorties. Also during this patrol an average of 50 sorties per day were flown during which the aircraft dropped 168 500 lb bombs, 24 1,000 lb bombs on enemy targets. As ever replacement aircraft were received although there was a shortage of Sea Furies and therefore only one was available.

HMS *Glory* departed on its third patrol stint on 12 March and arrived on station the following day. Flying started on 14 March with 50 sorties being achieved. The targets were as before although greater success was achieved this time around. During these missions four Sea Furies were launched operating in pairs, one would operate within easy reach of the carrier while the others would have a far ranging remit to operate in the wooded areas west of Anak. Reminiscent of conditions that would trouble the Americans in Vietnam the Communist forces would attempt to use the wooded areas for cover. Unlike the Americans the Sea Furies were successful in strikes against troops and the ox carts used for moving ammunition and stores. Further sorties struck against buildings in Sinchon while the Fireflies acted as spotters for bombardments after which they bombed a bridge near Taetan. The following day, with low cloud and reduced visibility, the number of sorties was reduced but they were effective in so far as the Sea Furies damaged and destroyed some well hidden junks. The Fireflies concentrated upon villages reported to contain enemy troops and a bridge at Ongjin. *Glory* would lose another Sea Fury, WE803, that afternoon when the aircraft piloted by Lt R J Overton was hit by anti-aircraft fire and subsequently crashed, the pilot was killed. While a sense of gloom overhung the carrier it did not stop the combat sorties and on 16 March even more missions were launched reaching a total of 62. Many of these sorties involved the Sea Furies assisting in looking for a downed American crew while the Fireflies concentrated on troop positions. While 16 March had been relatively quiet the next day, complete with clear skies and light winds, saw 106 sorties launched towards the Sok-to area as there were reports of enemy forces massing for an attack. Large quantities of bombs and rockets were expended, all of which appeared to have an affect on the enemy. The Sea Furies hit buildings at Koho-ri, rail tracks at Chinnampo plus ox carts, light shipping and a village reported to house a large concentration of troops. Recent reconnaissance sorties had shown that the rail link between Haeju and Chaeryong had been fully repaired and so the Fireflies concentrated upon upsetting the North Korean rail timetable. The Fireflies also bombed the village of Kasong-dong after which large explosions were seen. On 18 March HMS *Glory* withdrew for replenishment returning the following day although flying was cancelled due to foul weather. Operations resumed on 20 March although the tail end of the storm meant that a reduced number of sorties was flown. However the Sea Furies did manage to attack warehouses and bunkers plus sampans found on a beach near Chodo. Kangso was also attacked by the Sea Furies hitting targets with both cannon fire and rockets. The Fireflies also concentrated on troop movement areas although their targets were mainly the railway bridges at Sugyo-ri and the tunnels at Haeju. Missions were again curtailed the following day, 21 March, although some Sea Furies were launched to support a landing by South Korean forces at the village of Ponghwa-ri near the river Han. Villages in the region were attacked with rockets as were troop positions and mortar trenches. In order to keep the communist forces at bay the Sea Furies flew at 200 ft during which

With instruction being shouted in his direction the pilot of this wrecked Sea Fury sits stunned in his cockpit awaiting rescue. Looking at the extent of the damage the pilot was lucky to survive. (Rick Harding Collection)

they strafed a command post plus a group of enemy occupied houses which was holding up the advance. The Fireflies, on the other hand, hit a village at Chanyon although they had to bomb through gaps in the clouds, they were slightly luckier with the rail bridges at Sugyo-ri where two spans were downed. Overnight the weather deteriorated further which caused all flights to be cancelled. As *Glory* was due to return to Sasebo the carrier set course earlier than normal arriving there on 23 March and staying there until 31 March. The delay was due to a training requirement as the Sea Furies were modified to carry 500 lb bombs so the pilots had to undergo training. The first lesson involved starting a 45 degree dive from 4,000 ft and releasing at 2,000 ft. The second involved dropping the bombs at 1,500 ft which was more accurate.

Once the pilots had completed their training HMS *Glory* was ready to resume its operational patrol departing Sasebo on 31 March although transit time was extended as the Task Force speed had to be reduced because they were battering their way through rough seas. Flying began on 1 April but this time the Sea Furies were carrying 500 lb bombs fused for thirty seconds instead of rockets. During their first patrol the Sea

The deck crew rush towards the bow of HMS *Theseus* where a Sea Fury has managed to bounce into the aircraft ranged on the forward deck. The accident took place during the work up period prior to the carrier departing for Korea. (FAAM Yeovilton)

Furies bombed warehouses at Simpo and Kyomipo after which a heavily loaded junk was strafed in a tributary of the Taedong River. As this was the first time the Sea Furies had used bombs their accuracy was less than impressive in contrast to that of the Fireflies that completely flattened the target areas in Soho-ri and Sahyu-dong. The following day saw the Fireflies hitting the bridges at Yonan and Haeju but further missions that day were curtailed as the catapult became unserviceable again which left the carrier only capable of despatching Sea Furies armed with 20 mm cannon. On 3 April villages in the region of Sariwon airfield were bombed by No.804 NAS who moved onto a factory in Chinnampo then the rail yards at Chinji-ri. The result was that three loaded trucks were blown up. The missions in the afternoon concentrated on the gun positions near Chodo which was hampering Allied shipping in the area. It had been determined that these positions would need a direct hit to destroy them and the Fireflies hit them hard. However, one Firefly was damaged by anti-aircraft fire which caused the crew to ditch although they were successfully rescued. Another Firefly staggered back to the carrier with undercarriage and engine problems. On 4 April the Sea Furies launched their missions fitted with rockets instead of bombs and attacked an enemy held ridge north of the Imjin River. Although they

Pictured in flight is Fairey Swordfish Mk.II HS643-B photographed from another of the breed. Both were possibly based on the escort carrier HMS *Biter* at the time, of note is the well worn state of the paintwork. (John Ryan collection)

Swordfish LS326 photographed at a later date, note that the camouflage remains on the wings and tailplanes only. The aircraft wears the codes of No.760 NAS. (Aerophot)

Fairey Firefly AS.5 sports the striping applied for Korean War operations. WB271 204-R was originally despatched for possible use in the conflict however it ended up with the Royal Australian Navy before being recovered by the RN Historic Flight who restored it to flight status although it was tragically lost in a fatal crash in July 2003. (John Ryan collection)

Hawker Sea Hurricane 1b is a very rare specimen and is preserved by the Shuttleworth Collection. It currently sports the 7-L Markings of No.880 NAS. (BBA Collection)

Although this is a preserved aircraft Supermarine Seafire F.XVII SX336 has been finished in a very accurate scheme by the restorers and displays the immediate post war colours. (BBA Collection)

Pictured in happier times is Hawker Sea Fury FB.11 TF956 123-T resplendent in the marking applied to the type for service during the Korean conflict. The aircraft was sadly lost in a crash in June 1989. (Dennis R Jenkins)

When the task of hunting submarines was handed over to helicopters some of the redundant Fairey Gannets found themselves a new role, that of Carrier Onboard Delivery. Here XA466 assigned to *Ark Royal* prepares to touch down. (Bob Archer)

Sea Venom 21ECM XG608-CU is seen here on display at Culdrose in company with other aircraft of the period. (Trevor Jones collection)

Sporting the codes of No.806 NAS is Hawker Sea Hawk FGA.6 WV908 188-A that is currently owned by the Royal Navy Historical Flight based at Yeovilton. After a much needed refurbishment the aircraft is now back on the display circuit. (John Ryan collection)

Scimitar F.1 XD236 038 was being operated by the Fleet Requirements Unit when photographed, the aircraft was later lost in a crash in June 1968. (Adrian Balch via John Ryan)

Originally built as Sea Vixen FAW.1 XN696 was later converted to FAW.2 standard in company with many of its fellows. Here it is seen coded 751 heading for the Yeovilton runway. (Bob Archer collection)

Sporting the final FAA scheme is Buccaneer S.1 XN965 wearing the 636-LM coding of No.736 NAS, the Buccaneer training unit. Although the S.1 had a limited front line life it did fill a very important training niche. (Trevor Jones collection)

Prior to wearing the Silver Jubilee decorations the Phantoms of No.892 NAS wore marks commemorating the American bicentennial celebrations as sported here by XV588 013-R. (John Ryan collection)

Complete with the red chevron and Omega badge of No.892 NAS is Phantom FG.1 XT859 the final fighter squadron to serve aboard a Royal Navy aircraft carrier or so it was thought. (John Ryan collection)

Complete with practise AIM-9L Sidewinders is Sea Harrier FRS.1 XZ491 000 of No.801 NAS comes into land at Yeovilton. The aircraft would be lost in a crash in April 1986 although the pilot ejected safely. (Trevor Jones collection)

Caught on camera in the original grey and white finish is Sea Harrier FRS.1 XZ455 102-VL. This machine was later converted to F/A.2 standard although its career was cut short when it crashed in February 1996. (Trevor Jones collection)

Sporting titling declaring 25 years of service is No.899 NAS Sea Harrier F/A.2 ZH809 that also sports a smart paint scheme. (Trevor Jones collection)

Currently in private preservation is Sea Harrier F/A.2 ZH810 716 which sports the marks of No.899 NAS. Of note is the fixed flight refuelling probe bolted over the intake. (Trevor Jones collection)

The development batch of F-35 aircraft is now undertaking flight test development trials. Although not subject to the same hype as the F-22 this new generation aircraft has garnered interest from many armed services. (USAF)

Seen passing over the desert near Edwards AFB is the X-35 prototype. The production version is intended for use on board the new generation of aircraft carriers. (USAF)

About to touch down aboard HMS *Rothesay* is Westland Wasp HAS.1 XT785 48. Developed in tandem with the Scout for the British Army, the Wasp remained in service for many years until replaced by the Lynx. (BBA Collection)

Photographed aboard HMS *Antrim* is Wessex HAS.3 XS862 406-AN. As the vessel is in port the flight deck guard rail is in place. (Trevor Jones collection)

Prior to the adoption of the Sea King as the primary anti-submarine helicopter, the Royal Navy deployed the HAS.3 version of the Wessex aboard ship. This is XP142 404-FF normally based aboard HMS *Fife*. (Trevor Jones collection)

Wessex HU.5 XT486 437-RS would play its part in the Falklands war although when photographed it was on the strength of No.829 NAS based aboard HMS *Resource*. (Trevor Jones collection)

One of the most useful versions of the Sea King ever developed is the Westland Commando which is a stripped down version of the anti-submarine model and has been found to be very useful for moving troops and equipment. Here ZA293 VO poses for the camera. (Aerophot)

A formation of Sea Kings from HMS *Hermes* perform a flypast for the camera, soon after this was taken the carrier and its aircraft were off to war. (Aerophot)

Finished in the original colour scheme is Sea King HAS2 XV658 04-PW. It was on the strength of No.819 NAS based at Prestwick when photographed. The helicopter was lost in a crash in February 1983. (Aerophot)

Now withdrawn, Westland Sea King HAS6 ZG818 (2)71-N was based on HMS *Invincible* when photographed. (Aerophot)

Originally built as a Sea King HAS.1 XV704 183-L would later be converted to AEW2 standard in July 1982, although it would be lost during a fatal collision with another Sea King XV650 in March 2003. (Trevor Jones collection)

The Westland Commando was also used in Bosnia and other regions of the disintegrated Yugoslav republic, for this purpose the aircraft had a disruptive white pattern applied over the basic green finish with SFOR (NATO Stabilisation Force) titles. (Trevor Jones collection)

Although the Royal Navy was not heavily involved in Granby/Desert Storm the Westland Commando version of the Sea King was used extensively to fly personnel and stores around Saudi Arabia. (Bob Archer collection)

Westland Sea King HAS.6 ZA133 013 assigned to No.771 NAS takes off while another from the same units taxies out behind it. (NARA)

were met with extensive anti-aircraft fire the fighters managed to hit 80 per cent of the specified area. A later mission by Sea Furies bombed the barracks at Chinnampo. At the same time the Fireflies also bombed the villages at Yuchon-ni and Changyon. After all the aircraft had returned to *Glory* the carrier withdrew for replenishment.

Over 6-7 April the *Glory* squadrons continued to strike at enemy positions and supply lines returning home without loss. Flying was cancelled the following day due to heavy fog, however, this cleared overnight and the Sea Furies were able to get airborne and supply much needed close air support for the US Marine Corps while the Fireflies concentrated on Haeju. These missions on 9 April were the last for this patrol as the carrier departed station and headed for Kure arriving there on 11 April. Once secured across the jetty from *Unicorn* replacement aircraft and stores were transhipped.

Rested and replenished HMS *Glory* departed from Kure on 18 April for the carrier's final patrol of that commission. After arriving on station flying was severely curtailed by low cloud and poor visibility thus the maximum amount of sorties flown over the next four days was 22. Even so the Sea Furies did manage to find and destroy three junks near Haeju while the Fireflies managed to attack the railways at Chinnampo. During the fifth day of the patrol the catapult failed yet again after the first Fireflies had been launched. These were the only missions flown by the Fireflies that day. The Sea Furies were able to launch using RATOG and continued their attacks. Hard work by the ship's engineers had the catapult available on 21 April which allowed both the Sea Furies and Fireflies to launch as normal. During these operations the Sea Fury piloted by Lt Barlow was hit by anti-aircraft fire and he was forced to land on the beach at Paengyong-do.

On 22 April HMS *Glory* received a carrier onboard delivery Avenger of the US Navy whose passenger was Captain T Maunsell who assumed command of the carrier. While the ship's command was changing the air wing was attacking troop positions and some T-34 tanks found hidden at Chinnampo. The following day *Glory* joined the RFA *Green Ranger* for replenishment after which Captain Colquhoun departed having completed his hand over. Patrols and attack sorties resumed on 24 April. As before, the Sea Furies and Fireflies continued to attack briefed targets along the coast and in the Chinnampo and Haeju regions as well as acting as spotter aircraft for bombardments. Weather restricted operations over the following two days but, even so, both aircraft types were able to concentrate on their main targets: troop concentrations in their area of responsibility. Until withdrawal the weather played havoc with the flying programme and only a handful of sorties was flown per day until 29 April when HMS *Glory* departed for Hong Kong after handing over responsibility to HMS *Ocean*. While on station off Korea HMS *Glory* and the air wing had flown 4,835 sorties for the loss of 27 aircraft during both tours. Ammunition expended during these missions included 886,300 rounds of 20 mm cannon shells, 126 x 1,000 lb bombs, 3,114 x 500 lb bombs and 13,098 rocket projectiles. The recipients for many of these projectiles included 796 junks, 1,001 ox carts and 308 rail vehicles. After the strains of service off the Korean coast HMS *Glory* would lead a quieter life with the Mediterranean Fleet over the following five months.

HMS *Ocean* arrived at Sasebo on 5 May 1952 departing from there five days later for the Korean west coast. During this period the air wing managed to launch an average of 76 sorties per day although the calmness of the weather would aid this tally. During the first day of operations No.802 NAS lost a Sea Fury piloted by Lt. Scott which was ditched after a fire in the cockpit as he was undertaking fleet air patrol, fortunately he was quickly rescued. The unit lost another aircraft, WH591, that day when Lt McEnery was forced to crash-land on the beach at Paengyong-do. A further two were damaged whilst taxiing on the flight deck of *Ocean*. No.825 NAS also suffered a loss when the Firefly piloted by Lt Gadney suffered complete engine failure which forced the crew to ditch. Fortunately the crew was quickly rescued by a USAF Grumman HU-16 Albatross. The next day was also a sad one for No.802 NAS when the Sea Fury piloted by Lt McDonald was hit by anti-aircraft fire during an attack on artillery positions on the Amgak peninsula. On this occasion it is likely that the pilot was badly injured as the aircraft crashed without any attempt to escape. After five days of operations the carrier underwent a refuelling period. *Ocean* resumed operations on 16 May with the Sea Furies concentrating upon rail targets while the Fireflies attacked bunkers and other buildings and caused a massive explosion in one. The downside of this attack was that a Firefly was hit by anti-aircraft fire leaving the crew with no option but to ditch. The following day saw the carrier provide a mission surge with 123 being flown. All worked perfectly until the last land-on when the Firefly involved suffered a port undercarriage lock failure. The damaged aircraft was quickly dealt with so that much needed rearming could be carried out. The following day saw the sortie rate return to a slightly lower pace although No.802 NAS lost another Sea Fury, WE680, when that of Lt Peniston-Bird was hit in the port wing which burst into flames. After some amazing piloting from the cockpit coaming the pilot was in a position to bale out of his aircraft and he was successfully picked up by a USAF Albatross. On 19 May all aircraft from *Ocean* provided air

Sea Fury FB.11 WJ237 113-O was operating from HMS *Ocean* when photographed. This aircraft plus WE724 was involved in a dogfight with eight MiG15's during which some strikes were seen on the Korean aircraft. (FAAM Yeovilton)

support for a landing on the south coast of Ongjin. During these missions the Sea Furies toted 1,000 lb bombs using RATOG for launching in order to get the most aircraft off the deck in one go. During this process one Sea Fury proceeded down the flight deck and off the end without the rockets firing. A few seconds later the Sea Fury was seen to climb away without any problem, the pilot having ridden the ground effect under the wings until enough forward speed was available to allow a climb away. To the embarrassment of the pilot he later admitted to have forgotten to set the master switch. During these operations No.825 NAS lost a Firefly which was shot down by anti-aircraft fire. Once all the aircraft had returned HMS *Ocean* departed for Sasebo. Upon arrival *Ocean* received replacement aircraft and stores from HMS *Unicorn* although some types of ammunition were in short supply as there was only one supply ship for the Korean war zone.

HMS *Ocean* departed Sasebo on 28 May arriving in theatre the following day. As bombs and rockets were strictly limited for this period it was decided that the sortie count should be held at 68 missions per day.

Combat operations rarely stopped for such minor inconveniences such as snow. Soon the carrier's crew will turn too to clear the flight deck and prepare the aircraft for flight. Some of the later will include the judicious use of hot air to warm the airframe up and prevent fluid leaks caused by seal contraction. (FAAM Yeovilton)

On this basis the first sorties of the day were generally armed reconnaissance whose task was to find targets for that day's attention although the pilots engaged in these missions had to concentrate hard to penetrate the improved camouflage employed by the Communist forces. The first day's operations were hampered by fog but the following day saw an improvement in conditions and the carrier's aircraft were employed on attacking railway infrastructure, especially the bridges which had been rebuilt. As each day's set of missions were carried out the amount of bombs and rockets was reduced and by 31 May the Sea Furies were reduced to carrying out their patrols armed with 20 mm cannon shells only. When Operation Billhook was launched on 1 June the *Ocean* air group was dedicated to providing support to the South Korean forces landing near the Ponghwai area close to the Han river. During these operations one Sea Fury managed to destroy another when it ploughed into it on the flight deck. The following day saw restricted flying due to inclement weather while the next days flying was late starting as the fog was slow to clear. It was a bad day for the Sea Fury squadron as the aircraft,WE694, of Sub Lt Swanson was shot down. Fortunately, the pilot was seen to escape by parachute from his blazing aircraft. Then a ditching occurred near the carrier when the aircraft of Lt McEnery suffered engine failure. On the final day of the patrol the Sea Furies attacked bridges near Chinnampo while the Fireflies attacked hard targets near the Pungchon, Hanchon and Haeju areas after which the carrier returned to Kure.

HMS *Ocean* resumed operations on 16 June and the first order of business was to carry out an armed reconnaissance to spot potential targets. Even this was not without incident as Sub Lt Ellis had to ditch his Sea Fury, WF611, alongside the carrier as the aircraft's engine oil pressure dropped suddenly causing the engine to stop. The following day saw operations restricted in the Chinampo area due to fog and mist. The Sea Furies concentrated upon fixed military targets while the Fireflies turned their attentions to various building known to house stores and ammunition. The following three days were similar with the weather interfering with some missions, however, all nominated targets were attacked successfully. The Fireflies also discovered a number of electrical transformers, although no authority was forthcoming to attack them; the same problem existed for reservoirs and dams. On 21 June the carrier undertook its replenishment day receiving oil, aircraft fuel and other stores. While out of theatre one of the Fireflies underwent an engine change while another required an outer wing change: needed after a rocket projectile fin had gone through the lower skin.

Operations resumed on 22 June the weather being excellent for flying although not for the concentration of troops found by a patrolling Sea Fury which were given a good pasting by the carrier's aircraft. The primary mission for the following day involved six Sea Furies and four Fireflies attacking gun emplacements and a controller based on the Pungchon peninsula. The attack was successful with bombs, rockets and cannon fire destroying the target although all aircraft were subject to intense anti-aircraft fire, luckily, no aircraft were hit. Having been told to steer clear of electrical generating equipment the carrier's air wing was informed that these installations were now fair game. Thus on 24 June the Fireflies were let loose on seven transformers in the Changyon and Haeju areas while the Sea Furies also used their cannons to hit other transformers leaving them arcing and sparking. After the fireworks show HMS *Ocean* departed for Sasebo arriving the following day.

On 3 July HMS *Ocean* in company with *Unicorn* sailed with an escort of five destroyers, *Unicorn* being utilised as a spare deck for some new pilots destined to join No.802 NAS. Operations began the following day with the usual area patrol after which the Sea Furies attacked shipping along the coast and a coastal based gun. Further strikes were carried out against railway targets and electrical installations. This excellent day was marred by the loss of a Firefly and its crew after its engine failed soon after take-off for a test flight. The following day missions were flown against various targets using the usual range of weaponry against railway installations and various bridges. On 6 July HMS *Unicorn*, having completed its time as a spare deck, departed for Japan. Prior to leaving, the carrier helped launch that day's missions against the usual range of targets, a similar pattern occurring the next day after which *Ocean* departed for replenishment from RFA *Wave Sovereign*. A change of emphasis on 9 July saw the Sea Furies engaged in Operation Boodles against targets on the Sillyong- Myon peninsula, it was a bit of trickery which allowed the Communist forces to build up strength in the area so that the Sea Furies had plenty of targets to attack. As the Fireflies were not engaged in these missions they were briefed to attack the targets normally reserved for the Sea Furies as well as their own targets. Another change in operations the next day saw the Sea Furies and Fireflies acting in concert. the Sea Furies discovered some interesting camouflaged targets and called in the Fireflies to help them destroy them which both did. Having pasted the fixed targets both squadrons turned their attentions to a long convoy of ox carts carrying stores and ammunition which were successfully destroyed, many complete with large explosions.

On 11 July the *Ocean* air wing undertook its most difficult mission against Pyongyang the North Korean capital. Designated Operation Pressure Pump the attack utilised elements of the 5th Air Force, USAF, US Navy and USMC aircraft plus aircraft from the Royal Australian Air Force. Overall the air elements flew 1,254 sorties at targets in and around the city, the following day even more missions were flown. The success of these attacks reduced the city's value as a military target to almost nil. Sea Furies from *Ocean,* which were briefed to hit a large marshalling yard, concentrated their bombs on the more crowded areas of the yard while the Fireflies used rockets against more thinly populated areas. Although the area was heavily defended none of these guns managed to hit the attacking aircraft. The following day, after the excitement of Pressure Pump, the air wing resumed its normal range of missions and after the aircraft had returned the carrier departed for Sasebo. In the early hours of 21 July HMS *Ocean* sailed from Sasebo and began its operations the next day. This period of the Korean coast was to see the sortie rate drop because of inclement weather, mainly rain and rough seas. Although these conditions did reduce the number of missions flown those undertaken were successful even if the pilots were not always able

The crew are in position for leaving harbour as HMS *Ocean* departs for Korea. Down the centre of the flightdeck are aircraft from the air wing, the nearest of which is Sea Fury VW545 assigned to No.804 NAS, it would end up ditching off the Korean coast after engine failure in September 1951. (FAAM Yeovilton)

to see the results at the time. Electricity generating installations were the targets for the following day as were the usual range of rail and military targets. No.802 NAS was struck by tragedy on 24 July when they lost their commanding officer, Lt Cdr R A Dick DSC. During a low level strafing run against a sampan on the Taedong river the aircraft, WJ238, was hit by anti-aircraft fire which damaged the flight controls and caused the Sea Fury to crash. On 26 July *Ocean* undertook its replenishment day and resumed operations the following day. But, again, for much of the rest of the patrol most sorties were cancelled due to bad weather. On 27 July the war drastically changed for the piston-powered aircraft from HMS *Ocean* when MiG 15 jet-powered fighters attacked the carrier's aircraft. The intended targets were a flight of Fireflies on their way to the carrier when they were bounced by a flight of MiGs. Fortunately, the jets' pilots were bad shots as all four Fireflies aircraft managed to reach the carrier even though one sustained some damage. A further attack took place against a flight of Sea Furies, again gunfire damaged one of the fighters although it too managed to reach the carrier where the pilot executed a flapless landing. Aware that further attacks by North Korean fighters were likely it was the weather that delayed and cancelled many of the next day's sorties. The weather was even worse on 29 July and just

Nearly blotted out by a snow storm this Sea Fury is being prepared for a possible sortie later that day although given the snow accretion it is highly unlikely that it will go ahead. (FAAM Yeovilton)

a single Firefly mission managed to launch, although it was quickly recalled. Flying was also limited to two strike missions late the following day after which the carrier departed for Kure arriving there on 1 August. Replacement aircraft were received in port plus stores and ammunition were replenished, although there was a shortage of rockets for the Fireflies therefore the inboard launchers were removed and replaced by bomb carriers.

HMS *Ocean* and her escorts departed Kure on the evening of 8 August resuming operations off the Korean coast the following day. Unlike the previous patrol the weather was exceptionally fine which increased the sortie rate. This would be the day that the Sea Furies of No.802 NAS would tangle with MiG jet fighters. Having launched at 0600 hours in the morning Lt Carmichael, Lt Davis and Sub Lts Ellis and Haines departed *Ocean* and headed into the Pyongyang area to reconnoitre the railway line. Close to the village of Chinji-ri the flight spotted eight jet aircraft to the north. Quickly recognised as enemy fighters the Sea Furies dumped their external fuel tanks and assumed battle positions. Such was the pace of the battle that Sub Lt Ellis noticed streams of tracer passing each side of his aircraft. Calling 'Break' the Sea Furies broke off into a scissors break. It would appear from subsequent events that either the MiG pilots were inexperienced or they believed that their jet powered mounts would see them through without undertaking any clever manoeuvres. The result was that the Communist pilots were being shot at by the Sea Fury pilots from all angles thus Sub Lt Ellis was easily able to place hits on the wings of one MiG which limped away from the battle escorted by two others. Overall the dog fight lasted no more than five minutes after which the MiGs pulled away although there was an explosion on a hillside close by as an aircraft crashed. A call round the flight revealed that all the Sea Furies had survived and it was realised that the Fleet Air Arm had successfully shot down a jet fighter. Although Lt Carmichael as flight leader was accredited with the kill the other members of the flight were credited with a quarter each as it was impossible to ascertain who had fired the fatal shots. Overall this one fight had resulted in one

A nice sunny day and crowded flight deck makes preparing aircraft for their next missions far easier. Within a few hours the deck of HMS *Ocean* would be empty although those remaining aboard will be worrying about the strike force until they return. (FAAM Yeovilton)

destroyed aircraft with two others badly damaged. Further MiG reports were arriving at *Ocean* even as the Carmichael flight was heading home. One of the first to encounter this next wave was Lt Clark whose Sea Fury was hit by cannon fire in the starboard wing which began to blaze merrily. The pilot dropped the aircraft's drop tanks and by careful side slipping managed to put out the fire. Eventually the badly damaged Sea Fury touched down on the deck of *Ocean*. Escorting Lt Clark was his wingman Lt McEnery who claimed hits on the tail of one of the attacking MiGs. The next attack was against a flight led by Lt Hallam who eventually had to break clear although his aircraft was hit by a 37 mm cannon shell behind the cockpit which left the pilot with no other option but to make a wheels-up landing at Chodo. His wingman Lt Jones managed to return to the carrier while a rescue mission was launched to collect Lt Hallam. Lt Carmichael was awarded the DSC and would eventually become a Commander. While the Sea Furies were tangling with the MiGs the Fireflies were dropping their bombs on a village just south of Chinnampo with great success. The following day was just as eventful. As before the Sea Furies departed to carry out strikes against railway targets led again by Lt Carmichael when yet again MiGs were spotted. External drop tanks were quickly cleared away and another dog fight quickly developed. Eventually the Sea Furies managed to reach cloud thus ending the engagement although at least one MiG was seen to limp away trailing black smoke courtesy of pilots Davis and Ellis. While the MiGs had sacrificed altitude to engage the Sea Furies it was unlikely that this would always be the case. Thus it was proposed that in theatre USAF F-86 Sabres should act as escorts to the Royal Navy fighters. However due to increasing commitments the USAF was not able to provide cover for these flights, therefore, further sorties had to be timed to coincide with F-86 patrols over Korea. When the Sabres were not available the Sea Furies flew in formations of eight aircraft that were intended to give cover to the attack aircraft while presenting the MiGs with too many targets. Even with these restrictions the *Ocean* air wing carried on regardless hitting all sorts of strategic and tactical targets. On 11 August this sudden flurry of jet fighter activity by the north ceased and on 13 August the carrier underwent a day of replenishment. Flying resumed again on 14 August and was a great deal quieter than before as the air wing concentrated on military targets in the Ongjin area, many of which were mortar positions. Having attacked the military positions the Sea Furies turned their attentions to road and rail bridges. However, No.802 NAS did lose an aircraft after a RATOG launch. Sub Lt Clark had used his RATOG to gain height rather than forward momentum on this occasion but once the rockets had finished firing the aircraft stalled and

Even though the deck heating is having some effect the senior deck NCO's have given their troops brooms to help with clearing the snow. Once the flight deck is clear the aircraft can be prepared for their next sortie. (FAAM Yeovilton)

dived inverted into the sea. The pilot managed to escape and was successfully picked up by the plane-guard helicopter. Over the following days a similar pattern of missions was followed before the carrier departed on 18 August for Kure to avoid typhoon Karen. HMS *Ocean* arrived at Kure on the evening of 19 August mooring at the jetty opposite HMS *Unicorn* where replacement aircraft and stores were transferred.

With the squadrons fully re-stored with manpower and aircraft HMS *Ocean* put to sea on 26 August and resumed operations the following day. Bad weather dampened flying until 30 August when sorties were launched in support of landings near Paengyong-do. Further air support flights were undertaken over the Ongjin peninsula in support of further landings during which one Sea Fury was slightly damaged by ground fire. Other aircraft from *Ocean* continued to attack the usual range of targets and all aircraft returned safely after which the carrier withdrew for replenishment. Operations resumed on 1 September with the Sea Furies attacking bridges while the Fireflies concentrated on buildings thought to contain stores, ammunition or troops. Over the two following days *Ocean*'s aircraft continued their usual pattern of sorties although there was a new twist to these operations as a North Korean came on air

Sea Fury FB.11 WJ231 was assigned to No.802 NAS aboard HMS *Ocean* during the Korean War. It survived its adventures over Korea being finally declared for scrap in 1962. However in a further twist the aircraft ended up at Wroughton store marked as WE726. Eventually the Sea Fury was restored in its correct colours for display at FAAM Yeovilton. (BBA Collection)

posing as an American operations controller, however the pilots were suspicious as they were controlling a gunnery shoot for a Royal Navy Frigate. Flying on 4 September was cancelled as Typhoon Mary was moving in the vicinity of South Korea. Combat flying resumed the following day and all missions were completed without loss. Once the last aircraft had returned the carrier departed for Sasebo and arrived on 6 September. After a seven day sojourn in harbour HMS *Ocean* left Sasebo to resume patrol duties. On 14 September flying resumed with the Sea Furies and Fireflies spending much of their time searching for targets worthy of attention. Over the following few days a similar pattern of events occurred until on 17 September the Sea Furies struck at sluice gates controlling water flow at the mouths of the Haeju and Yonan rivers. All strikes were successful and the gates and supporting walls were destroyed by bombs. Over the following two days the air wing continued to strike their designated targets but on these occasions the crews were warned about the possibility of MiGs in the area although none were encountered. A replenishment day occupied 20 September. The next day MiGs were reported to be much in evidence and, therefore, some missions were diverted away from their primary targets. On 21 September No.802 NAS would have the Sea Fury of Lt Graham struck off charge due to the amount of anti-aircraft fire damage it had suffered whilst another would be totally destroyed when it ploughed into the flight-deck barrier. On 24 September the carrier undertook its final sorties of the patrol and then departed for Kure arriving on 25 September. Mooring alongside the jetty opposite *Unicorn* the usual process of exchanging aircraft and replenishing stores was undertaken.

HMS *Ocean* left Kure on 2 October in company with the usual selection of escorts and arrived on station the following day. While the weather was good, strong winds reduced flying operations until 11 October, although some missions, mainly reconnaissance, were undertaken. Replenishment day was 9 October from RFA *Wave Sovereign* and the carrier resumed limited flying the following day. Strikes were undertaken against lorries in the vicinity of Chinnampo with at least one being totally wrecked. Further trucks and sampans were attacked later that day with great success while the Fireflies concentrated their rocket fire upon nominated buildings and left at least two blazing fiercely. The weather improved during the morning of 11 October and missions were flown from mid morning with the air wing concentrating upon fixed and military targets. The Sea Fury piloted by Lt Brown was hit by anti-aircraft fire which wrecked the aircraft's hydraulics and left the pilot with no other option but to crash-land at Suwon. The weather was much better on 12 October, thus the first mission was launched in the early hours. Eight Sea Furies gave the local trucks a hard time by destroying at least two and damaging the others. Further truck concentrations at Chinnampo were attacked by the Fireflies. The final day of this patrol saw the Sea Furies concentrating upon road infrastructure while the Fireflies attacked various troop concentrations near Ongjin, although they had to curtail their activities as MiG fighters were reported en route. It later emerged that these aircraft were being launched from bases in Manchuria where they were controlled by ground controllers. On 13 October HMS *Ocean* left its patrol zone for Sasebo and arrived the following day. HMS *Ocean* departed from Sasebo on the carrier's final patrol on 23 October, resuming flying operations the following day. As before the usual range of reconnaissance missions were undertaken to establish the enemy's operations in the carriers absence. From the reports compiled after the aircraft had returned it appeared that the North

Koreans were rebuilding all the previously damaged infrastructure surrounding them all with a range of anti-aircraft guns. Flights were delayed the following day as the aircraft were covered in a mix of salt and exhaust smoke caused by the variegated winds over the carriers deck. Truck hunting and attacks on road infrastructure continued and the Sea Furies successfully destroyed. The following day coastal shipping was given close attention with a variety of junks and sampans being destroyed and damaged. During these sorties Lt Mather's aircraft, WE708, was hit by ground fire which caused the engine to shut down. Lt Mather attempted to glide out to sea but he was too low and was forced to land in a paddy field; he was later rescued and his Sea Fury was destroyed by other aircraft from *Ocean*. On 28 October HMS *Ocean* refuelled from RFA *Wave Chief* before restarting operations the following day. Both the Sea Furies and Fireflies were briefed to look out for and attack troop movement or concentrations although the Sea Furies still continued their truck busting activities. The final day of Korean operations for HMS *Ocean* was 30 October although launches were delayed due to fog. Once airborne the Sea Furies attacked bridges and barges while the Fireflies concentrated on sampans. During these sorties No.802 NAS lost another Sea Fury, WE684, when the aircraft of Lt. Jenne suffered an engine failure and the pilot ditched in the sea but was rescued by a plane guard helicopter. A second aircraft experienced a rough running engine which required the pilot to nurse his Sea Fury back to the ship. Inspection of the fuel system filters revealed water contamination in the fuel system. Further investigations revealed contamination in most of the remaining Sea Furies although the Fireflies were clear. HMS *Ocean* left the area for Sasebo arriving on 1 November. As a reward for the carrier's operations in Korean waters the squadrons were awarded the Boyd Trophy. On 4 November HMS *Ocean* met up with HMS *Glory* off Hong Kong where both took part in Exercise Tai-Pan.

HMS *Glory* began its third and final tour off the Korean coast having first received five Sea Fury FB.11s and three Fireflies from *Ocean* before that ship turned for home. This meant that No.801 NAS commanded by Lt Cdr P B Stuart would start with 21 Sea Furies while No.821 NAS commanded by Lt Cdr J R N Gardiner had its strength increased to 13 machines. As well as the strike aircraft *Glory* also accepted a pair of Dragonfly plane guard helicopters. To improve the capability of the Firefly the wing-mounted radar was removed and replaced by an extra fuel tank. *Glory* arrived in Sasebo on 9 November for refuelling and sailed for the Korean coast the following day as part of CTE 95.11.

This was the time of the Truce Talks but they were making little positive progress. Therefore, in order to avoid compromising the talks the operating area for the *Glory* air wing was carefully delineated on the maps given to the crews. The carrier's first missions saw the Sea Furies armed with 500 lb bombs and 20 mm cannon while the Fireflies flew with a full load of cannon shells and eight 60 lb rockets although at times the inner rails were removed and replaced by bomb carriers. The first day's flying was severely hampered by persistent rain and drizzle but, even so, the Sea Furies departed to attack lines of communications while the Fireflies were either given selected pre-planned targets to attack or those given on the day by the 'Sitting Duck' destroyer operating close inshore to observe enemy movements. Most flights for the first few days undertook these types of sorties although they were seriously hampered by weather. However, when the weather cleared on 18 November problems arose; it was noticed that anti-aircraft activity had increased markedly and the first fatality occurred on that day when Lt Neville-Jones of No.801 NAS, flying TF971, was shot down, his aircraft crashing into marshy land. A further aircraft, a Firefly, was also hit by enemy fire although in this case the pilot managed to fly his limping aircraft out to sea before ditching, both crewmen were successfully rescued. During this period of operations the *Glory* air wing suffered damage to nine Sea Furies and six Fireflies and was glad to withdraw to Sasebo for

Although de Havilland had provided the Royal Navy with the Sea Mosquito it was not a complete success, therefore the company tried again with the Sea Hornet. Although this was a good machine it was not widely used. However the few units that flew the type did provide much needed cover for other areas of operation. (Rick Harding Collection)

With much of its air wing ranged on deck HMS *Ocean* swings at anchor prior to departing for sea. On the bow are Sea Furies while just aft of the island is the Sea Otter rescue aircraft. The carrier's Fireflies are sitting on the after flight deck. (FAAM Yeovilton)

replenishment and time to replace or repair its aircraft. *Glory* left Sasebo on 28 November, although with a different Captain as Captain Maunsell was taken seriously ill, he was replaced by Cdr Bromley-Martin who took over as acting captain. While incoming intelligence revealed that the communist forces were massing to invade the islands of Sok-to and Sumni-do it was not possible for the air wing to undertake any missions against these concentrations as the weather for the first three days was atrocious. If this was not enough a change in the wind direction, now from the north, resulted in a severe temperature drop that caused leaks in various fluid systems on those aircraft parked on deck. During this period of operations each day's flying would see 28 Sea Fury and 24 Firefly sorties launching each day. During the missions of 6 December the Sea Fury piloted by Lt Marshal was hit in the engine which caused the coolant system to leak, eventually the engine spluttered to a halt, but once again the pilot was rescued within minutes after ditching. When *Glory* left the area to return to Sasebo the air wing had managed an average of 47 sorties per day which was good, considering the weather, however, the downside was that nine Sea Furies and a single Firefly had been damaged by ground fire.

On 14 December *Glory* got a new commander: Captain E D G Lewin DSO, DSC and Bar who arrived just in time as the carrier departed the following day. Combat flying resumed on 17 December with the Sea Furies still had to concentrate upon busting railways and paying special regard to tunnels. The Fireflies resumed their previous role although the continuing wind from the north played havoc with the coolant systems which forced the cancellation of many sorties. Other problems encountered included faulty 20 mm cannon ammunition, the first indication of which was an explosion in one of the guns of the Sea Fury of Lt Leahy which blew the access panels off the top of the wing and blew a large, jagged hole in the bottom of the wing (even with this amount of damage the pilot managed to make a safe but shaky landing aboard *Glory*). Lt Leahy was also flying VW659 when a failed RATOG launch saw him and his Sea Fury ending up in the sea after departing *Glory*. A further problem with ammunition occurred on 20 December when a Firefly piloted by Lt Fogden suffered an explosion which caused the aircraft to crash into the sea. Unfortunately, the crew was lost. It was later discovered that this ammunition had been manufactured in 1943 and was suffering from ageing so the crews were told to use their cannon only in self defence. On the following day No.801 NAS lost another Sea Fury, WF627, when the aircraft of Lt Mitchell suffered ground-fire damage to the engine and a successful rescue was completed after Lt Mitchell ditched. HMS *Glory* departed from Korean waters on Boxing Day having achieved an average daily sortie rate of 61 per day. The carrier's first port of call was Iwakuni where three Fireflies were lightered aboard; a fourth was flown on later. From Iwakuni the carrier set course for Sasebo arriving there on 28 December. For the next five days the carrier re-stored and rearmed and a belated Christmas and combined New Year party was held for all hands.

The next patrol period began in the early morning of 4 January 1953 when HMS *Glory* sailed to undertake a foreshortened patrol period off the coast of Korea. Shortages of cannon ammunition meant that care had to be taken with its expenditure and for strafing purposes only really important targets could be attacked. The first patrols of 5 January resulted in two losses. The first overtook VR922, a Sea Fury piloted by Sub Lt Foster, whose electrics failed completely and this was followed by engine problems that would result in the pilot making a wheels-up landing at Paengyong-do. The second concerned the Sea Fury of Lt Mather which was hit by ground fire and burst into flames soon afterwards. The pilot was left with no option but to bale out, he was later captured by Communist forces. Prior to his capture a full rescue mission was launched but this resulted in a double tragedy when the Sea Fury of Sub Lt Rayner was seen to crash into a hillside and the Sea Fury of Sub Lt Simmonds, WE689, was seen to spin into the ground. The following day was no better when the Firefly piloted by Lt. Heaton was hit by ground fire. The result was a seriously malfunctioning engine although with careful nursing the pilot managed to reach the island of Kirn-do where he and his observer abandoned their ditched aircraft and were rescued some minutes later. The final day of operations, 11 January, saw the Sea Furies in action again, this time against ammunition dumps in the Haeju and Ongjin areas and most dumps disappeared with a satisfactory explosion. Once all the chicks had been safely gathered in *Glory* headed for Kure sailing via Iwakuni to collect replacement aircraft and off load those requiring repairs. After nine days in port the carrier departed Kure and arrived off the Korean coast on 21 January where the USS *Badoeng Strait* had previously been on station. Fortunately, a full programme of missions was possible during this patrol as, at last, usable and safer ammunition was now available. While the carrier had a full complement of aircraft and ammunition illness amongst the pilots meant that the daily sortie rate was very low which was not helped by periods of inclement weather. Even with these difficulties both the Sea Furies and Fireflies continued attacking various designated targets before the carrier headed for Sasebo on 29 January.

HMS *Glory* was two days late in departing Sasebo because, after reports of North Korean submarines operating in the area, an escort of destroyers was needed. To support the destroyer screen the carrier flew off Fireflies on anti-submarine patrols. *Glory* arrived on station on 7 February but, unfortunately, much of this patrol was a wash out due to inclement weather. During this patrol the Fireflies flew with rockets for the first segment, switching to bombs for the latter part of the patrol. In addition, each day the squadron was obliged to provide a single aircraft complete with 250 lb depth charges for anti-submarine patrols. For the Sea Furies the biggest worry was the MiG 15. The first attack from MiGs was on a No.801 NAS patrol when the jets dived on the patrol from a great altitude. Although the Sea Furies were fired on the jets passed through the formation at such a speed that no hits were scored. Early morning strikes were launched on the mornings of 8 and 14 February utilising four Sea Furies and a similar number of Fireflies, their purpose was to catch North Korean transport as it completed its journeys south. On both occasions the ploy was successful as trucks were noted as being damaged and destroyed. However, the carrier air wing lost a Sea Fury on 9 February when the Sea Fury piloted by Sub Lt Hates was hit by anti-aircraft fire which damaged the engine oil feed system. After struggling with his ailing aircraft Sub Lt Hates reached Taedong estuary where he successfully ditched and was rescued. Two further Sea Furies were lost on this patrol, the first being that of Lt MacPherson whose aircraft, WH620, was hit by ground fire during a strafing attack on an ammunition dump. The pilot made no attempt to escape and was killed when his aircraft crashed into a hill. The second loss concerned Sub Lt Bradley who had called the carrier to report an engine problem,

With a Sea Fury sitting on the flight deck catapult and full strike ranged behind it HMS *Ocean* ploughs through a fairly calm sea off the coast of Korea. (BBA Collection)

unfortunately the engine failed and the ditching attempt proved fatal. The Firefly squadron also suffered casualties but fortunately none were fatal. Two were landing-on accidents while the third was as the result of engine coolant loss that required the crew to ditch, both crews were recovered successfully. Although HMS *Glory* was scheduled to continue flying on 15 February excessive winds and a deteriorating weather forecast saw the carrier setting course for Kure arriving there two days later. While in port the carrier landed two Sea Furies and a similar number of Fireflies for repair and received others in return.

HMS *Glory* departed Kure on 25 February arriving on station the following day. It was on this patrol that the aircrews were given an extra item to take with them in their aircraft: an emergency radio purchased from USAF stocks and known as Dodo. As well as a morale booster this radio worked and had already been responsible for the rescue of numerous American airmen. As ever, the Korean winter weather conditions played havoc with flying operations, reducing sortie rates throughout the patrol. During this patrol the Fireflies concentrated on troop formations and their associated stores' dumps. Once they had frightened the troops the Fireflies turned their attention to road and rail links. HMS *Glory* underwent replenishment on 3 March returning to station the following day to take part in Operation Paperchase which was scheduled to end on 6 March. Both squadrons would take part in this operation the purpose of which was, in co-ordination with American air units, to drop leaflet bombs over the major conurbations in North Korea. *Glory* departed the area after the leafleting missions and arrived at Sasebo two days later. After a seven day break the carrier plus escorts sailed once again and resumed operations on 16 March. While the weather was warming this brought with it another problem: sea fogs which limited flying operations. The first operation was against a railway bridge which photoreconnaissance had noted as well defended by anti-aircraft guns. While the attack Sea Furies started their run-in another section of aircraft used the gunners fixation on the strike force to destroy the gun positions successfully, the same fate befell the bridge. Flying resumed on 21 March after a day cancelled by weather and another for replenishment. The missions launched that day were aimed at suppressing road and rail transport during which a Sea Fury, WJ242, piloted by Lt Wheatley suffered engine failure, the result being an emergency landing at Paengyong-do. The next day saw the Sea Furies acting in the anti-aircraft suppression role during an attack on the radio station at Sariwon. As before both targets were successfully destroyed with no losses. Flying was seriously disrupted over the following three days, so much so that *Glory* was ordered to depart for Kure. When *Glory* tied up at Kure the other side of the jetty was occupied by HMS *Unicorn* and the opportunity was taken to swap the two defective Fireflies and a similar number of Sea Furies for more serviceable items.

Departing from Kure on 3 April the carrier was able to resume operations the following day. Fortunately the weather was improving and, therefore, an intensive flying programme was put in place. As before, the air wing concentrated on its usual range of targets, however, while much of the weather was good heavy coastal fog caused the cancellation of 130 sorties. On 5 April the *Glory* air wing managed to fly 107 sorties, this being the maximum possible with a full complement of serviceable aircraft and pilots plus flight deck crews that were more than equal to the task. During this surge all the carrier's pilots flew a minimum of four sorties with all aircraft performing admirably except for one Sea Fury which suffered a damaged tailplane during a flight deck movement. Overall, No.801 NAS achieved 71 sorties and No.821 NAS achieved 52, the remainder being flown by the ships officers. *Glory* departed for Sasebo on 11 April and arrived the following day.

The next patrol began on 19 April and on the 20th *Glory* resumed operations against the usual range of targets. Tragedy struck on 25 April when the Sea Fury, WJ245, piloted by Lt McGregor was hit by ground fire while attacking a bridge near Sariwon. The aircraft crashed before the pilot could make an attempt to escape. A second Sea Fury, WJ248, was lost that day when the aircraft of Sub Lt Keates was shot down while attacking some caves near Changyon reported to contain ammunition. HMS *Glory* would depart for Kure on 27 April arriving there two days later. During the time in harbour replacement aircraft were transferred to *Glory* while the damaged machines were sent across to *Unicorn*.

HMS *Glory* sailed from Kure on 5 May to undertake its final patrol of the Korean war. Attacks concentrated upon troops and their supplies. One unusual hazard was that when strafing ox carts carrying fuel and ammunition this was normally accompanied by flying manure as part of the explosion. Again, the weather played its part in cancelling sorties although when they did fly the aircraft were effective. During this patrol only one aircraft was lost: the Sea Fury piloted by Lt Sherlock suffered a hit to the engine which resulted in a coolant leak. Fortunately the pilot was able to ditch and was safely recovered within minutes. On 14 May HMS *Glory* carried out its final missions before departing the area for Iwakuni. During the voyage five Fireflies and three Sea Furies were flown off to Iwakuni to be available for HMS *Ocean* which was due to relieve *Glory*. On 17 May *Glory* arrived in Sasebo finding *Ocean* already in residence. Transfers of stores and aircraft survival equipment occupied both vessels until *Glory* departed for Britain. After arriving in Britain HMS *Glory* entered Portsmouth for a much needed refit. For the remainder of its career the carrier acted in the ferry role before being paid off in 1956 and was placed on the disposal list the following year.

HMS *Ocean*, under the command of Captain C L G Evans DSO, DSC sailed from Sasebo on 16 May and arrived on station the following day. Making up the air wing was No.807 NAS with Sea Furies commanded by Lt Cdr T L M Brander DSC plus No.810 NAS with Fireflies commanded by Lt Cdr A W Bloomer. As with *Glory* the replacement carrier would concentrate upon the usual range of targets although missions did not begin until 23 May due to bad weather. Over the next three days the air wing launched a full range of attacks without any losses before departing for replenishment on 26 May. The sorties launched on 28 May had to divert to the airfield at Seoul as bad weather precluded the aircraft from returning to base. Once back aboard the carrier they were quickly refuelled and rearmed being launched against rail and road bridges. On 30 May *Ocean* departed for Sasebo arriving the following day. While in port the carrier and its crew not only prepared the vessel for its next patrol they also took part in celebrations to mark the coronation of Queen Elizabeth II.

With its bomb racks cleared and everything out and down Sea Fury VW697 R-102 of No.804 NAS prepares to land on HMS *Glory*. Of note are the cannon blast and oil streaks under the aircraft. (FAAM Yeovilton)

On 9 June *Ocean* arrived on station although missions for that day were cancelled due to inclement weather. A similar situation prevailed the following day, operations being limited to one bridge strike. The following day was better with all targets being hit without loss. Replenishment occupied 13 June and the carrier resuming flying the following day: the Sea Furies concentrated on close air support duties while the Fireflies attacked various troop concentrations and fixed storage targets. On 17 June only a handful of missions were flown before the weather closed in and the *Ocean* set course for Kure arriving there two days later. Six days later the carrier was back on station and was ready for operations on 27 June. Over the following three days the Sea Furies concentrated on close air support missions while the Fireflies attacked their usual range of pre-briefed targets. The carrier would lose it first aircraft on 30 June when the Sea Fury, WE724, of Sub Lt Hicks suffered an engine failure which saw him ditching near Paengyond-do from where he was quickly rescued. After replenishment *Ocean* resumed operations on 2 July. The same type of Missions were resumed with good results and the carrier departed for Sasebo on 16 July arriving the following day. The fourth patrol resumed on 15 July although the carrier lent three Fireflies plus crews and ground crews to an airfield near Seoul. Their purpose was to intercept the well known 'bed check charlies' that were flying over into American controlled territories and bombing targets of opportunity. The USAF had already tried, and failed, to stop these flights with their own night fighters. Although the Fireflies were not able to shoot down any of these interlopers their efforts did succeed in chasing many of these intruders away. The first day of flying for the air wing was severely hampered by fog, one Firefly managed to make it back to *Ocean* with six gallons of fuel remaining after three attempts at landing. The weather cleared that afternoon, however, the catapult became unserviceable and thus all the flights needed RATOG to launch. During one of these take-offs the Sea Fury piloted by Lt Mulder ended up in the sea after firing the RATOG early which meant he was unable to gain sufficient flying speed. A further loss saw a Firefly crash on take-off but, unfortunately, in this case the crew were killed.

Further losses took place on 16 July when the Sea Fury piloted by Sub Lt Mulden suffered brake failure and taxied into another Sea Fury and two Fireflies badly damaging them all. Although the air wing was short of aircraft they did manage to launch a limited number of sorties all of which returned home without loss. Replenishment took place on 19 July and the carrier resuming flying operations the following day. Further sorties were launched the following day although they were curtailed by bad weather. On 23 July HMS *Ocean* sailed for Kure arriving there two days later to await the arrival of *Unicorn* and a tranche of replacement aircraft. The Korean War Armistice was signed on 27 July 1953. HMS *Ocean* would remain in Japanese and Korean waters flying sorties that kept an eye on the North Koreans and their Chinese Allies. During these patrols *Ocean* was frequently accompanied by HMS *Unicorn* with Sea Furies operating off both flight decks. Two Sea Furies would be lost: WH622, piloted by Lt Pugh, ending up in the sea while departing *Ocean* whilst Lt Halliday was badly injured when his just landed Sea Fury, WJ240, was hit at high speed by the following aircraft WH623. Although badly injured Lt Halliday was rescued from his severely damaged aircraft whilst the following aircraft was lost overboard but the pilot was rescued successfully. HMS *Ocean* left the far east and set course for Britain and Devonport in late 1953 for a much needed refit. While HMS *Ocean* would continue in service in a support role HMS *Unicorn* returned to Britain in November 1953 She was being paid off into the reserve on arrival and was finally for scrap in 1958. Thus ended the Royal Naval involvement in the Korean War.

Chapter 8

From Suez to the Falklands

After the Korean War many of the *Colossus* class carriers were withdrawn from use and placed in reserve causing the Royal Navy to shrink yet again. HMS *Glory* would finish its working life at the beginning of 1956 having acted as the base ship for a swarm of helicopters acting in the relief role over a deeply snowbound Scotland. A few of the surviving fleet carriers would also go to the breakers' yards during this fleet rundown. One of these was HMS *Illustrious*, being paid off in December 1954. Also destined to disappear were two of the modified *Illustrious* class carriers: *Implacable* and *Indefatigable*. The former was paid off in September 1954, having acted as a troop ferry ship, while the latter was also retired during the same month. *Indefatigable* would be retired in October 1953, its withdrawal being hastened by an explosion which caused serious damage below the island, killing eight crew and wounding a further 32. During the subsequent fire and rescue ten gallantry awards, including two George Medals, were given in recognition of the crew's bravery.

The maintenance carriers were also decimated, HMS *Perseus*, having served with distinction in Korea was de-stored by the end of 1954. The original intention had been to tow the carrier to Belfast for conversion to a submarine depot vessel. Arriving in Belfast in early 1955, the carrier was worked on until work was suspended in 1957 and it was placed on the disposal list; finally being broken up in 1958. One of shortest carrier careers was that of HMS *Pioneer* which had been commissioned in 1945. After service as a ferry vessel in the Far East the *Pioneer* was finally disposed off for scrap in September 1954. HMS *Unicorn* would also be retired during this period having served with honour during the Korean War. Arriving at Devonport in November 1953 the vessel was paid off and sold for scrap in June 1959.

In October 1951 the dictator president of Egypt, General Gamal Abdel Nassar, unilaterally seized control of the Suez canal in abrogation of an Anglo-Egyption Treaty of 1936 which gave Britain access to the canal and its established bases in the area for a period of 20 years. The seizure of the assets of the Universal Suez Canal Company had been precipitated by the withdrawal of the financial support by America, Britain and the

Although developed during wartime the Blackburn Firebrand TF.II did not enter service until war's end. This aircraft DK383 OC is part of No.708 NAS. Although a big and beefy machine the Firebrand did not live up to its promise as it was a handful to fly and difficult to land due to visual restrictions. (BBA Collection)

International Bank that was required for the construction of the Aswan Dam. The cause of this withdrawal was Egypt's move towards the Eastern Bloc for the purchase of weapons and other materials. Both Britain and France were alarmed by the threatened closure of the canal as this waterway was deemed essential for the transport of oil and it gave access to the trade markets of India and the Far East.

In response, Britain, France and Israel together decided to launch an armed seizure of the canal. Planning of the operation began in late July 1956 when the Israeli Prime Minister David Ben-Gurion, the French Prime Minister Guy Alicide Mollet and the British Defence Minister met in secret in the French town of Sevres near Paris. During this meeting the British Prime Minister, Sir Anthony Eden, was kept informed of events and decisions reached throughout the conference.

In response to Egypt's move General Sir Charles Keightley was appointed as commander in chief of all British and French forces on 11 August for the forthcoming military operations. Supporting the General would be Air Marshall D H F Barnett as the Air Task Force Commander. The rear echelon command for the Royal Navy was supplied by the Commander in Chief Mediterranean Fleet who moved, with his staff, from Malta to Episkopi, Cyprus on 30 October. As this was a joint Anglo-

EK726 was a Firebrand TF.V that had originally been built as a TF.IV. This aircraft was retained by Blackburn's for trials work. Even in its Centaurus powered form the Firebrand was not a great success. (BBA Collection)

French operation an ultimatum was issued to the Egyptian government to withdraw its forces, however Nassar had sabotaged the canal by sinking 49 ships along its length. Even as the Anglo-French forces were moving towards a war footing Israel had already launched its own attack on Egypt codenamed Operation Kadesh on 29 October. American disapproval of British and French actions saw the French Navy carrier group sighting units of the US Navy just north of Egypt. The Americans would make their presence felt throughout the entire operation. When the Anglo-French ultimatum expired the US Navy sailed two destroyers into Alexandria and the carrier group moved slightly closer to the area of operations. On 1 November the C-in-C Mediterranean Fleet sent an urgent signal to the Admiral of the 6th US Navy asking that he and his carrier go and play somewhere else as the British had no desire to inflict damage on the ships and equipment of a close ally. Further reports of American interest were received on 3 November when submarines were detected. However, a flow of signals between the British and American navies soon saw the submarines being ordered to patrol on the surface.

The Royal Navy sent the aircraft carriers HMSs *Albion, Bulwark* and *Eagle. Albion* had just completed a full refit and had sailed from Portsmouth on 15 September 1956 with Nos.800 and 802 NAS with Hawker Sea Hawks, No.809 NAS with eight Sea Venom FAW.21s and No.849 NAS 'C' Flight with Douglas Skyraider Airborne Early

Warning(AEW) aircraft aboard. Also sent to support the Suez operations were the carriers HMS *Ocean* and *Theseus*. Flying operations would begin on 1 November when Operation Musketeer began with air attacks. Aircraft from *Albion* would cover the parachute drops by the 3rd Battalion of the Parachute Regiment on El Gamil airfield near Port Said on 5 November. After the airfield had been captured and made secure, helicopters from *Ocean* and *Theseus* plus *Albion*'s Skyraiders undertook relief missions into the airfield taking in vital supplies and flying out the wounded. The vital supplies included beer; it had been discovered that by removing the rear observer seats at least 1,000 cans of beer could be carried, a load most welcomed by the troops. *Albion* would return to Grand Harbour, Malta, after hostilities had ended.

HMS *Bulwark* sailed for Musketeer duties on 6 August and embarked Nos.804, 897 and 810 NAS with Seahawks en route. During its part in Operation Musketeer the *Bulwark* aircraft flew over 600 sorties in support

The replacement for the Firebrand in FAA service was the Westland Wyvern S.4. Powered by a Python turboprop, this much underrated aircraft was a very capable strike machine. VZ758 was on the strength of No.813 NAS based at Ford although its seagoing base was HMS *Eagle*. (BBA Collection)

Running its powerplant aboard HMS *Eagle* is Wyvern S.4 VZ749 272-E part of No.813 NAS. Of note is the Dennis the Menace artwork under the cockpit. (Rick Harding Collection)

The de Havilland Sea Vampire was one of the first jets to land aboard an aircraft carrier. Although not really suited for carrier operations the Sea Vampire paved the way for the aircraft that followed. (Rick Harding Collection)

of the various segments of the Anglo-French landings before departing the area for a much needed refit in Portsmouth. The newest carrier in the fleet, HMS *Eagle*, with the Flag Officer Aircraft Carriers, Vice Admiral Manley Power, aboard had been undertaking exercises off Malta when warned for Musketeer duties. Aboard *Eagle* were No.898 NAS with Seahawks, Nos.892 and 893 NAS with Sea Venom FAW.21s operating eight and nine aircraft respectively, No.830 NAS with Westland Wyverns plus No.849 NAS 'A' Flight operating Douglas Skyraiders in the AEW role. *Eagle* would be in position to undertake its share of the air cover duties during the landings of 1 November. The Sea Venoms began operations on 1 November with a surprise attack on the Egyptian airfields in the canal zone. No.893 NAS was responsible for the destruction of many of the MiG 15s on Almaza airfield near Cairo while the other Sea Venom squadrons also shot up the other airfields nearby. Alongside attacking ground targets the Sea Venoms also supplied Combat Air Patrols(CAP) over the fleet against possible retaliation that never materialised. Continued operations by the Sea Venoms were carried out against various ground targets using both cannon and rocket fire.

When the Port Said landings began on 3 November the Sea Venoms provided top cover. This was integrated into the 'cab rank' holding pattern from which aircraft were sent to attack targets of opportunity. It was during one of these attacks that the Commanding Officer of No.893 NAS , Lt Cdr R A Shilcock, attacked and sank an Egyptian 'T' boat that was attempting to close in on the fleet. During the entire period of Musketeer only one Sea Venom was lost: WW281 of No.893 NAS which crash landed on HMS *Eagle* during which the cross deck nylon-barrier was used for the first time. Fortunately the crew escaped, although the navigator, Flt Lt R C Odling was badly injured while the pilot Lt Cdr Wilcox suffered minor injuries. The aircraft was written off. During the ceasefire period the Sea Venoms acted as top cover for the troop withdrawals.

In the early hours of 1 November the Sea Hawks began their briefed objective of destroying the Egyptian air assets either on the ground and the air (while avoiding the possible heavy flak if possible). Surprisingly, the Egyptian Air Force did manage to get a patrol of MiG15s airborne, although, given the lack of training in combat techniques and a lack of ammunition, combat was not engaged. Fortunately, the flying time to the targets was only in the region of 30 minutes as the carriers were only 60 miles offshore. As the Sea Hawks closed in on Almaza Air Base the pilots were astonished to see the shiny silver MiGs parked in long rows on the airfield hard standing. Although the local defence gunners did their best to shoot down their attackers the Sea Hawks swept in firing their

Sea Vampire TG328 was the aircraft modified to undertake the flexible deck trials aboard HMS *Warrior*. Although in principle a good idea in the weight saving stakes in reality it was unworkable due to the increased handling requirements. (FAAM Yeovilton)

cannons at the parked aircraft. As the aircraft passed off to the north they left behind a shambles of exploding MiGs. Although the Sea Hawks had used a High-Low-High flight plan to reach and leave their targets the aircraft arrived over their carriers with little fuel available should a diversion have been needed. The successful first day attacks on the EAF air assets had the desired effect of giving the attackers air superiority, however, the anti-aircraft gunners obviously caused problems because, by day five of the attacks, many of the Sea Hawks were sporting minor repairs after being hit sometime during the campaign. Only one abort was called during Musketeer which was against Cairo West. This was fortunate because this part of the airfield was being used as the evacuation point for American citizens leaving Egypt. During Musketeer the Sea Hawk pilots flew a minimum of four sorties a day, they also paid the anti-aircraft gunners the compliment of attacking them once they had completed their missions.

No.830 NAS commanded by Lt Cdr C V Howard embarked on HMS *Eagle* in April 1956 with a strength of nine Westland Wyvern S.4s. When the carrier was warned that it would be needed for Operation Musketeer the Wyverns had the obligatory yellow and black stripes applied to the fuselage and wings. When offensive operations began on 1 November the Wyverns were briefed to attack the airfield at Dekheila, once a home to the Fleet Air Arm. Eighteen sorties were flown by the squadron, their remit was to strafe and bomb the airfield and its aircraft during which eighteen 1,000 lb bombs were dropped and 420 rounds 0f 20 mm were fired. During this attack some light flak was encountered although none of the Wyverns were hit. The second day of operations saw the number of aircraft missions drop to 15 during which Dekheila was attacked again and military vehicles south of Cairo were attacked. On 3 November the squadron suffered its first casualty when Wyvern, WN330, piloted by Lt McCarthy was hit by anti-aircraft fire while attacking the bridge at El Gamil near Port Said. Fortunately the aircraft was still controllable and the pilot was able to glide his aircraft towards *Eagle* before ejecting and was quickly picked up by the rescue helicopter. No.830 NAS flew no sorties during the fourth day but resumed operations on day five. Instead of attacking airfield and structures the Wyverns were assigned to the support of Army units. A total of 16 individual sorties were flown during which rockets and bombs were dispensed as required. It was during these missions that the squadron's senior pilot Lt Cdr W H Cowling was forced to eject from WN328 when the engine was hit by flak. Again the pilot was able to glide towards *Eagle* before ejecting safely being rescued quickly by the carrier's rescue helicopter. Overall, three strikes were launched from *Eagle* during which the squadron dropped seventeen 1,000 lb bombs, fired 176 rockets with 60 lb warheads and 2,250 rounds of

This Supermarine Attacker FB.2 WK333 was on the strength of No.803 NAS normally based aboard the carrier HMS *Eagle*. The Attacker was the first jet aircraft to enter service with the FAA in any quantity. (Rick Harding Collection)

20 mm cannon ammunition were fired, all being used during that day's 473 sorties. The final day of operations on 5 November saw the squadron flying 17 individual sorties during which they were employed on 'cab rank' duties for which they all sported long-range fuel tanks and bombs or rockets. During Musketeer the squadron lost two aircraft while others suffered minor damage to their tailplanes and engine installations. Aircraft deployed by No.830 NAS included WL888, WN325, WN326, WN328, WN330, WN336, WP337, WP338 and WP341. Although No.830 NAS would receive two replacement Wyverns its life was short as the squadron was disbanded in January 1957.

As mentioned before, also sent to support the Suez operations were the carriers HMS *Ocean* and *Theseus*, both veterans of the Korean war. *Ocean*, having returned to Devonport for refit, had been used as a troop ferry during 1955, moving troops and their equipment to Cyprus. When the Suez crisis started to develop *Ocean* in company with *Theseus* transported the 16th Parachute Brigade to Cyprus. As the helicopter was now the favoured transport the carrier was quickly returned to Britain for conversion for their operation. During October 1956 with No.845 NAS and Whirlwinds aboard, and in company with *Theseus*, she undertook commando assault exercises in the English Channel. At the completion of these exercises No.845 NAS had transferred to *Theseus* while *Ocean* had embarked the Joint Service Experimental Helicopter Unit. Both vessels arrived in Grand Harbour, Malta, at the close of October 1956.

During the attack on Port Said the troops of 45 Royal Marine Commando were landed by helicopter. This was the first time that vertical replenishment had been used in action, this method of deploying troops and materials meant that 415 men and 23 tons of stores were landed in one and a half hours. After this last military adventure *Ocean* would return to Britain where it would enter Devonport to be converted for the training role. *Theseus* had also undergone a quick conversion for the operation of helicopters. It too would be involved in the Port Said landings although its career would end when it returned to Britain in December 1956.

Hostilities ceased at midnight of 6 November after pressure was put on both British and French governments by the United States acting through the United Nations, whose Security Council recommended the placement of an Emergency Force to safeguard the canal and ensure the withdrawal of the combatants. Much to the chagrin of the British and French, who had been making good progress along the canal, they were forced to withdraw. During this short sharp conflict the Fleet Air Arm had lost two Hawker Sea Hawks, two Westland Wyverns and a pair of Whirlwind helicopters. The final fallout of this debacle was the

Utilised by No.800 NAS based at Ford, Attacker WA472 was later passed onto second line units for training purposes eventually ending up with Airworks for target purposes. The aircraft is currently with FAAM Yeovilton. (Rick Harding Collection)

The de Havilland Sea Venom FAW.21 was used during the Suez campaign for ground attack and air defence purposes. XG675 was used by two frontline squadrons before passing onto second line units for training purposes. (BBA Collection)

Seen here in its ECM Mk.2 form, Sea Venom WW221 was originally built as an FAW.21 although it was soon upgraded to FAW.22 standard. Other modifications included the fitment of ejection seats and modified wings. In between time the aircraft served with Nos. 893 and 831 NAS. (BBA Collection)

resignation of the British Prime Minister Sir Anthony Eden who resigned from office in January 1957.

After Suez the size of the Royal Navy was reduced as Britain's global responsibilities became less demanding. The final carriers left over from war service were retired which left the Royal Navy with new-build vessels only, although some of these had been authorised during the Second World War and a handful were already under construction at the cessation of hostilities. The main classes of aircraft carrier left in service, post Suez, included the *Centaur* class light fleet-carriers that comprised *Albion*, *Bulwark*, *Centaur* and *Hermes*, a half sister to the *Centaur* class, the *Colossus* light fleet-carriers including *Glory*, *Ocean*, *Triumph*, *Venerable*, which eventually entered service with the Argentine Navy as 25 *de Mayo*, *Vengeance*, which currently serves with the Brazilian Navy as the *Mineas Gerias* and *Warrior*, operated by the Royal Canadian Navy before joining the Royal Navy. There were also the fleet carriers *Ark Royal*, *Eagle* and *Victorious* Another light fleet-carrier class were the *Majestics* which included the *Bonaventure* of the Royal Canadian Navy, originally it was due to be named *Powerful* of the Royal Navy, *Leviathan* whose construction was stopped at the 80% complete point, *Magnificent*, which was the first Canadian carrier, *Melbourne* and *Sydney* of the Royal

Australian Navy and *Vikrant,* originally ordered as HMS *Hercules* of the Royal Navy before being sold to India.

From 1956 there were significant changes applied to the aircraft carriers of the Royal Navy; some were practical and adopted for use while others were slightly fanciful. The fanciful included the flexible carrier deck which was tested on HMS *Warrior* soon after its return from the Royal Canadian Navy. In March 1948 *Warrior* entered Portsmouth to have a thick, flexible, rubber deck fitted, in theory this would allow operational aircraft to land on aircraft carriers. The aircraft that would use this system would need strengthened under surfaces to cope with the landing although this would be countered by the removal of the undercarriage units which equalised the weight. The original trials had been carried out successfully at RAE Farnborough. The aircraft type chosen to carry out these trials on *Warrior* was a modified de Havilland Sea Vampire F.21, the pilot of which was the well known test pilot Lt Cdr

Pictured aboard the carrier HMS *Eagle* is Hawker Sea Hawk F.1 WF145. This aircraft spent its entire working life engaged in proving equipment and weapons for use in other aircraft. (FAAM Yeovilton)

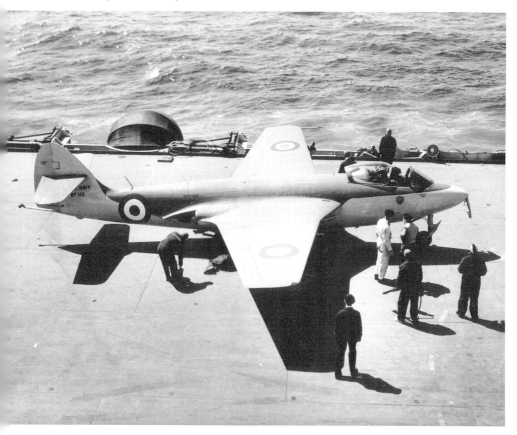

Sea Hawk FGA.6 XE364 was assigned to No.899 NAS when photographed complete with a full load of rockets. The aircraft and the squadron would both take part in operations over Suez. (FAAM Yeovilton)

E M Brown. Although these trials were successful and Lt Cdr Brown was awarded the Boyd Trophy for his work in this project it was subsequently seen as an aeronautical and naval dead end as the support needed to operate these types of aircraft was far more than that needed for conventional machines.

The first significant change to the aircraft carrier was the angled flight deck. Originally carriers had a flight deck that ran fore and aft, the disadvantage being that aircraft needed to be moved around the deck park to allow recovery and launching while strong barriers were needed to protect the aircraft in the forward deck park from damage and destruction should a landing-on aircraft miss the arrester wires. Invented by Captain D R F Campbell the angled deck and its landing area was offset from the carrier's centreline by eight degrees to port thus removing the need for protective barriers which were lethal to the crews of jet aircraft. Another advantage of this type of deck was that an aircraft that missed the arrester wires could undertake 'bolter' and go round again for another attempt. HMS *Theseus* would be the vessel chosen to trial the angled deck layout during February 1952. Although this was only a painted layout set at three degrees to port aircraft were only able to carry out approaches as the arrester wires were still set fore and aft. The success of these trials led to the adoption of the angled flight deck as a standard for the world's navies. Coupled to the angled deck were two other inventions that are still in use today. The launch catapult, up to the end of WW2, was normally hydraulic, however, as jet aircraft arrived in service with their increased weights this type of catapult was at its maximum with no further chance of further development. Invented by Cdr C C Mitchell the first use of the steam catapult was in the carrier HMS *Perseus* during 1949. As the catapult was seen as a significant invention the trials were undertaken in great secrecy off Rosyth and Belfast. During 1951 HMS *Perseus* continued trialling the steam catapult, later that year the US Navy was invited to send representatives and

Having utilised the Grumman Avenger in the airborne early warning role the FAA chose the Douglas Skyraider to replace it. During the Suez campaign the Skyraiders were used to collect walking wounded having delivered such vital supplies as beer. (Will Blunt Collection)

The Supermarine Scimitar F.1 finally gave the Fleet Air Arm a supersonic fighter that was capable of delivering a nuclear weapon. Scimitar XD231 was being operated by No.807 NAS when photographed. (Will Blunt Collection)

The Scimitar was also capable of utilising a photoreconnaissance nose, the trials for which had been undertaken using this aircraft, XD268 156-V. Having trialled the reconnaissance nose the aircraft was on the strength to No.803 NAS aboard HMS *Victorious*. The aircraft was also involved in Bullpup missile trials and as seen here it was involved in bridle catching trials, the test installation for which was under the forward fuselage. (Will Blunt Collection)

aircraft to the carrier. During these combined trials more than 1,000 dead loads and 127 active aircraft, USN and RN, both piston and jet powered, were successfully launched. At the completion of these trials *Perseus* underwent a refit during which the steam catapult, deckhouses and workshop equipment were removed. The only visible signs that a steam catapult was fitted were the rails and the top part of the shuttle. Under the deck were a pair of parallel cylinders which housed pistons that were fixed to the shuttle while sliders were also incorporated that opened and closed slots in the cylinders as the shuttle moved under steam power. Steam was fed from the ship's boilers into an accumulator that allowed the launch party to adjust the operating pressure depending on the weight of the aircraft. When the aircraft was attached to the shuttle by a strop it was held in place by a 'hold-back' near the tail. When the catapult was released the aircraft's engines, running at full power, coupled with the fed-in steam pressure overcame the force of the hold-back which allowed the aircraft to accelerate rapidly up to a speed of 135 knots within a distance of 150 feet. At the end of their run the pistons would be stopped by water rams and the shuttle was motored back ready for the next launch. A fully trained crew could launch an aircraft every two minutes. However, jet aircraft, with their greater speeds, were difficult to control during landing. Originally, landings were controlled by a Landing Signals Officer(LSO), or batman, who would guide the aircraft onto the deck or wave them off if their approach was incorrect. The increased speed of jet aircraft made the LSO redundant as his ability to correct and react to an approaching aircraft was too slow. The answer was the mirror landing-aid invented by Cdr H C N Goodhart. This system was centred around a curved mirror that was mounted on a stable platform on the midships port side of the flight deck where the effects of the ship's pitch would be minimised. Either side of the mirror was a line of green lights which provided the pilot with a datum. A bank of lights, each with multiple power supplies, was mounted on the port aft side, these being angled in such a way as to reflect a light beam along the angled deck which incorporated a three degree glide slope. The mirror height could be adjusted to account for the length of each aircraft type's arrester hook. Although the technology sounds complicated in reality all the pilot had to do when approaching was keep the spot of reflected light, the 'meatball', in line with the green datum arms. The meatball position acted in the natural sense thus if the meatball was lower than the green arms then the aircraft was too low, if too high then the aircraft was too high. Very little changed with this method of handling landings, the only major change being the introduction of a vertical bank of lights for the mirror. This change, although minor, meant that the meatball was more positive as the light was radiated not reflected.

The first aircraft carrier to sport all these modifications was HMS *Albion* which had them all incorporated during construction. *Albion* entered service in May 1954. Other carriers fitted with these modifications were HMS *Ark Royal* which entered service in 1955 although the deck was set at five degrees. During the carrier's refit and modernisation from 1966 to 1970 it was fitted with a flight deck set at eight degrees, a side mounted flight-deck lift and improved steam catapults, all of which would allow the *Ark* to operate its complement of F-4 Phantoms and Buccaneers more efficiently. Other fleet carriers modified with an angled flight deck included HMS *Eagle* which was rebuilt between 1959 and 1964. This was an improvement on the 1954 to 1956 refit which introduced a five and a half degree deck and mirror landing aid. HMS *Eagle* would also be the recipient of a Type 984 three dimensional radar and was also the first carrier to be fitted with computer aided action-information system. HMS *Hermes* was another fleet carrier completed with an angled flight deck set at eight degrees plus aircraft operating aids. Although laid down in 1945 the vessel was not ready to launch until 1952. A programme to complete the vessel was begun in 1957 but it was not completed until 1959 which made it comparable to the recently modernised *Victorious*. The final fleet carrier that sported an angled flight deck was the *Illustrious* class carrier HMS *Victorious*. After its war service *Victorious* would be little utilised; however, in March 1950 the vessel entered Portsmouth Dockyard to undergo major modernisation. The vessel that eventually emerged was virtually brand new, not only were the engines and boilers replaced, the island was rebuilt and all the major modifications needed to operate modern jet aircraft were incorporated. Although this made *Victorious* the most modern carrier in the fleet it would actually have been cheaper to construct a new carrier. The *Majestic* class aircraft carriers operated by the Commonwealth navies were also fitted with these modifications. Included in this group were *Bonaventure,* RCN, *Melbourne*, RAN and *Warrior*, RCN. Another member of the *Centaur* class that was involved in carrier trials was HMS *Bulwark*, although *Bulwark* only had a painted angled deck its claim to fame was its use as the trials vessel for the mirror landing aid. Another *Centaur* class carrier fitted with an angled deck plus all the aids was the name ship although this vessel had its deck set at angle of six degrees.

The number of carriers remaining in the Royal Navy by 1960 had reduced as Britain's foreign policy changed necessitating a change in the role of the aircraft carrier. By 1960 HMS *Albion* was scheduled to enter

After the Scimitar, the squadrons were equipped with the de Havilland Sea Vixen. Here an FAW.2 is seen departing HMS *Eagle*. (Will Blunt Collection)

Portsmouth for conversion to commando carrier status. *Albion* was recommissioned in August 1962 and embarked No.845 NAS with Westland Wessex helicopters, No.846 NAS with Westland Whirlwinds and No.40 Royal Marine Commando. After working-up exercises were completed the carrier was allocated to the Far East Fleet. During November 1963 the carrier was on a visit to Mombassa when the Brunei revolt began. *Albion* was quickly alerted to move to the area and the vessel sailed via Singapore to pick up extra stores and equipment. In theatre the ships helicopters were used to move Royal Marines and troops from British and Commonwealth units. Stores and vehicles were also delivered ashore by helicopters to bases in Borneo including Labuon, Kuching and Taiwan. *Albion* remained in theatre until returning to Portsmouth for a refit in April 1964.

HMS *Bulwark* entered Portsmouth Dockyard in January 1959 for conversion to commando carrier status. Prior to that the vessel had been deployed to Aden after trouble had flared up there. *Bulwark*'s conversion would only take a year and the carrier was recommissioned in January. Once the initial ships work-up had been completed No.848 NAS and its Whirlwinds were embarked as was No.42 Royal Marine Commandos.

The catapult bridle drops away from underneath Sea Vixen FAW.1 XN657 491-C as it departs from the carrier HMS *Centaur*. In common with many of its type this aircraft was later modified to FAW.2 standard. (Will Blunt Collection)

While *Albion* would be involved in the Brunei crisis *Bulwark* would become ensnared in an operation that had warnings for the future. In July 1961 the carrier was visiting Karachi when orders were received to move rapidly to the Persian Gulf to provide protection for Kuwait as Iraq forces were threatening to cross the border. Known as Operation Vantage the carrier landed its Royal Marines and their equipment in support of the Kuwait armed forces. Air cover and support were provided by the HMS *Victorious* air wing. This show of force convinced the Iraqis that invading Kuwait would not be to their advantage thus their armed forces were pulled back from the border. Unfortunately, in 1990-91 it was a much harder task to remove the Iraqis.

HMS *Centaur* remained as a bona fide aircraft carrier throughout the 1960s. Having been involved in Exercise Jet 60 during March 1960 the carrier, and its crew, would soon be in action for real as their brief was to use all means possible to contain the activities of arms smugglers moving weapons into Western Aden in an operation codenamed Damon. After three weeks enforcing this blockade *Centaur* returned to Portsmouth for a refit which began in August. After five months in the hands of the dockyard maties the carrier was recommissioned and embarked No.807 NAS with Scimitars, No.893 NAS with Sea Vixens, No.849A. NAS with Gannet AEW3s and No.824 NAS with Whirlwinds for plane guard duties. During 1961 *Centaur* replaced *Victorious* in the Persian Gulf, assisted with flood relief operations in Kenya and assisted with the rescue of the crew of the Greek tanker *Stanvac Sumatra* which had broken in half in the South China Sea. During 1962 the carrier was involved in Exercise Jet 62 and Exercise Riptide before returning to Portsmouth for a refit. Back in action in January 1964 HMS *Centaur* embarked No.45 RM Commando, two Westland Belvederes plus all the equipment for the troops. Their destination was Aden where units of the Tanganyika Rifles had mutinied. The arrival of these extra troops and the availability of the carrier's air wing soon quelled the fighting. However, Aden continued to cause trouble and *Centaur* had to return to Aden, this time it was rebelling tribesmen in the Radfan desert. *Centaur* returned home for the last time in December and finally paid off in December 1965.

HMS *Hermes,* being a late starter, embarked No.804 NAS with Scimitars, No.890 NAS with Sea Vixens, No.849C NAS with Gannets and No.814 NAS with plane guard Whirlwinds. During the 1960s Hermes would see little combat action; its only operation being undertaken in June 1967 when it was required to cover the British withdrawal from Aden.

The fleet carriers led a fairly quiet life during the 1960s. HMS *Ark Royal* would spend much of its time taking part in various exercises before entering Devonport Dockyard for a complete rebuild that would allow the carrier to operate F-4 Phantoms. Prior to its paying off the carrier had been involved in the Beira Patrol which had been put in place to stop supplies reaching Rhodesia after Premier Ian Smith had declared a Unilateral Declaration of Independence. The *Ark* would be relieved by HMS *Eagle* in January 1966. On station *Eagle* would spend the next five months mounting air patrols in an effort to stop ships entering the port of Beira in Angola. Although numerous vessels were identified only two oil tankers were turned away. Given the current situation in this benighted country maybe trying to defeat the Smith Administration was a wrong option. It would be HMS *Victorious* which had the more exciting decade. During 1961 the carrier assisted *Centaur* during flood relief operations in Kenya and this was followed by a high speed dash with all despatch to the Persian Gulf to provide air support for *Albion* in Kuwait emergency. The Middle East seemed to have an attraction for *Victorious* as the carrier passed through the Suez Canal in June 1967 just before the Arab-Israeli War started. While the fighting continued the carrier was held at Malta in case any intervention was needed to rescue any British citizens. *Victorious* returned to Portsmouth for a refit in June 1967. It was during this refit that the carrier suffered some minor damage after a fire. This was the excuse the politicians needed to withdraw the carrier from use, although very senior Naval Officers were against this decision as *Victorious* was in overall excellent condition and was regarded as the best carrier available.

As the Royal Navy entered the 1970s the available carriers were the fleet carriers HMS *Eagle* and *Ark Royal*. The commando carriers were more numerous consisting of *Albion*, *Bulwark* and *Hermes*. HMS *Ark Royal* was recommissioned in 1970 and spent much of the following decade involved in numerous exercises around the world. Two items are worthy of note: in November 1970 the carrier launched the hot air balloon *Bristol Belle* piloted by Lt Adams its destination being Malta. This would be the only time that the Royal Mail was delivered by this method. The second item of note took place in May 1971 when Harriers from the RAF undertook trials from the carrier, a precursor of things to come. HMS *Ark Royal* returned to Devonport in December 1978 to pay off for the final time, its air wing flying off to St Athan. The withdrawal of the *Ark* marked the end of the conventional carrier in Royal Navy service. HMS *Eagle* would also spend its last decade of service taking part in various exercises before arriving in Portsmouth in January 1972 to pay off. The carrier would spend its final few years moored at Plymouth where it acted as a spares source for *Ark Royal*. HMS *Eagle* was finally sold for scrap in 1978.

The commando carrier fleet would also be reduced during this period, one of the first to go was *Albion*. During the early 1970s *Albion* had undertaken exercises in the Mediterranean before proceeding to Singapore to assist in the British withdrawal from Singapore in October 1971. The following year saw the carrier involved in various exercises before arriving in Portsmouth in November 1972 to pay off. HMS *Bulwark* also spent the 1970s involved in various exercises before entering Portsmouth in March 1978 for refit. It had been intended to withdraw the carrier at this point, however, delays in commissioning the new *Invincible* class through-deck cruisers required that HMS *Bulwark* be refitted for further service. *Bulwark* continued in use until March 1981 when it entered Portsmouth for the final time for decommissioning. The longest serving commando carrier would be HMS *Hermes* which was, like its compatriots, involved in various training exercises until entering Devonport Dockyard for conversion to an anti-submarine carrier, although it was still capable of carrying out commando duties. When recommissioned in December 1976 the carrier worked-up in the English Channel operating Harriers prior to the type's deployment with the forthcoming *Invincible* vessels. Exercises kept *Hermes* busy until December 1979 when No.700A NAS embarked with its Sea Harriers for intensive flight trials. At the beginning of 1980 *Hermes* would enter Portsmouth Dockyard for modifications that centred around the installation of a 12 degree ski jump plus all the paraphernalia needed to operate Sea Harriers. The work was completed by June 1981 after which

When the Fleet Air Arm acquired the Blackburn Buccaneer it gained an aircraft that was capable of travelling at high speed and low level whilst delivering a nuclear weapon on a designated target. (Rick Harding Collection)

the carrier underwent a full work-up, all of which paid off in 1982. At the completion of its efforts during Operation Corporate HMS *Hermes* continued its usual round of exercises before being sold to the Indian Navy in 1986 and renamed *Viraat*.

While the Royal Navy lost its last fleet carrier at the end of 1978 the principle of providing aerial fleet defence had not been totally abandoned. Although building and equipping replacement fleet carriers was not a viable option due to the lack of available funds an alternative was available. It had already been proved that the Hawker Siddeley Harrier could be operated from aircraft carriers therefore funding was found to develop a sea going aircraft, the Sea Harrier FRS1, and the platform to fly them from. The class of ship developed was the *Invincible* class anti-submarine carrier originally described as a through-deck cruiser. A total of three vessels was ordered, the first vessel to be laid down was the class name ship. *Invincible* was laid down in 1973 and launched in May 1977 with completion occurring in June 1980. Commissioning took place during the following month. From the outset the vessel was intended to operate a mix of Sea Kings and Sea Harriers, however, it was better at operating the latter as the inboard set of the

The Buccaneer S.1 was replaced by the S.2 variant which was a far more capable machine courtesy of the Rolls Royce Spey engines that were more powerful and reliable than the previous Gyron Juniors. (Rick Harding Collection)

island superstructure restricted aircraft movements somewhat. Even with this design fault the carrier would give good service during the Falklands War. It was fortunate for the Royal Navy that the misguided Nott report was not implemented and the vessel was not sold to Australia for £175 million.

The second ship in the order would become HMS *Illustrious*. Laid down in October 1976 the ship was launched two years later commissioning in June 1982. It had been intended that *Illustrious* should not be accepted until November at the earliest, however, the Falklands War accelerated the programme. This carrier was also the first to incorporate improvements courtesy of the Falklands experience, the most obvious of these were the platforms for the Vulcan Phalanx close range air defence system and an improved command and control system.

HMS *Ark Royal* was the third and final ship of this order. Laid down in December 1978 the ship was launched in June 1981 and commissioned in November 1985. As the last of the class to complete, *Ark Royal* included all the improvements that operational experience with the other two carriers had suggested. During construction a larger ski jump, similar to that aboard *Hermes*, was installed and set at 12 degrees and some forty feet further forward. The *Ark Royal*'s hull was also strengthened which cured the vibration found in *Invincible* at full speed. A new bow was also fitted which allowed room for the bow mounted Vulcan Phalanx Close-in weapons System. Two others were installed on a sponson at the port rear quarter and outboard of the island on the starboard side.

Starting a war has often been seen as a way of supporting an ailing government or hiding the truth from the electorate. The war over the Falkland Islands fitted both the categories well, in Argentina the ruling military Junta had become unpopular, not only was inflation running rampant, but stories of disappearing citizens were finally being accepted as true by the populace. A similar situation existed in Britain where the Thatcher government had started to become unpopular and was facing a general election. The first move would be made by the Junta in Argentina whose intention to conquer the Falklands, or Islas Malvinas as the Argentinians called them, had first been mooted in January 1982. Initial preparations were undertaken at this time by the senior officers of all three services and enough intelligence was garnered in Buenos Aires by British operatives that signalled a possible invasion. While the available Malvinas invasion plans were being scrutinised by the senior officers of all three services the Argentine Air Force was still running logistics flights into and out of Britain and Israel picking up weapons and ammunition.

On 19 March a party of Argentinean demolition workers arrived on the island of South Georgia to begin the removal of scrap materials. This, coupled with a problem with a LADE airliner at Port Stanley airport, gave the Argentine Junta all the excuse they needed to launch Operation Rosario, the retaking of the Malvinas. The invasion fleet arrived off the East Falklands on 30 March although the planned landings were delayed for 24 hours due to bad weather. Just after midnight the invasion began and, although they put up a spirited resistance, the small detachment of Royal Marines was ordered to surrender by the island's governor, Rex Hunt, in order to reduce the loss of life. By mid afternoon 1 April the islands were in Argentinean hands. Consolidating their position on the islands was achieved quickly, the Army positioned itself in various strong points overlooking Port Stanley and around Stanley airfield. The airforce meanwhile would ship in various aircraft types suited to the counter insurgency role: Pucaras, MB.339s, Bell 212s and a single Puma helicopter. Also established was an air bridge that saw a constant stream of transports bringing in supplies and ammunition plus extra anti-aircraft guns and personnel. Eventually some 9,800 soldiers were deployed while six MB339s, four Beech T-34C Mentors, 35 Pucaras and numerous helicopters were deployed by the air force plus the crews to man and maintain them. While the army and air force provided the greater majority of equipment and manpower, operational control was vested in the Argentine Navy. Ironically, after the invasion the navy played a limited part in defending the newly captured territories and was kept in harbour for much of the time, their only major adventure in South Atlantic waters would see the cruiser *General Belgrano* sunk by a hunting Royal Navy submarine.

By 7 April 1982 it had become obvious to the Junta and senior military officers that they had grossly underestimated the strength of the British reaction having laughed raucously at the informed British public who had thought that the Falklands were off the north coast of Scotland somewhere. While there was a certain amount of geographic humour involved the Argentine Junta were fully aware that the British armed forces were preparing to retake the Falklands and the other islands. In response the Argentine Air Force stepped up the frequency of resupply flights, not only were standard stores requirements satisfied, but an AN/TPS-43F surveillance radar was flown in to improve the islands air traffic control facilities. This system would also play a great part in detecting the various British aircraft undertaking attacks and reconnaissance over the islands. As the decision had been taken not to base any interceptors at Stanley, the only airfield that might have handled them, due to the lack of hardened protection another solution was needed. This would be a massive deployment of anti-aircraft guns and missile batteries that, after a few teething problems, would become a fairly well integrated defensive system although their coverage was limited to Goose Green plus Post Stanley and environs.

On 27 April long range radar on the islands detected the faint first traces of the British task force en route to the Falklands. Realising that this might be the last clear chance to reinforce the garrison a further 14 attack aircraft were despatched to the islands.

While Argentina had been preparing various scenarios covering the capture of the Falklands it should come as no surprise to find that the British Chiefs of Staff had commissioned a report covering the possibility of Argentina invading the islands as the South Americans had laid claim to these pieces of real estate for many years. The report was finally available for inspection in September 1981 and covered the possibility of repulsing such an attack, remote given the time and distance, or more likely a counter attack to throw any invading forces off the islands. While the former premise was theoretical only the latter was seen as a distinct possibility therefore further work was undertaken to develop the counter invasion plan. From the outset it was realised that the whole hinged around having a large enough naval force to transport troops and

After using the Avenger and the Skyraider the FAA employed the Fairey Gannet AEW.3 to provide AEW coverage for the fleet. This would be the last fixed wing AEW type employed by the Royal Navy before the big carriers were withdrawn. (Rick Harding Collection)

equipment plus provide surface and air cover. An added bonus would be the possibility of using the Ascension Islands as a midway stopover point. From the outset any such operation would require the concentration of massive resources and would take a long time to organise due to the long lead time required to collect personnel, equipment, stores and ammunition together plus requisitioning civilian shipping to carry everything. The naval force would require a minimum of an *Invincible* class carrier, at least four escort ships and the use of at least two hunter killer submarines for long range patrols. In the event the naval requirements were vastly understated as the actual invasion fleet required the greater majority of the extant British Fleet.

When Argentinia landed their scrap merchants on South Georgia on 1 March 1982 the official government line was that this was no more than an incursion to recover metals and not, as predicted, the opening moves

Pictured just before touching down on HMS *Ark Royal* is this MDD F-4 Phantom of No.892 NAS. The Phantom not only provided air defence capabilities but it was also capable of undertaking strike and attack missions. (BBA Collection)

of a Falklands invasion. By 29 March the scrap merchants were still on South Georgia therefore vessels of the home fleet were withdrawn from their normal duties to join the ice patrol ship HMS *Endurance* whose province was the South Atlantic. The ships allocated were the Royal Fleet Auxiliary ship *Fort Austin* and the submarine *Spartan*, both of which sailed from Gibralter. A further submarine, *Splendid*, was ordered to leave from Faslane the following day to provide increased support. While this small force was sailing for the cold waters of the South Atlantic the Admiralty, in concert with the Ministry of Defence, had started the planning for the deployment of a larger force should it be needed. Heading the Admiralty was the Chief of the Defence Staff, Admiral of the Fleet Sir Terence Lewins GCB, MVO, DSC, while the overall commander of the military operation would be Admiral Sir John Fieldhouse GCB. The in-theatre commander would be Rear Admiral J F Woodward, Flag

Officer First Flotilla, who was tasked with preparing a suitable group of ships at his Gibralter base. Even as the fleet was being assembled it was reported that the Argentine Navy appeared to be carrying out naval exercises some 800 miles from the Falklands. While on the face of it this appeared to be no more than manoeuvres, the task of assembling the British naval force was speeded up although the instruction to do it covertly was somewhat optimistic as hiding the presence of a large warship out of its usual beat could not be missed by the most inept of spies. The arrival of the Argentine invasion force on East Falkland on 2 April changed the situation dramatically.

The British response would be designated Operation Corporate and would be one of the fastest assembled operations ever put together, requiring the full co-operation of all the British armed forces, the Merchant Navy, all the defence manufacturers plus many other smaller organisations and individuals. While the military side was coming up to full speed the diplomatic battle was in full swing, although the Argentine government was proving intractable. The events of 2 April would engender widespread anger amongst the British populace and was fuelled, to some extent, by the media. Given the strength of feeling in the country and with the support of all the political parties it was almost inevitable that the military option would be exercised. The first move involved Admiral Woodward departing from Gibralter with ten warships that had just been restored after taking part in Exercise Springtrain. In Britain a much greater task force was being assembled around the carriers HMS *Hermes* and *Invincible* later to be named as part of Task Force 317 which included all surface ships, land and air forces. Submarine forces were designated Task Force 324. Exercising overall tri-service control was Admiral Fieldhouse who was based in the command centre at Northwood. Assisting the Admiral was Air Marshall Sir John Curtiss, KCB acting in the Air Commander role while his land counterpart was, initially, Major General J J Moore CB , OBE, MC who would later be replaced by Lt General Sir Richard Trent KCB as General Moore departed on 20 May to take up the appointment of Commander Land Force, Falkland Islands. Submarine forces were under the command of Vice Admiral P G M Herbert OBE.

The scale of the task facing the British Armed forces should not be underestimated as the maintenance of ships, aircraft and vehicles had to be completed quickly as all were required for frontline use. This meant that 12 hour shifts and seven day working was instituted immediately. While the diplomatic battle raged on between Argentina and Britain another diplomatic mission was undertaking more subtle negotiations with friends and allies in order to extend the range of the British forces.

The result was that the Americans would make available the airfield and its facilities at Wideawake on Ascension Island while also providing much needed weaponry.

On 12 April Britain put in place a 200 mile Maritime Exclusion Zone around the islands letting it be known that there might be submarines in the area. The submarine announcement had the desired effect as the majority of supplies and equipment originally destined to be moved by sea had to be broken down and loaded onto pallets to await movement by air, thus causing shortages of vital stores late in the campaign. The first stage of recapturing the Falklands involved retaking South Georgia which was accomplished as Operation Paraquat between 20 and 26 April with elements from all forces being heavily involved. Task Force 317.9 commanded by Captain B G Young aboard the destroyer *Antrim* met with *Endurance* and both proceeded to South Georgia. Arriving off the island troops were put ashore by helicopters from No.845 NAS *Endurance* Flt and No.737 NAS, *Antrim* Flt. However the ground forces had to be withdrawn the following day as severely inclement weather arrived exposing the troops to unnecessary danger. The withdrawal was not without loss, however, as the two Wessex helicopters of No.845 NAS were destroyed. *Antrim* was back in action on 25 April when the ship's helicopter spotted the Argentine submarine *Santa Fe* and attacked, causing severe damage. The following day the Argentine forces surrendered South Georgia, presenting the Royal Navy with a harbour closer to the Falklands. It also sent a strong message to the Argentine Junta that not only was Britain prepared to fight to regain the Falklands but with the capture of South Georgia and other moves within South America that mainland Argentina was also open to attack.

The main vessels of the Task Force would be the carriers. HMS *Hermes*, having served as a commando carrier, had undergone extensive modifications at Portsmouth Dockyard during 1980 which allowed it to operate Sea Harriers as well as helicopters. The most obvious modification was the fitment of a 12 degree ski jump fitted to the bow which assisted the Sea Harriers to operate from the carrier. Selected to act as the flagship of the Task Force, *Hermes*, with Nos.800 and 899 NAS, Sea Harriers, Nos.826 and 846 NAS with Sea Kings aboard, departed from Portsmouth on 5 April 1982. The vessel's aircraft complement was later increased by the addition of some Lynx helicopters from No.815 NAS and Harrier GR.3s of No.1 Squadron RAF. Accompanying Hermes was HMS *Invincible,* the name ship of a the three strong class of light carriers. Launched in May 1977 the vessel was commissioned on 11 July 1980 and undertook numerous exercises as part of its work-up period. Originally

As with all modern types the Phantom required a training unit; this being No.767 NAS. In this portrait FG.1 XT868 153-VL carries out a spirited flypast using full afterburner. (BBA Collection)

planned as a pure anti-submarine vessel the carrier was capable of operating the Sea Harrier and the Sea King, the former being launched courtesy of a bow-mounted ski jump. *Invincible* was docked at Portsmouth in December 1981 when ordered to prepare for the Falklands. The air group assigned to the carrier included No.899 NAS with Sea Harriers and No.820 NAS flying Sea Kings. During the conflict further Sea Harriers of No.809 NAS were added to the carriers inventory to increase the type's attack flexibility.

This was the force that set sail for the Falkland Islands and was intercepted on 21 April by long range Argentine reconnaissance aircraft. Two days later the British Government issued a definitive statement that extended the Maritime Exclusion Zone and turned it into a Total Exclusion Zone which became effective by the end of the month. The premise of this new order was that any Argentine vessel or aircraft entering the Zone and deemed a threat would be destroyed. The establishment of a base on Ascension Island allowed a build-up of stores and equipment, not only for the forthcoming fighting but as replacements for any losses. Supplying the base required that a fleet of 70 ships be almost permanently at sea shuttling between Britain and Ascension.

Hermes and *Invincible* used their transit time usefully undertaking air combat and ground attack work-ups although there was a cessation when passing through the Bay of Biscay where the usual bad weather was encountered. Having passed through the bay the work-up for combat continued during which period the Sea Harriers were painted

Photographed at the end of its landing run, this Phantom still has the arrestor wire attached to the hook. The Phantom was given the same range of modifications as its RAF counterparts, the most obvious of which was the fin tip mounted ARI 18228 passive warning receivers. (BBA Collection)

dark sea-grey on all light covered surfaces while the national markings were also toned down, aboard *Invincible* the Sea Harriers were repainted overall in a lighter grey. It is reported that some aircraft aboard *Hermes* were painted using mops and brooms as this vessel, unlike *Invincible* had no spray painting facilities. The irony was that the rough painted aircraft had a more durable finish than the spray painted machines, a bonus in the South Atlantic and its rough conditions. It was during this period that decisions concerning the Sea Harriers' weapons loads for different mission were confirmed. In the fighter role the aircraft would carry a pair of AIM-9L Sidewinders plus 200 rounds of 30 mm cannon ammunition while in the attack role the Sea Harriers would retain their cannon added to which would be a selection of 1,000 lb bombs, either conventional or retarded, 2 inch rocket pods or 600 lb cluster bombs. Actual live firing and bombing took place on 16 April as the fleet neared Ascension. Nine

Sea Harriers took off in the early morning to undertake live attacks against surface splash targets while a Sidewinder was launched against a LEPUS flare which was successfully destroyed. The Task Force arrived off Ascension on 17 April where all hands turned to and replenished the ships. Although intended that the stop period would continue until 20 April the fleet was forced to depart due to a submarine warning which turned out to be false. The warning saw the fleet leaving two days earlier than planned; a great effort had been made by personnel on both the island and ships which meant that only a handful of sorties were needed to be made by helicopters to deliver the last few necessities. As soon as the fleet was en route a standing deck alert of two Sea Harriers armed with Sidewinders was instituted. For the remainder of the aircraft at least two sorties a day were flown, partly as training and partly to provide an airborne component for fleet defence. The first exercise of the alert aircraft took place on 20 April when the air defence radar picked up an inbound aircraft heading towards the ships. The alert aircraft were scrambled and headed towards the intruder that turned out to be a Boeing 707 of the Argentine Air Force on a reconnaissance mission. After a period of aerial cat and mouse the Boeing departed but returned at various times over the following few days. Eventually through diplomatic channels the Argentine government was informed in the nicest possible way that should their reconnaissance aircraft return it would be at risk and in great danger of being shot down. As can be imagined this warning was taken seriously and the flights ceased.

The Task Force reached the edge of the British exclusion zone on 30 April and prepared for their missions scheduled for 1 May. That day's proceedings started in the early morning of 1 May when 'Black Buck 1' flown by a Vulcan B.2 operating from Ascension Island attacked Stanley Airport. Before the *Hermes'* Sea Harriers launched to attack targets at Stanley and Goose Green the combat air patrol (CAP) had already been launched by *Invincible*. The attack group of nine aircraft destined for the selected targets in the Port Stanley Area departed during the mid morning. When closing on the East Falkland Island the nine aircraft split into two groups of five and four respectively, the latter attacked the air defence positions around the airfield perimeter using the toss bomb method to release their bombs. The aircraft from the first attack remained in the area to confuse the defenders and hopefully allowing the other five aircraft to sweep in fast and low to continue the attack on the airfield and its facilities. Of the five remaining attackers two dropped 1,000 lb retarded bombs onto the runway to follow up the attack of the Vulcan while the other three dropped cluster bombs (CBUs) on the facilities around the airfield. Having caught the Argentine forces unawares the

Argentine defences exploded into life as the Sea Harriers departed and fired missiles and cannon shells at the Harriers. Given the violence of the Argentine reaction it was remarkable that only one Sea Harrier was hit: ZA192 which suffered a 20 mm cannon hit to the fin.

The next wave of three aircraft from *Hermes* departed straight after the main force had gone. Their target was the grass airfield at Goose Green which was home to a detachment of Pucaras. Travelling at high speed and low level the three aircraft passed over MacBrides Head turning west to travel down Falkland Sound before passing over Darwin and on towards Goose Green. Passing over the airfield the Sea Harriers released their CBUs which damaged the grass runway and scattered shrapnel over the entire area. All three attackers returned safely, the only defending fire encountered being sporadic rifle fire. This was the mission made famous by the BBC Reporter Brian Hanrahan whose phrase, "I counted them all out and I counted them all back" has gone down in aviation folklore. The attack on Goose Green had two purposes: to disable the runway and to damage and destroy the resident Pucaras. In both cases the attack was successful courtesy of a Pucara that had nosed over on take-off. This meant that three Pucaras were airborne, and needed somewhere to land, while the next section of aircraft were waiting to depart when the Sea Harriers struck. The result of the bombing run was one Pucara destroyed and two more damaged. After returning to *Hermes* the Sea Harriers were refuelled and re-roled into the air defence role in preparation for possible retaliatory attacks.

Although no fighter bombers attacked the Task Force the *Hermes* air defence radar picked up two bogies inbound at high altitude. In response, the alert Sea Harriers were quickly launched and vectored towards the intruders. The launch of the *Hermes* flight was detected by the Argentine aircrafts' radars and they turned towards the rapidly climbing Sea Harriers. With both sets of fighters rapidly closing the incoming Argentine aircraft were quickly recognised as Daggers, modified versions of the Dassault Mirage, and they were the first to fire. The Daggers were at 33,000 ft with the Sea Harriers some 13,000 ft below them. A Shafir missile launched by a Dagger was aimed at one of the Sea Harriers which immediately broke away launching chaff and diving into cloud below. The missile fortunately missed. While the Daggers were concentrating on the Sea Harrier piloted by Lt Hale they were losing altitude; both factors which allowed the second Sea Harrier, piloted by Lt Penfold, to achieve an optimum firing position for a Sidewinder launch. The missile hit Dagger C-433 which exploded killing the pilot, the other fighter, now outnumbered, dived away rapidly.

The shape of things to come, an RAF Harrier GR.1 hovers alongside the commando carrier HMS *Hermes*. Note the application of Royal Navy titles to the rear fuselage.
(BBA Collection)

The Sea Harrier FRS.1 provided the air defence and attack capability for the British fleet during Operation Corporate. Here ZE694 003-R sports the overall grey finish adopted for operations over the islands. (BBA Collection)

Having played the opening hand the Task Force awoke on 2 May to await possible retaliation. The first Argentine move was a Grumman Tracker of the Argentine Navy which was detected at a distance. A Sea Harrier of No.801 NAS was sent to investigate and came across five vessels some 150 miles away. These were later confirmed as the aircraft carrier *25 de Mayo* and its escorts. Tagged as hostile the Task Force prepared for a possible incoming A-4Q Skyhawk raid. The weather now played its part as a thick fog rolled in and blanketed the area thus deterring the Argentine attack. While the threat of air attack receded this was the day that the cruiser *General Belgrano* was sunk by a British submarine.

The fog persisted throughout the following day and stopped all flying. The next day, 4 May, began with another 'Black Buck' Vulcan raid on Stanley airport which was precursor for another day of intense airborne attacks. *Hermes* restarted its missions just after dawn launching an armed reconnaissance mission that covered Fox Bay, Port Howard and Pebble Island, all known to be Argentine strong points. The planned attack took place against Goose Green and the mission consisted of three Sea Harriers. Take-off was scheduled for mid afternoon the weapons load consisted of two aircraft, ZA192 and XV450, carrying CBUs while a third, XZ460, carried 1,000 lb retarded bombs. As before the attack was undertaken fast and low. During the run-in XV450 was hit by cannon fire and crashed in a fireball in the vicinity of the airfield; the pilot, Lt Taylor, was killed. The other two aircraft continued their attacks before joining up and heading back to *Hermes*. Having shown that the Sea Harrier was capable of carrying out accurate attacks at low level it was time for a change of tactics due to the loss of Lt Taylor and his aircraft, both were valuable assets. In a similar parallel to the later Gulf War the tactics changed to medium- and high-level bombing, both methods being within the capabilities of the Sea Harriers avionics suite.

From 5 to 8 May *Hermes* undertook no attack missions due to inclement weather although the CAP was maintained at all times. Missions resumed on 9 May, the first was against Stanley airfield. Two Sea Harriers were allocated to this sortie and their weapons load was a single 1,000 lb bomb on the centreline pylon. Having arrived over the airfield the Sea Harriers found the area obscured by thick cloud. The pilots decided to return to *Hermes* but the pilot of ZA191 detected a radar return some 60 miles away on the surface of the sea. The companion aircraft, XZ460, dropped through the cloud to discover the Argentine trawler *Narwhal* below. The requested permission to attack the ship was granted. Both Sea Harriers bombed the trawler and strafed it although one bomb missed whilst the other lodged in the forecastle without exploding, the bomb fuses having been set for high level. By this time the trawler was losing headway although it was continuing on its way. A further pair of Sea Harriers would turn up and all four strafed the vessel until it came to a halt. *Hermes* despatched a Sea King and boarding party which discovered evidence of intelligence gathering. An attempt to tow the vessel away was doomed to failure as bad weather intervened, allied to the battle damage this caused the trawler to sink.

Inclement weather again precluded any attack missions on 10-11 May although normal service was resumed on the following day. No.800 NAS was tasked with bombing Stanley airfield to which end four Sea Harriers were despatched each with a 1,000 lb bomb carried on the centreline pylon. The briefing meant that the bombs had to be dropped outside the range of the defending Roland missiles, consequently, the bombs were dropped from 18,000 ft. Of the four bombs dropped one failed to explode, another was not spotted and the remaining two missed the runway. Although the attack was deemed a failure there was a secondary, psychological effect as the defending forces were never fully aware of when and where the next bomb might fall. A further attack was mounted by No.800 NAS; two aircraft departing from *Hermes*. The controlling vessel was HMS *Brilliant* which was acting in concert with HMS *Glasgow*, the latter bombarded Argentine positions near Port Stanley. Just as the Sea Harriers began their run-in the attack was called off by *Brilliant* which was subsequently attacked by A-4Q Skyhawks of which two were shot down by Seawolf missiles while a third crashed while taking avoiding action.

Flying operations started again on 15 May having been hampered during the previous two days by bad weather. Attacks resumed against Stanley airfield again from high level although with a resultant loss of accuracy. The high-level option was only used in the morning, the more accurate toss bombing option being adopted as standard from that afternoon. Adding to the Argentine misery was the newly adopted practice of carrying a 1,000 lb bomb by the outbound CAP aircraft which could be dropped on likely targets sometime during the mission. Not only did this increase the chance of damage to vital Argentine resources it also added to the sense of uncertainty. The following day saw yet another armed reconnaissance undertaken which revealed that off Port King was the supply vessel *Rio Carcarana* while alongside the pier at Fox Bay was the *Bahia Buen Suceso*. Both were too good to miss so two sets of Sea Harriers were launched to attack the ships. As the *Rio* was in clear water Sea Harriers XZ459 and XZ494 were tasked to bomb the ship. The attack was successful; the ship becoming enveloped in smoke and fire which caused the crew to abandon ship, it was sunk later by a Westland Lynx. The second vessel, the *Bahia*, could only be strafed because it was close to civilian settlements. The pilots of XZ500 and ZA191 raked the ship from stem to stern causing the crew to abandon it. Although not severely damaged the *Bahia* remained tied up in Fox Bay until the end of hostilities. All four Sea Harriers returned to Hermes unscathed although ZA191 had suffered some minor damage to its rear fuselage courtesy of the defenders' gunfire.

The Sea Harriers undertook further reconnaissance flights during 16-17 May in preparation for the intended landings. On 18 May the Sea Harrier strength aboard *Hermes* was increased by the arrival of four extra aircraft from No.809 NAS which had been despatched from the *Atlantic Conveyer*. All four machines, XZ499, ZA176, ZA177 and ZA194, were quickly given their *Hermes* dark grey overcoats. Also arriving from *Atlantic Conveyer* were four Harrier GR.3s of No.1 Squadron RAF and these were augmented by a further pair two days later. While the arrival of the ground attack Harriers was a welcome addition, their presence put a great strain on the aircraft accommodation and thus a few helicopters were moved to other ships within the Task Force.

While the fixed wing element underwent massive developments in capability, so did the helicopter. Not only did it offer anti-submarine capabilities due to its ability to hover but also air-sea rescue and the ground insertion of troops were added tasks. The first helicopter to exemplify these skills was the Westland Whirlwind depicted here by XL853. (BBA Collection)

On 21 May Operation Sutton was launched, an innocuous designation that covered the amphibious landing at Port San Carlos and San Carlos water. Anticipating the possibility of a strong Argentine attack in response to these landings the Sea Harrier CAP was increased over the islands which meant that at least ten Sea Harriers were on patrol over the islands. This airborne line presented the Argentine air forces with a dilemma, do they attack through a defending line where they stood a good chance of being shot down, or do they abort their mission? Fortunately a measure of common sense meant that the Argentine pilots chose that staying alive to fight another day was a better bet.

Even so six Daggers attempted attacks upon the picket ships, *Antrim*, *Broadsword* and *Argonaut*, losing one of their number in the process to a ship-launched missile. A two aircraft CAP was vectored onto the departing Daggers although when the Daggers saw the Sea Harriers

Following on from the Whirlwind, Westland then provided the services with the Wessex which covered all the roles previously offered by the Whirlwind. (BBA Collection)

Obviously helicopters the size of the Whirlwind or Wessex could not be carried on the flight decks of the smaller vessels such as destroyers and frigates, therefore Westland would provide the Wasp based on an earlier Saro prototype. (BBA Collection)

arriving they accelerated away. Even so, the CAP did fire a rather hopeful Sidewinder at the fighters but it failed to make contact. A second CAP of XZ492 and XZ496 was launched by *Hermes* in mid afternoon and was vectored onto an attacking force of three Skyhawks. In the subsequent engagement two out of the three Skyhawks were shot down. The third Skyhawk was damaged by another Sidewinder and was last seen limping for home with black smoke trailing behind it. A further CAP of XZ455 and ZA176 was launched in late afternoon and vectored by *Brilliant* towards four incoming Daggers detected near King George Bay. The Sea Harriers dropped in behind the Daggers flying fast and low and XZ455 fired at C-409 and achieved a direct hit on the fighter. Although the Sea Harriers carried on firing cannons at the Daggers no further hits were recorded and the Sea Harriers returned to *Hermes*.

Even as the previous CAP was returning to *Hermes* a second pair were launched, XZ457 and XZ500. Their area of patrol was the southern end of Falkland Sound. Having closed on Darwin the Sea Harriers were alerted to the presence of the Skyhawks that had just bombed the frigate HMS *Ardent*. The Skyhawks (A-4Q0660 and A-4Q0665) turned away and were passing Swan Island when they were spotted by the waiting Sea Harriers. Opening their throttles the two Harriers dived down onto the fleeing Skyhawks. The pilot in XZ457 launched a Sidewinder at A-4Q 0660 and the impact blew the little delta apart although the pilot did manage to eject. A second attempted launch against another A-4Q failed as the missile hung-up so cannons were used against another Skyhawk. The shock of the guns firing must have jolted the weapons connectors as a second launch attempt was successful although it responded by flipping about the sky completely missing its target. The cannon fire must have had some affect as the pilot of 0665 turned towards Stanley airfield with fuel venting out of punctured tanks. Having nursed the aircraft close to safety the pilot was dismayed to be told that the port main undercarriage had hung-up thus he was left with no other option but to eject. A third Skyhawk, 0667, was very unlucky as the pilot of XZ500 had decided to use cannons after problems occurred with an attempted missile launch. With remarkable accuracy, a burst of cannon fire entered the Skyhawk just aft of the cockpit which punctured the dorsal fuel tank and caused the engine to disintegrate. The result of this flaming violence was the total failure of the entire machine and the unfortunate pilot was killed in the resulting explosion.

Bad weather over the South American mainland stopped that day's planned air attacks but the respite allowed the British forces to consolidate the landings. Although the bad weather kept the air attacks at bay the *Hermes* still launched its CAP aircraft for the day. The morning

CAP used Sea Harriers XZ460 and XZ499 whose beat was the southern part of Falkland Sound. Closing in on their patrol area the pilots of the Sea Harriers spotted the Prefectura patrol vessel *Rio Iguaza* trying to sneak through the Sound towards Goose Green with a vital load of supplies. While XZ460 provided cover overhead the pilot of the other Sea Harrier strafed the vessel. Such was the effect of the cannon fire that the badly damaged boat had to be beached at Button Bay close by Bluff Cove house.

On the following day, 23 May, the Sea Harriers proved to the resident Argentine helicopter force that flying low and slow through any available cover is no defence against a well flown Sea Harrier. The *Hermes* CAP, consisting of ZA192 and ZA191, took off just after lunch and were flying over West Falkland near Shag Cove House when both spotted what looked like a helicopter in the vicinity. A quick pass revealed it to be an Argentine Puma, further observation revealed another two Pumas and an escorting Augusta A-109 Hirundo. The helicopters had departed from Port Stanley and were headed to Port Howard carrying much needed munitions for the garrison. The buzzed Puma crew immediately took evasive action although the violent manoeuvre coupled with the Sea Harriers' jet wash caused the pilot to lose control and the helicopter crashed into a nearby hillside. Fortunately the crew managed to escape just before the Puma exploded. Although the A-109 was supposed to act as a defending gunship for the Pumas its crew had other ideas and had landed near a stream in a ravine close by the crash site. Spotted by the pilot of ZA191 a quick strafing pass saw the helicopter explode, fortunately, the crew had already abandoned their machine to its fate. Having disposed of two helicopters the Sea Harriers began searching for the remaining aircraft. The other two Pumas had quickly landed blending quite well into the landscape changing the fight into a cat and mouse game. The Sea Harriers loitered in the area flying low and slow to conserve fuel. Eventually, one of the Pumas, assuming the Sea Harriers had departed took off to search for survivors of the crashed Puma. The pilot of ZA191 was not able to fire at the newly emerged Puma as the aircraft had run out of ammunition, however the other Sea Harrier had enough left to leave the aircraft unflyable. Both Sea Harriers had to depart as they were both were low on fuel. However, they did contact the replacement CAP which claimed the Puma for themselves. While dealing with helicopters was fairly easy the few Argentine air raids were far more difficult to cope with. The Argentine forces had learned from the previous experience that the Sea Harriers were quick to respond to incoming raids, thus by careful observation, reconnaissance and careful

One of the primary roles assigned to the utility Wessex was that of troop carriage, here troops embark aboard the helicopter before lifting off the carrier. (BBA Collection)

studying of radar returns that days raids could be planned around the position of the defending fighters. Even with such care a pair of Daggers was spotted by the pilots of ZA177 and ZA194 close to Pebble Island. The lead aircraft spotted the Sea Harriers diving to attack and quickly accelerated away. The trailing Dagger was not so quick as a Sidewinder launched from ZA194 destroyed C-437 and killed the pilot. The final *Hermes* mission was against Stanley airfield where arrestor gear had been spotted being installed on the runway's end. Although it was highly unlikely that the Argentines would base high speed jets on such a vulnerable base it was decided that another attack on the runway was due. Four Sea Harriers were armed with three 1,000 lb bombs each, the take-off time for the mission slipping from early to late evening. The first three aircraft, XZ496, XZ500 and XZ455, launched and attacked the runway successfully using the toss bomb method. The mission was marred with tragedy as Lt Cdr Batt flying ZA192 was killed when his Sea

With the disappearance of the fixed wing AEW capability from the FAA inventory the solution was to utilise some older Sea King airframes to carry a radar unit externally in an inflatable radome. (US Navy)

Harrier crashed soon after take off. A follow-up mission took place on 24 May and comprised two Sea Harriers armed with 1,000 lb air burst bombs while four Harrier GR.3s also took part armed with 1,000 lb retarded bombs. The two Sea Harriers undertook a toss-bomb attack which was enough of a distraction to allow the Harriers to sneak in and drop their bombs on the runway. Although the runway was not put out of action all six aircraft returned to the carrier unharmed.

A further CAP was launched just after lunch consisting of Sea Harriers XZ457 and ZA193 coming under the control of HMS *Broadsword* which had moved in company with HMS *Coventry* to the north of Pebble Island to improve radar coverage. Having been airborne for 45 minutes Broadsword reported incoming aircraft heading towards San Carlos. Closing in on the Argentine aircraft the Sea Harriers dropped down to low level just behind three of four Daggers reported. The pilot of XZ457 launched both Sidewinders hitting two of the Daggers both of which exploded while his compatriot in ZA193 managed a tight aspect lock onto the other Dagger, the launched missile destroying the target. The fourth Dagger pilot seeing what had happened to the rest of the flight jettisoned his bombs and departed the area at high speed.

The following day, 25 May , was not only Argentina's national day it was also the day that *Broadsword* was damaged, *Coventry* was sunk and the transport vessel *Atlantic Conveyer* was hit by an Exocet missile which mortally wounded the ship and it sank. The loss of the naval vessels was a combination of brave flying by the Argentine pilots and a dose of bad luck on the part of the Royal Navy. The incoming raid had been detected by both ships' radars during the early evening. A CAP was scrambled consisting of XZ496 and XZ459 and they were vectored towards the incoming Skyhawks. As the Argentine aircraft came close to the navy vessels they split into pairs. The response by the Sea Harriers was to take on a pair each. XZ496 had closed to within three miles before being warned off by *Broadsword* whose missile radar had locked onto the inbound bogies. The Sea Harrier pulled clear only for the pilot to watch in horror as the Skyhawks dropped their bombs, the missile control system had failed at the critical moment. *Broadsword* was lucky as three bombs missed the ship and the fourth penetrated the hull without exploding. *Coventry* was far less fortunate. Again the intercepting Sea Harrier was warned away as both *Coventry* and *Broadsword* attempted to shoot down the Skyhawks. It was while manoeuvring that *Coventry* broke *Broadswords* radar lock on the Skyhawks. Now clear to attack the Skyhawks dropped their bombs on *Coventry*; three penetrated the hull where they exploded causing so much damage that the ship eventually rolled over and sank. Very short of fuel the frustrated Sea Harrier pilots returned to *Hermes*. The attacks came to a head in the early evening when a pair of Super Entendards were detected heading towards the carriers. Obviously, protecting the source of the Task Force air defence assets was of vital importance and so ten Sea Harriers were launched to intercept the incoming raiders. The result of this attack was the loss of the *Atlantic Conveyer* while the Etendards escaped without loss.

On 29 May a strategy change took place which saw the adoption of a policy of random bombing of Stanley airfield. It was hoped that not only would this demoralise the defenders it would also disrupt the C-130 supply flights. During the day every CAP mission dropped a bomb load on known positions and missions were interspersed by deliberate raids and the constant shelling of the area by the British warships in the area. The following day the weather had cleared slightly which allowed a concentrated attack to be undertaken against Stanley airfield. A late evening CAP consisting of ZA176 and XZ499 were airborne when the final Exocet attack of the war took place, fired at maximum range the missile passed through the fleet without hitting anything eventually falling into the sea. Although the CAP Sea Harriers gave chase they could not catch the aircraft and they turned back towards *Hermes*. Upon landing aboard the carrier they found that they had missed all the excitement as a Skyhawk attack had resulted in two of the four raiders shot down by ships' missiles, the other two escaped.

Further Argentine air raids were thwarted on 1 June, the target being the British positions on Mount Kent. Although the CAP Sea Harrier managed to reach the inbound bogie which was identified as a Canberra the pilot could not make an interception due to fuel constraints. Even so the appearance of the Sea Harrier caused the Canberra to jettison its wingtip fuel tanks, fire off chaff and make off towards the mainland as fast as possible. The weather changed for the worse the following day and brought with it low cloud and fog which reduced visibility greatly. The conditions lasted until mid morning of 5 June when a CAP was launched. As soon as they had departed *Hermes* the weather closed in again and the two Sea Harriers had to land at the newly opened Forward Operating Base (FOB) at Port San Carlos.

The following day saw flying limited again due to bad weather and reduced visibility however 7 June brought fine weather which allowed flying operations to resume again. On 8 June both Sea Harriers and Harriers were detached to the San Carlos FOB which increased the on station time for all aircraft, however this most useful of assets would be quickly closed again when one of the Harriers suffered a serious technical failure and crashed on the runway. This was the most tragic day for the British forces. The RFA vessels *Sir Tristram* and *Sir Galahad* were both anchored near Fitzroy unloading troops and equipment. Argentine observers had seen these activities and called up an air strike. The response from the mainland was to despatch eight Skyhawks and six Daggers although the latter was reduced to five when one of the Daggers malfunctioned. The remaining five would never reach Fitzroy as they attacked HMS *Plymouth* whose spirited defence drove the attackers away although the ship was damaged in the process. Of the eight Skyhawks only five would reach Fitzroy, the others had to return to base due to technical faults. The remainder managed to bomb the RFA vessels with considerable loss of life. All five escaped undamaged as the CAP cover was trying to help *Plymouth* and no proper air defence perimeter was available. The *Hermes* Sea Harriers did manage to even the odds somewhat when the dusk CAP of ZA177 and XZ499 over Choiseul Sound noticed a landing craft being attacked by Argentine Skyhawks.

The carrier HMS *Centaur* ploughs through a calm sea, visible on the flight deck are Sea Hawks, Sea Venoms and Fairey Gannets. (Rick Harding Collection)

Diving down at high speed completely unnoticed the first Sea Harrier managed to get in behind the formation loosing off both Sidewinders quickly. Both hit their targets which were destroyed. The pilot then attempted to use his cannons. Although outside the capabilities of the avionics parameters the splashes allowed the other Sea Harrier to fire a Sidewinder that successfully shot down another Skyhawk. The fourth Skyhawk dumped its external stores and headed for home as quickly as possible. Both Sea Harriers returned home undamaged.

On 9 June the FOB was available for use which was a bonus for No.800 NAS as *Hermes* was by now standing off the Falklands by 260 miles. Except for an incoming alert there was little trade for the Sea Harriers and their next adventure did not takie place until 11 June. Incoming intelligence had reported a small formation of Pucaras attacking troop positions on Mount Kent. In retaliation a flight of four Sea Harriers was prepared with each Harrier carrying three 1,000 lb bombs fused for air bursting. After departing from *Hermes* the Sea Harriers set course for Stanley airfield, as they started their approach the defenders let loose with everything they had. Their efforts were in vain as all four aircraft successfully toss bombed their loads before turning away for home. All

After its career as a full blown carrier had ended HMS *Albion* found a new career as a commando carrier. For this role the capability to carry helicopters replaced the earlier jet aircraft while extra accommodation was incorporated into the hull. (Rick Harding Collection)

bombs exploded over the airfield causing fires in various installations and destroying a Pucara. By this time the Argentine air attacks were few and far between, possibly the Junta had realised that their Malvinas expedition was close to ending. Only one more raid would take place over the night of 13-14 June when a pair of Canberras escorted by a pair of Daggers were detected heading towards the British positions near Port Stanley. As they passed close to HMS *Exeter* its Sea Dart missiles downed one of the Canberras and the pilot ejected safely. At one minute to midnight on 14 June 1982 the Argentine forces on the Falkland Islands officially surrendered. Although the fighting was officially over *Hermes* remained on station to provide CAP cover just in case a rogue air raid was undertaken. During the fighting No.800 NAS flew 1,126 sorties, 1,299 flying hours plus fourteen AIM-9L Sidewinders were launched of which one malfunctioned and another was launched out of range. HMS *Hermes*, having been relieved by *Invincible*, finally anchored in Portsmouth harbour on 21 July to a rapturous welcome.

The other Sea Harrier unit deployed with the Task Force was No.801

NAS which was deployed aboard HMS *Invincible* during the fighting. On 2 April the squadron's commanding officer, Lt Cdr N D Ward, was contacted by the MoD and told to prepare the squadron for embarkation. Unlike No.800 NAS whose personnel were already available Lt Cdr Ward was faced with recalling all his manpower as the unit was on block leave. As the armed forces are normally a well organised machine the recall proceeded smoothly, even Yeovilton came up to speed, quickly authorising the transfer of four Sea Harriers from No.899 NAS to bring the operating complement up to eight machines.

HMS *Invincible* departed from Portsmouth on 5 April setting course for Ascension Island. During the transit intensive flying was carried out to bring all the pilots up to the same state of readiness, it also gave the maintainers the chance to sort out any niggling technical problems with the aircraft. During the work-up each aircraft was moved into the carrier's spray bay where a smooth coat of dark sea grey was applied, all unit markings being obliterated in the process. Although the *Invincible*'s Sea Harriers looked smarter their finish was not as durable as that applied by the *Hermes* crew using the older method of hand painting. In common with the *Hermes* pilots those of *Invincible* undertook live weapons firing and drops also practising with the Blue Fox radar system in order to be as proficient as possible during combat. In company with *Hermes* the *Invincible* departed Ascension Island earlier than planned heading south. The *Invincible* CAP of two No.801 NAS Sea Harriers came on line on 20 April this being maintained until the end of hostilities.

In the early hours of Saturday 1 May 1982 HMS *Illustrious* entered the Total Exclusion Zone. Two hours after arrival the first Vulcan 'Black Buck' raid peppered the Stanley airfield environs. Although there was no retaliation by the Argentine forces on the islands it was expected that some would arrive from the mainland. Anticipating this four of No.801 NAS Sea Harriers were launched to provide a CAP in the vicinity of Port Stanley. The first interception took place during mid morning when a pair of Daggers were reported inbound towards the carriers. The *Invincible* CAP consisting of ZA175 and XZ498 were vectored towards the bogies finally ending up within 5,000 ft of the Daggers. After much manoeuvring both sets of aircraft ended up facing each other, although neither side fired, the Argentine fighters dropped their external tanks and accelerated away from the Sea Harriers. During this first day numerous incoming radar returns were reported by the Royal Navy air defence radars although most of the potential raids appeared to either turn back at West Falkland or were flying too high to be easily intercepted. *Invincible* launched a mid afternoon CAP consisting of XZ495 and ZA175 their first trade being four T-34 Mentors detected by the radar of HMS *Glamorgan*. As the Sea Harriers approached the turbine trainers they saw that the Argentinian's intended target was a Royal Navy Sea King. Moving into the attack position the Sea Harriers used their cannons against the Mentors which were rapidly climbing into the cloud base. Although the Mentors were a juicy target their tendency to dive in and out of the cloud meant that they were not worth the effort to keep chasing especially as *Glamorgan's* radar had just painted two high speed, high level aircraft inbound. Climbing up towards the two aircraft, identified quickly as Mirages, the Sea Harriers lured the Mirages towards them before turning 180 degrees and heading for the intercept. The Argentine pilots fired their missiles at long range although they were seen to drop away. Soon after firing, the Mirages turned away and departed for home at high speed. After a day chasing visible shadows it was time for the pilots of No.801 NAS to achieve some success.

Glamorgan would signal *Invincible* that two high level aircraft, later identified as Mirages, were heading towards the fleet. A CAP was quickly launched in the early evening consisting of XZ452 and XZ453 and were directed towards the incomers. The two Mirages were also under radar control from Port Stanley and were vectored towards the Sea Harriers. Heading towards the Mirages the Sea Harriers split their forces, one continued towards them while the other manoeuvred to get in behind them. The splitting of the forces allowed the circling Sea Harrier to shoot down the first aircraft while the head-on attacker fired a Sidewinder at the remaining Mirage. Although this aircraft seemed to escape it had been badly damaged by the missile. The pilot elected to try for Stanley airfield, unfortunately the Argentine anti-aircraft gunners shot the aircraft down, killing the pilot. Having shot down two aircraft No.801 NAS would manage a third that day when ZA175 and XZ451 were vectored towards three incoming targets that were quickly identified as Canberras. The pilot of XZ451 quickly launched a Sidewinder which hit one of the Canberras, later identified as B-110, in one of the engines and the resultant explosion set fire to the wing. Although the aircraft seemed to be in control it eventually dropped away and crashed into the sea. The second Sea Harrier also fired at the Canberras, but, although neither of the two aircraft was shot down one of the bombers was seen to shed pieces into the night sky. However, it was in a good enough condition to escape back to its home base after jettisoning its bomb load. During the following day there was little trade for *Invincible's* Sea Harriers and flying was restricted on 3 May due to a thick sea fog. On 4 May during the early afternoon some incoming targets

Reckoned to be a better vessel than the *Ark Royal* by many senior naval officers it was a great surprise when HMS *Eagle* was laid up after a minor fire. It was utilised as a spares source for *Ark Royal*. (Rick Harding Collection)

With Buccaneers and Phantoms ranged on the foredeck HMS *Ark Royal* proceeds at speed. At this stage in the carrier's career the vessels island was festooned with radar and communications aerial, a stark contrast to those vessels just after WW1. (Rick Harding Collection)

were detected although their traces were intermittent. As the traces continued and got stronger the vessels close to the Falklands went on full alert. The incoming aircraft were Super Etendards and one of their launched missiles hit HMS *Sheffield* causing its loss while the second fell into the sea. Low cloud would restrict flying to close in CAP around the ships. On 6 May *Invincible* would suffer its greatest loss, a CAP consisting of XZ452 and XZ453 was vectored towards a reported aircraft sighting. Both aircraft descended into thick cloud and were never seen again. While neither aircraft was ever recovered it was postulated that both aircraft had flown into the sea or more likely collided in the cloud with such violence that neither aircraft or pilot was in a fit state to escape.

No interceptions were made over the next couple of days, even though the Argentine armed forces kept the CAP fighters quite busy. On 9 May a single Sea Harrier helped with the capture of the Argentine intelligence vessel *Narwhal*. On 14 May *Invincible* joined *Hermes* in providing disruptive bombing of the Argentine positions on the Falklands. By 15 May *Invincible* had moved until it was some 80 miles east of Port Stanley, from here it despatched CAPs whose aircraft dropped their bombs as ordered on Argentine positions. A welcome arrival on 18 May saw the arrival of four No.899 NAS Sea Harriers which boosted the vessels air wing strength. On 19 May four Sea Harriers departed *Invincible* heading towards the Mount Kent area where Argentine helicopters had been spotted. Early morning low cloud and mist had led to the mission being rescheduled for early afternoon. Although the mountain was reached without incident cloud around the slopes meant that the Sea Harriers had to bomb through gaps in the cover. Although all bombs were dropped no helicopters were destroyed. Flying during 20 May was restricted to a minimum as all aircraft had to be prepared for the next days amphibious landings codenamed Operation Sutton. Joining with No.800 NAS the *Invincible* squadron was surprised by the lack of Argentine reaction. It would be mid afternoon before Argentine aircraft put in an appearance. A pair of Pucaras was intercepted by three Sea Harriers just after the former had rocketed an observation gunnery post near Goose Green. The lack of speed of the Pucara meant that the Sea Harriers had difficulty in intercepting them, even so A-511 was shot down, the pilot later becoming a prisoner of war.

Argentine Daggers proved to be the greatest problem later on that day. Having strafed HMS *Brilliant* a pair would head for the mainland. *Brilliant* got its own back soon afterwards when the ship's radar picked up three inbound Daggers heading towards Falkland Sound. The *Invincible* CAP, already airborne, was vectored onto the incoming aircraft. The pilot of ZA190 dropped in behind Dagger C-404 and fired a Sidewinder which destroyed the Argentine fighter bomber. The pilot of ZA190 also fired on Dagger C-403 and the missile hit the wing which caused the aircraft to spin away uncontrollably although the pilot did manage to eject. The third Dagger, C-407, was spotted by the pilot of ZA175 whose missile destroyed the aircraft although yet again the pilot ejected safely.

On 29 May *Invincible* was operating off the east side of the Falklands when orders were given to turn the carrier into wind due to increasing winds and a steadily increasing sea state. Unfortunately for the pilot of ZA174 he was taxiing out to the take-off point as the carrier heeled slightly to change course. This combined with a slippery deck saw the aircraft slide off the deck although the pilot fought to save it. Eventually the pilot was left with only one option which was to eject. He did so and was picked up almost immediately by one the ship's Sea Kings. On 1 June the Sea Harrier force finally managed to intercept and shoot down an Argentine C-130E inbound to Stanley airfield with a load of vital

Until the arrival of the new carriers in the near future, *Ark Royal* was the pinnacle of the development of the aircraft carrier for the Royal Navy. (BBA Collection)

supplies. A pair of Sea Harriers under the control of HMS *Minerva* was directed to the transport that was flying as low as possible above the sea to confuse the radar. The Mk.1 eyeball is a different matter and the Sea Harriers soon picked up the C-130. A Sidewinder was launched which dropped into the sea, however, the second missile impacted the starboard wing between the engines. The missile strike was followed by a cannon attack which damaged the tail flight control surfaces, eventually the Hercules went out of control before crashing into the sea. Unfortunately, this was the day when No.801 NAS lost another Sea Harrier although this time the cause was a surface to air missile. XZ456 was passing Stanley airfield when the missile blew the rear section of the fuselage off. As the aircraft went out of control and the pilot ejected safely although he was destined to float about in his dinghy before being picked up by a Sea King helicopter. During 4-7 June bad weather and dense fog virtually stopped flying. It was not until 8 June that flying restarted and No.801

NAS found itself chasing various contacts without any success, although their compatriots from *Hermes* had greater success, this being some revenge for the loss of Sir *Tristam* and Sir *Galahad*.

When the fighting ceased on 14 June after the Argentine surrender it was calculated that No.801 NAS had flown 599 missions during which 56 1,000 lb bombs were dropped, 12 AIM-9L missiles were launched and over 3,000 cannon shells were fired.

Invincible departed for Ascension Island for a period of rest and recuperation returning south to relieve *Hermes* on 1 July. *Invincible* was relieved by *Illustrious* on 28 August, the former heading north and finally arrived in port on 17 September. En route to harbour the Sea Harriers were flown off to RNAS Yeovilton.

When the Falklands War erupted HMS *Hermes* was modified with a ski ramp jump on the bow so that the Sea Harrier could be operated at greater efficiency. After service with the Royal Navy *Hermes* was sold to the Indian Navy as the *Vikrant*. (Rick Harding Collection)

Chapter 9

From the Falklands to the Future

After the Falklands War had ended the Royal Navy carrier fleet underwent further reductions in size. HMS *Hermes* was the first to be affected and left active service in 1983. Prior to entering Portsmouth for a much needed refit in December the carrier had undertaken a farewell cruise including exercises off both Norway and the United States. HMS *Hermes* would come off refit in April 1984 and undertook a full range of sea trials before she returned to Portsmouth where the vessel became the harbour training ship; although in contrast to many vessels assigned to this role *Hermes* was kept at a readiness state of thirty days. After *Hermes* had swung at anchor for a while the Indian Government purchased her in 1986 and, therefore, the carrier moved to Devonport for a pre delivery refit and modification programme. This was completed in early 1987 and the vessel was subsequently renamed *Viraat*. After arriving in India the ship was assigned to the Western Fleet where it operates a mix of Sea Harriers and Sea Kings up to a maximum of thirty aircraft.

The departure of *Hermes* left the Royal Navy with the three light aircraft carriers of the *Invincible* class, namely *Ark Royal, Invincible* and *Illustrious*. Having returned from the Falklands conflict *Invincible* entered Portsmouth for a much needed refit that included the fitting of a Vulcan Phalanx Close-in Weapons System (CIWS). Refit complete *Invincible* began a round of exercises and visits that was interrupted by a period in the Singapore Dockyard in January 1984 due to a vibrating propeller shaft. The repairs were good enough for the carrier to return to Portsmouth for full repair work to be undertaken, this kept *Invincible* out of action from March 1984 to March 1985. Exercises would keep the vessel occupied until September 1986 when the carrier became a cadet training vessel. During the preceding year the Royal Air Force would deploy the Harriers of No.1 Squadron aboard the ship for Exercise Hardy Crab, a harbinger of things to come. After its time as a training ship *Invincible* entered Devonport Dockyard in May 1986 for a major refit and modernisation until recommissioned in May 1989.

A new air group was embarked in August comprising No.800 NAS with Sea Harriers, No.814 NAS with Sea Kings and 'A' Flight of No.849

Having shown that the Sea Harrier was more than capable of providing the fleet with air defence and attack capabilities in its FRS.1 form, the decision was taken to improve certain parts of the aircraft. This mainly centered around adding an air-to-air radar which in turn increased the number of weapons available to the type. The opportunity was also taken to modify the rear fuselage structure, as the original had a tendency to suffer from stress cracking. Here a pair of Sea Harrier F/A.2's from HMS *Invincible* pose for the camera. (Trevor Jones Collection)

NAS with Airborne Early Warning (AEW) Sea Kings. In February 1990 HMS *Invincible* was re-roled for the troop carrier/assault vessel task to take part in Exercise Cold Winter for which No.42 Royal Marine Commando plus Nos.845 and 846 NAS with the Commando version of the Sea King was embarked. The Commandos and their helicopters would be disembarked in August 1991 to be replaced by the normal air group. Exercises and visits occupied *Invincible* until November 1992 when it returned to Portsmouth for a refit. This was completed with a shakedown cruise in April 1993. After a period undertaking exercises *Invincible* was tasked with sailing to the Adriatic in July 1993 to relieve HMS *Ark Royal*. The latter had been taking part in Operation Grapple enforcing the No Fly Zone over Bosnia and supporting the British forces operating with the United Nations in the former Yugoslavia. HMS *Invincible* was replaced by *Ark Royal* in January 1994 returning to Portsmouth for a period of leave and a refit. *Invincible* returned to active duty in August 1994 embarking an air group that consisted of No.800 NAS with Sea Harriers, a flight of Sea Harrier F/A.2s from No.899 NAS,

While Sea Harrier F/A.2 ZH808 was built from the outset as this variant, many of the earlier FRS.1 airframes were converted to the later standard. (BBA Collection)

No. 814 NAS with Sea Kings and A Flight of No.849 NAS with AEW Sea Kings. Once the air group was embarked *Invincible* departed for the Adriatic where it took over from *Ark Royal*.

Invincible would later have a change of location, this time the venue was Iraq where the ship took part in the Armilla Patrols that had started in 1980 when the hostilities between Iraq and Iran escalated into full scale warfare. While the Royal Navy carriers had little real involvement with Operation Granby/Desert Storm they had a greater influence on events afterwards. In October 1997 Iraq was entering another phase of non co-operation with the UN weapons inspectors which was only diffused by the intervention of a Russian delegation. A further flare-up occurred in January 1998 and as this was seen as more threatening than usual it was decided to send a strong show of force to the Gulf. *Invincible* undertook exercises in the Mediterranean as part of Operation Deliberate Guard in company with the frigate HMS *Coventry*, the destroyer HMS *Nottingham* and the Royal Fleet Auxiliary (RFA) *Fort Victoria*. Aboard the carrier was No.800 NAS with Sea Harrier F/A.2s, these being augmented by a detachment of RAF Harrier GR.7s plus the usual selection of Sea Kings for AEW and anti-submarine work. As *Invincible* was needed in a hurry the carrier and its escorts passed through the Suez Canal where they joined up with the carrier battle group led by the aircraft carrier USS *Nimitz*, later replaced by the USS *George Washington*, the British operation was codenamed Bolton. Joining this show of force were the Royal Navy vessels *Bridport*, *Inverness*, *Sandown*, *Herald* and the RFA *Diligence*. It was also thought that the submarine HMS *Spartan* was also deployed. Eventually the UN Secretary General Kofi Annan would broker an agreement although as tensions remained high *Invincible* remained on station until it was relieved by HMS *Illustrious* in March 1998.

In October 1998 *Illustrious* was on station in the Gulf again just in time for the Iraqi Government to reduce its level of co-operation again. The response was Operation Desert Fox that began on 15 December and continued for the next three days and nights as wave after wave of air strikes was launched. HMS *Invincible* would return to the Gulf on 9 January in company with HMS *Newcastle* and the RFA *Fort Austin*. At the end of January 1999 HMS *Invincible* was redeployed to the former Yugoslavia to take part in Operation Allied Force. Allied Force continued until 10 June when the air strikes were suspended by NATO. After this period of operations HMS *Invincible* returned to Portsmouth for a much needed period of rest before resuming its usual round of exercises and visits.

After its service in the Gulf HMS *Invincible* returned to Portsmouth for a much needed refit which began in 2000. During this maintenance period the Sea Dart defence system was removed as it was thought that

For reasons best known to themselves, the MOD decided to retire the Sea Harrier Force earlier than expected in March 2006, especially as the youngest airframe was only eight years old and the F-35 Lightning II was still several years in the future. Whatever the political reasoning, the carriers still needed an aircraft presence, this now being provided by the Joint Force Harrier based at Cottesmore as shown by this RAF Harrier. (Trevor Jones Collection)

Prior to their replacement by the F/A.2 the carriers utilised the FRS.1, here a pair of the earlier aircraft begin landing on HMS *Invincible*. (US Navy)

such a missile defence system was better operated by the normal Type 42 destroyer escort. The resultant space was available for further stores and ammunition which improved the vessels offensive capability. *Invincible* undertook a final period of cruises and exercises plus UN nominated duties before she returned to Portsmouth on 3 August 2005 to be paid off. After 25 years of Royal Naval service the carrier is now being held in a state of minimum readiness, it will officially retire in 2010. In a twist to the normal scrapping procedure, after decommissioning the people of Barrow on Furness are campaigning hard to have the ship preserved under their care as *Invincible* never visited the town where it was built.

HMS *Illustrious* was too late to undertake any part in the Falklands campaign even though the completion and trials work were pushed forward in an attempt to make the vessel ready for war service. *Illustrious* undertook its sea trials in January 1982 and was commissioned at sea in June, the first Royal Navy ship ever to do this. After sea trials and working up the carrier was despatched to the South Atlantic where it would relieve the *Invincible* off the Falklands complete with its air group which consisted of No.809 NAS with Sea Harriers, No.814 NAS with Sea Kings and 'D' Flight of No.824 NAS with AEW Sea Kings, the unit was later renumbered No.849 NAS. Two months after arriving the air defence of the Falkland Islands Protection Zone was handed over to the RAF F-4 Phantoms based at RAF Stanley. Once the hand over had been completed HMS *Illustrious* departed for Britain in company with HMS *Amazon* and *Brambleleaf*. On the journey home the carrier paid calls on destinations in both North and South America. As *Illustrious* neared Britain No.809 NAS flew off to Yeovilton to disband and the carrier itself arrived in Portsmouth during December. During its deployment the vessel had been at sea for 143 days, covered 43,560 miles with 7,127 deck landings made.

Whilst in Portsmouth the dockyard maties returned to the ship to complete those parts that had been left unfinished before sailing. After two months in the dockyard *Illustrious* returned to sea to undertake sea trials after which it returned to Portsmouth for a rededication service. Now complete and recommissioned *Illustrious* undertook its uncompleted missile and systems trials. During this phase the entire air group consisted of a single Wessex of No.845 NAS that was used for replenishment purposes. After a month of testing and rectification *Illustrious* was ready for active sea duty. To that end in May 1983 the carrier took aboard No.899 NAS with Sea Harriers and the Westland Commandos of No.846 NAS. Air defence training and Sea Dart firings off

While the Sea King has provided great service to the Royal Navy, it was obvious that a replacement for anti-submarine duties was needed. The answer was the EH.101 Westland Merlin that has started to equip the A/S squadrons. (BBA Collection)

While the Sea King is slowly being replaced in A/S usage by the Merlin, the troop version, the Commando, will take longer to replace. Here a Commando with disruptive white camouflage over green lands aboard a US carrier with one of the Invincible class carriers in the background. (US Navy)

Aberporth lasted until the end of the month when No.810 NAS with Sea Harriers and No.820 NAS with Sea Kings all coming from *Invincible* were taken aboard as both ships passed Plymouth. During the remainder of that year and for much of 1984 HMS *Illustrious* was engaged in the usual round of exercises and visits although there would be a break in July when a specially instrumented Sea Harrier was embarked for Sea Eagle missile trials. The target for these trials would be the decommissioned destroyer HMS *Devonshire* which was successfully sunk. Having disposed of the *Devonshire* the carrier would deploy for Exercise Remount, an amphibious operation. After a period in Portsmouth for a minor refit in August the ship would resume the usual round of peacetime exercises which was interrupted in March 1986 when there was a serious fire in the forward starboard gear room. As the carrier had to enter Portsmouth Dockyard for repairs the resident air group was flown off to their respective air bases. Three months later the carrier was at sea again although it suffered another fire, this time in the port-outer

Olympus gas-turbine engine. With the defective power plant replaced *Illustrious* spent much of its time in the Far East before returning to Portsmouth at the end of 1986.

HMS *Illustrious* returned to sea duty at the start of 1987 spending much of the year engaged in exercises and visits. A similar programme was followed throughout the following year and up to June 1989 when the carrier was paid off into the reserve for two years. Having sat in Portsmouth for two years *Illustrious* was moved to Devonport to undergo major modifications which kept the carrier out of action until May 1994 During this period the Sea Dart system and its various extras were removed and replaced by extra storage space. After the completion of sea trials the carrier participated in the Review of Ships in the Solent to commemorate the 50th Anniversary of the D-Day landings. After a further period of sea trials and the usual subsequent rectification the vessel was declared ready for operational use. In March 1995 *Illustrious* was deployed to the Adriatic to relieve HMS *Invincible*, aboard the carrier was No.801 NAS with Sea Harrier F/A.2s, No.820 NAS with Sea Kings and 'B' Flight of No.849 NAS with its AEW Sea Kings.

In 1998, in a break from its usual peacetime duties, *Illustrious* was deployed to the Persian Gulf to take part in Operation Southern Watch. After a period at Portsmouth in 2000 the carrier deployed to Sierra Leone leading Task Force 342.1 to undertake Operation Palliser in company with *Ocean, Argyll, Iron Duke* and *Chatham*. Their purpose was to assist UN forces in restoring order in the region. Having completed this deployment the carrier found itself off the coast of Oman in 2001 to take part in Exercise Saif Saree II. During this exercise the two towers of the World Trade Center in New York were destroyed by terrorist action. In response *Illustrious* remained in the Gulf for a possible deployment to Afghanistan although this was delayed until all forces were in place. Replaced in theatre by the helicopter carrier HMS *Ocean*, *Illustrious* returned to Rosyth Dockyard for an extended refit. During this period the vessel was modified so that it was possible to switch quickly between the light carrier and helicopter assault carrier roles. One of the carrier's first operations after returning to sea duty in 2006 was to sail to the Lebanon to assist in the evacuation of European citizens during the Israeli offensive. During 2007 and 2008 the carrier was involved in various exercises, deployments and visits although the ship and crew did find time to make a television series in 2008.

Laid down in December 1978 and originally to have been named *Indomitable*, a third *Invincible* class light-carrier eventually became the fifth HMS *Ark Royal*. The ship was launched at the beginning of June 1981, although it would take the next four years for the carrier to be

The winner of the JSF competition was the Lockheed Martin F-35. Here the X-35B version of the aircraft, which should actually be designated XF-35B, undertakes an STOVL landing. (USAF)

officially recorded as being completed. Some of the delay was due to the need to incorporate modifications to *Ark Royal*, their incorporation was either for operational reasons or to rectify faults discovered during the operational use of the other two carriers of the class. One of the most obvious changes was the adoption of the 12 degree ski jump which had been trialled on HMS *Hermes*. The incorporation of this increased jump improved the operational capability of the assigned Sea Harriers and it has to be questioned why the smaller version was ever fitted to the two earlier ships. Other changes included strengthening of the aft hull section, which immediately cured the vibration problem that *Invincible* in particular was prone to. Improvements to the vessel's defensive systems were also incorporated and centred around the Vulcan Phalanx CIWS, to allow the bow mounted CIWS to be installed. The bow had been modified during construction while two further mountings were incorporated on a sponson on the port rear quarter and one outboard of the island on the starboard side. Internal modifications were restricted to providing more accommodation plus an improved suite for command and control usage.

In June 1982 some key members of *Ark Royal*'s future crew were assigned to the Swan Hunter yard at Wallsend, not only would they learn a lot about their new posting but their input regarding ergonomic matters was much appreciated. Three months later the carrier was in dry dock for the installation of propellers, rudders and stabilisers after which *Ark Royal* was towed to the Walker Yard as Wallsend was urgently required for another vessel. It would be May 1984 when the ship's engines were turned under load for the first time although contractors' sea trials did not begin until October. After returning to the Walker Yard for rectification the carrier would not return to sea until April 1985 for final machinery trials although for this trip a Westland Wessex from

With the flags of all the purchasing nations along the fuselage the first F-35, AA-1, undertakes a high speed run for the camera. (USAF)

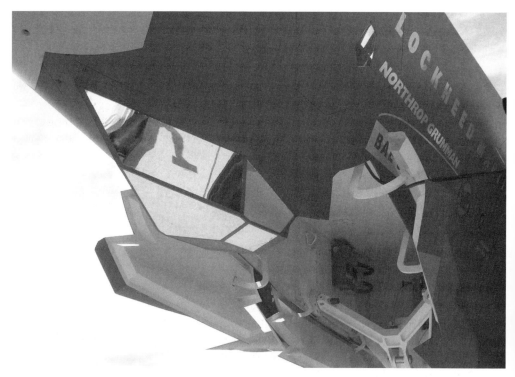

At the heart of the F-35 attack system is the EOTS, Electro-Optical Targeting System, which gives the aircraft an excellent passive attack capability. (USAF)

No.707 NAS was aboard for use in the air delivery role. After a few days at sea the ship returned to the Walkers Yard where the Royal Navy acceptance team carried out their final checks before the carrier joined the fleet. The ship's company would board in June 1985 and the vessel departed almost immediately with its first strike aircraft aboard, a Fairey Swordfish. At the beginning of July *Ark Royal* began its approach to Portsmouth during which a Sea Harrier of No.899 NAS was landed aboard, both aircraft representing significant periods in the history of the Fleet Air Arm.

HMS *Ark Royal* sailed from Portsmouth in July to undertake its shakedown cruise with the Wessex helicopters of No.845 NAS embarked. During the period at sea the air handling side of the ships operation was given a thorough work-out. These trials completed, the ship returned to Portland for further working-up exercises. At the beginning of November the carrier was officially commissioned into the Royal Navy, departing soon afterwards for Gibralter. When in the Mediterranean *Ark Royal* undertook a full range of exercises during which the carrier stopped at the point where a previous *Ark Royal* had been sunk to lay a commemorative wreath. The carrier arrived in Portsmouth just in time for Christmas leave. During this period in harbour the air wing was assigned comprising No.801 NAS with its Sea Harriers plus No.820 NAS with Sea Kings both from HMS *Illustrious*. Sea and air trials kept the crew and their vessel fully occupied until June when the final piece of the air wing puzzle was added; this being the AEW Sea Kings of 'B' Flight No.849 NAS. Over the next 18 months *Ark Royal* was involved with various exercises and visits before she returned to Portland for a minor refit. This completed the carrier resumed its sea going duties; its first exercise in November 1987 being Purple Warrior which was notable for the integration of the Harriers from No.1 Squadron RAF into the air wing. No sooner had the air augmented ship gone to sea than it had to return to port for repairs after the port-inner Olympus gas-turbine engine failed. In late January 1988 *Ark Royal* sailed again picking up the air group on the way.

Until January 1991 the carrier and its air group were involved in the usual round of exercises around the world although the situation would change in August 1990 after the invasion of Kuwait by Iraqi forces. *Ark Royal* would be deployed to the eastern Mediterranean in company with *Sheffield, Regent* and *Olmeda*. Their purpose was to secure the area of sea between Cyprus and the war zone in order to deter any Iraqi aggression. Working in close co-operation with the US Navy force which consisted of the USS *Virginia, Philippine Sea* and *Spruance* the ships spent 51 days at sea although they saw no action. At the conclusion of Operation Granby the carrier set course for Portsmouth calling in at various Italian ports along the way. *Ark Royal* would spend much of April May 1991 undergoing refit before returning to sea at the end of May.

The carrier was engaged in various exercises and visits until April 1993 when it was designated as commander Task Force 612.02 in the Adriatic in support of UN forces operating in the former Yugoslav Republic. During this deployment the carrier's Sea Harriers were declared to NATO and the UN commanders as laser-guided bomb capable. *Ark Royal* would remain on station, except for periods of leave, until returning to Portsmouth in November 1994 where the vessel was paid off into the reserve while it awaited its planned 1997 modification and maintenance period. HMS *Ark Royal* finally entered Rosyth for its major modifications which included the removal of the Sea Dart missile system and the plating over of the fore deck which allowed more aircraft to be carried on deck. The carrier recommissioned in 2001 and resumed its sea duties which once again included exercises and visits. In 2003 *Ark Royal* was involved with the invasion of Iraq which saw the ultimate demise of Saddam Hussein, although in this case the air group consisted of helicopters instead of Sea Harriers. Unfortunately, during this operation two of the Sea Kings collided which cost six lives. It was during this deployment that the Merlin HMA1 was first deployed.

After Iraq *Ark Royal* entered extended readiness and then, once HMS *Illustrious* had resumed active duty, underwent a refit. *Ark Royal* re-entered service in October 2006 and began a ten week work-up period after which the ship was utilised mainly in the helicopter support role while HMS *Ocean* underwent a refit. During the refit improved aviation facilities were provided, an enhanced communications mast replaced the original, the Bowman command and control communications system was installed, a SCOT 5 satellite communications system and a towed sonar decoy system was fitted as was an electronic charting system and display. The overall changes allowed for increased carriage of troops plus their equipment, which meant that 400 troops could be housed, and facilities for RAF Chinooks were also included. In November a new first was achieved when a British Army AH-64 Apache landed aboard. The carrier would undergo a further refit in 2007 finally rejoining the fleet as flagship in May 2007.

Illustrious and *Ark Royal* both had Joint Tactical Information Distribution Systems (JTIDS) fitted including communications links 10, 11 and 14 these being supplemented by multi function consoles with flat screen displays. The Satellite Communications (SATCOM) system installed in these vessels has the capability to handle a maximum data transfer rate of 2Mb/s. British Aerospace Systems (BAES) then upgraded the JTIDS to include Link 16 plus upgrading aircraft detection and control and a new Identification Friend or Foe (IFF) system was installed. Upgrades were also carried out on the ships countermeasures systems which included the Thales Defence Type 675(2) jamming unit, and a UAT(8) electronic support measures system which also is a Thales product although it was originally manufactured by Racal. Further protection was added by the installation of the Hunting Engineering Sea Gnat which consists of eight 130mm six barrelled launchers that can fire chaff and infra-red decoy charges into the air. The original BAES Type 909 G/H Band fire-control radar has been replaced by the Type 996 system while *Ark Royal* has the Type 992. The original system was removed when the Sea Dart missile defence system was removed. Both replacement radars operate in the E/F Bands while BAES also supplied the Type 1022 search radar that operates in the D Band. Further radar systems included the Types 1006 and 1007 navigation radars, both types operate in the I Band. HMS *Ark Royal* will be subject to further modifications when a new communications and radar mast, developed by QinetiQ in co-operation with Babcock Design and Technology, is installed. This will enable all the

Surrounded by thrown up dust this STOVL development of the F-35 touches down at Edwards Air Force Base. (USAF)

aerials for detection and communications to be housed within the mast. It will be noted that *Ark Royal* is the only one of the three vessels that has further upgrades planned for it; this is due to the age of the vessel, it is the youngest, plus the fact that the hull was built from the outset with the strengthening modifications already integrated. Both *Ark Royal* and *Illustrious* will remain in service until 2016, although the former may remain in use a little longer if required, when the two new carriers are scheduled to enter service.

While the carriers have not been heavily involved in operations since the Falklands, where they were engaged in the support role, their aircraft have been. In October 2007 the Naval Strike Wing (NSW) deployed to Kandahar Airfield in Afghanistan where they took over from No.IV Squadron. Although their duties are in support of the International Security Assistance Force (ISAF) in reality the NSW undertakes most of its sorties within Regional Command South which mainly covers the area patrolled by Britiah Forces in Helmand Province. As the outgoing unit was already well settled into the routine of operations over Helmand it was possible for the NSW to come up to speed quickly during the hand

Entering Portsmouth is HMS *Invincile* returning from patrol off the Falkland Islands, at this point the air group had flown off to Yeovilton. (Ian Smith Collection)

over period thus ensuring that their contribution to Operation Herrick was a positive one. Tasks for the NSW are provided by the Combined Air Operations Centre and require the unit to fly a fixed number of patrol sorties per day which include close air support and tactical reconnaissance while other aircraft are kept at a high state of readiness in case extra air power is needed.

The story of the replacement carriers for the *Invincible* class has its roots in the 1960s and the proposed CVA-01 fleet carrier design. In 1960 the Admiralty proposed that a new group of fleet carriers capable of operating future and proposed aircraft be constructed. The need for new vessels was becoming more obvious as bigger and heavier aircraft were entering service and the current crop of in use vessels were going to struggle should aircraft bigger than the Buccaneer and Phantom enter service. As always with such a major spend, various points of view needed consideration, the initial design put forward by the Naval Constructors was rejected by the Chief of the Defence Staff, gone were the days when the Royal Navy could put forward its own estimates and have them approved with little argument by Parliament.

After much wrangling a definitive proposal document was issued in

January 1961: the Admiralty accepting that the new vessel would displace around 50,000 tons and be capable of launching both strike missions and fleet air defence. The intended air wing was split equally between fighters and strike aircraft, totalling approximately 40 aircraft. Unfortunately for the Admiralty, the cost of the new carrier programme was raising concerns from the Treasury and the Air Ministry, the latter was determined to gain all the funds from the carrier programme so that its proposed airfields on islands plan could go ahead (the premise was that placing airfields on strategically located islands would render the need for carriers and their aircraft obsolete, their replacement being RAF aircraft moved as required to cover the fleet). However, this idea came unstuck when a map was discovered that showed that the Royal Air Force had shunted Australia slightly northwards by 600 nautical miles to cover a gap in the air coverage. Throughout 1962-1963 the CVA-01 carrier concept was continually under cancellation pressure, although senior naval officers continued to back the idea even though the designs were becoming more complicated and expensive. This support resulted in the proposed modification and refit of HMS *Ark Royal* being cancelled because, although it was nominally a fairly new vessel, it did contain some fabrications that were far older than the carrier, having been manufactured during WW2 when quantity not quality mattered.

In July 1963 the new carrier was formally announced by Peter Thorneycroft to Parliament at an estimated cost of £56 million. The design

Seen turning at speed is HMS *Invincible* the first of the class to be launched and the first to be placed in reserve. (US Navy)

HMS *Ark Royal* enters San Francisco harbour with the crew in the review position around the flight deck. *Ark Royal* could be the last of the class to retire. (US Navy)

work was already under way when the carrier was announced, which was fortunate as the Naval Constructors Department was short of qualified personnel. Adding to the delays were concerns about the capabilities of British shipyards to build a vessel of the size of CVA-01. A change of government in 1964 to Labour control saw that party's usual response to the Armed Forces coming into play thus CVA-01 was put under pressure again by the Treasury and the RAF, the latter determined to protect its TSR-2 and later its F-111K programmes. In the event both aircraft programmes were eventually cancelled, the RAF receiving McDonnell F-4 Phantoms instead. In order to keep the carrier project alive stringent weight reducing measures were applied. By December 1965 the full tender documents had been completed and the start of procurement for long lead items had begun. The CVA-01 carrier programme was formally cancelled on 22 February 1966 using some very dubious figures and statistics to prove that the carrier was too expensive for British needs. This would leave the remaining fleet carriers to soldier on, the last being HMS *Ark Royal*. Replacing the fleet carriers were the *Invincible* light carriers that fortunately were reinforced by HMS *Hermes*. The Falklands war, which involved the *Hermes* and *Invincible* was fortuitous for the Prime Minister, Margaret Thatcher, and more importantly the Royal Navy as without the carriers the Falklands could not have been retaken. Although the *Invincible* class of ships has given sterling service it had been postulated by various naval experts that this class of small carriers would not be able to undertake such an operation again.

At the present time, the much needed renewal of the *Invincible* class has allowed the Royal Navy to propose that the next class of aircraft carriers was larger, and therefore more capable, as a larger and more flexible air wing could be embarked. The newly proposed aircraft carriers for the Royal Navy, the Carrier Vessel Future (CVF), consists of two ships: HMS *Queen Elizabeth* and *Prince of Wales,* delivery being expected in 2014 and 2016 respectively. Obviously the purchase of these new vessels will, as always, depend on the whims of various political parties, it would not be the first time that much needed military equipment was cancelled. Fortunately, events in both the Gulf and the former Yugoslavia showed that an aircraft carrier was able to place force projection where it was needed and that their deletion from the fleet would make the defence and attack role impossible.

The initial announcement of the CVF programme was made on 25 July 2007 by the Secretary of State for Defence to Parliament. Construction and delivery of the vessels will be under the control of the Aircraft Carrier Alliance (ACA), within which are the main contractors including British Aerospace Systems/Vosper Thorneycroft, Thales, Babcock and the ships division of BAES. Ordered after the 1998 Strategic Defence Review it is intended that the two new carriers will replace the three *Invincible* ships. However, such a strategy has its detractors, many of whom are worried that at certain points in their career 50 per cent of the force will be laid up for refitting and modification and, therefore, should anything happen to the in-service vessel the Royal Navy could face difficulties in prosecuting its tasks. This raises shades of the past when Dennis Healey was quoted as saying that the lowest number of aircraft carriers with which the Royal Navy could operate flexibly and efficiently was three ships. Another minor point raised by more traditional naval personnel is that of the ships' names as many have suggested that more famous names should receive precedence.

The concept behind the CVF, although dressed in more modern language, is to deploy offensive air power in support of operations over sea and land. To undertake these missions the new carriers will operate a mix of aircraft that can cover all requirements, all being grouped under the title Joint Force Air Group. At the centre of this group will be the

Lockheed Martin F-35 Lightning II, originally designated the joint strike fighter. This aircraft is capable of short and vertical take-off and landings. Until the new aircraft is ready for use the current fleet carrier aircraft is the Harrier GR.9 (the earlier Sea Harrier F/A.2 was retired in March 2006). Replacing the Sea Harrier were the Harrier GR.7 and GR.9 which were allocated to the Joint Force Harrier based at RAF Cottesmore. This organisation acts as the parent to the three Harrier squadrons based in the UK; these being the Naval Strike Wing, No.1(F) Squadron and No.IV Squadron. Although there is a strong cadre of naval pilots within the Harrier Force doubts have already been expressed over the availability of new pilots to fly the F-35 as many of the Sea Harrier pilots are no longer available either through retirement or reallocation of duties. The helicopter side of the air group will be the Westland Merlin while provision will be made to launch Unmanned Aerial Vehicles to provide extra capabilities where needed.

When the ACA began the design process for the CVF one of the first sets of plans that were dusted off were the final set for the CVA-01. Eventually, using extensive computer modelling the design group produced a series of six designs, the final selected design was 'Design Delta'. This particular design was seen as offering the best blending of current and future needs for the fleet. Once the design had been chosen, extensive testing using both computers and the good old water tank were carried out on the hull shape. With this completed the really difficult part of the process was begun. Given that the projected life of these vessels is set between 40 to 50 years the design has to be flexible enough to operate the F-35 aircraft and possibly later more conventional aircraft that require launch and arrest facilities. Changes from previous carrier designs include placing the engine rooms higher up the hull which allows for shorter length intakes and exhausts and reduces the vulnerability of the engineering spaces in particular and the hull in general. Unlike earlier carriers this vessel has been designed from the outset to be environmentally friendly and therefore an integrated waste management system is included. The carrier island is also different from previous efforts in that it is split into two distinctive sections, the intention of which is to improve flight deck management. The ACA also took advantage of technology developments so that more aircraft can be carried and operated for a crew size that is close to the size of those aboard the *Invincible* class.

In December 2005 the Ministry of Defence approved the funding for the demonstration phase for the detailed designs for the carrier. This was followed in April 2006 by the placing of contracts with the ACA members including BAES Naval Ships, Thales, Vosper Thorneycroft(VT) Group,

HMS *Illustrious* proceeds on patrol, of note is the modified ski ramp on the bow and the lack of aircraft on deck except for the standby Sea King. (US Navy)

Babcock and BAES Instyle. When this phase had been completed the contracts for actual construction were placed in July 2007. Construction will take place mainly in British shipyards thus the Govan yard, now part of BAES, will construct hull block 4; hull block 3 will be constructed at Barrow, VT at Portsmouth will be responsible for hull block 2 while bow block 1 will be under the control of Babock who are also designated as the final assembler. Other contractors involved with building these carriers include BMT Defence Systems for naval architecture, EDS for systems integration, Lockheed-Martin for programme management and engineering, QinetiQ covering computer modelling and simulation, Rolls Royce covering propulsion, Strachan and Henshaw for waste management, Swan Hunter involved with construction and VT Group covering construction and naval architecture.

The maritime division of QinetiQ was responsible for designing the hull which is intended to have an in-use life of 50 years. The initial configuration of the carrier is intended to have a bow-mounted ski jump, although the flight deck and the compartments under it are expected to be capable of accepting conventional launch and take-off gear as the F-35 has an expected service life of 20 years. As with all such projects there are

With a pair of AIM-120 AMRAAM missiles on its under fuselage pylons, Sea Harrier FA.2 ZH803 of No.800 NAS prepares to depart for another mission. (BBA Collection)

cost cutting exercises which are the norm, in the case of the CVF this has resulted in the deletion of armour plate from the hull and the armoured bulkheads. Hopefully, this will not have a deleterious effect upon either carrier at any time. The carrier is intended to support 40 aircraft which should be capable of launching 420 sorties over a five day period. The projected single 24 hour sortie rate is 110 missions. The design maximum launch rate is 24 aircraft in 15 minutes while the recovery time for the same number of machines is 24 minutes. The use of a twin island configuration will reduce the turbulence over the flight deck. The forward island is concerned with ship handling while the aft section is solely concerned with aircraft control. The two islands will also be the mounting points for the ships radar systems, that on the forward island will mount a multi-function unit while the aft island will carry the air surveillance radar. The flight deck, although not angled, is wide enough to support simultaneous launches and recoveries. Aimed at assisting heavily loaded aircraft to get off the deck, the fore part of the deck has a 13 degree ski jump installed. It is planned that the deck will have three runways, two will support the V/STOL F-35 aircraft plus a longer one for launching more heavily laden machines. Vertical landing pads will be provided at the rear of the flight deck to cope with F-35s undertaking vertical landings while further forwards it is intended to install blast deflectors to cope with the F-35 engines running at full power. Moving aircraft from the hangar to the flight deck is courtesy of a pair of 70 ft deck edge lifts both on the island side of the ship.

Communications will include the Joint Tactical and Distribution System including links 10,11,14 and 16. Included in the build will be the mountings for the CIWS, although, when this will be installed is not known at this time. Also in the running when the budget allows or circumstances require is the ASTER missile defence system that would be housed in two lots of 16-per-launch cells. Other systems that will be installed include IFF plus navigation and bridge systems developed by Northrop Grumman Sperry Marine. Ships propulsion will be a mix of gas turbines and diesels, the MoD having decided against the nuclear option due to the cost. Rolls Royce will be responsible for the design and manufacture of the propulsion system known as the Integrated Electric Propulsion system.

The vital statistics of the new carrier class includes a displacement of 65,000 tonnes which places the ship between the US Navy *Nimitz* class and the French Navy *Charles de Gaulle* carriers which also makes them three times bigger than the current 20,000 ton *Invincible* class. The design has a maximum speed of 25 knots. When both carriers are in service the Royal Navy will have its air strike edge fully restored and be able to undertake missions in support of British forces and interests globally, not bad for a service that was flying stick and string biplanes some 90 years ago.

Appendix 1

Carrier Details

Activity Class Escort Carrier

Builder	Caledon Shipbuilding Company
Machinery	2 x shaft Burmeister & Wain diesels, 12,000 bhp = 18 knots
Displacement	11,800 tons standard 14,250 tons deep load
Dimensions	512 ft overall x 66 ft beam x 25 ft 1 in draught
Armament	2 x 4 ins HA 6 x twin 20 mm Oerlikon, 8 x 20 mm Oerlikon
Endurance	4,500 miles @ 18 knots
Flight deck	498 ft x 66 ft steel
Arrester wires	2 x 15,000 lb rated @ 60 knots 3 x 15,500 lb rated @ 55 knots
Hangar	87 ft x 59 ft x 21 ft
Catapults	none
Aircraft	15 maximum

D94 *Activity*

Archer Class Escort Carrier

Builder	Sun Shipbuilding & Drydock Corp
Machinery	1 x shaft 4 x Busche diesel engines 8,500 shp = 17 knots
Displacement	10,220 tons standard 12,860 tons deep load
Dimensions	492 ft overall x 111 ft 3 in beam x 26 ft 3 in draught
Armament	3 x 4 in US Mk9 6 x twin 20mm Oerlikon, 7 x 20mm Oerlikon
Endurance	7,000 miles @ 10 knots
Flight deck	438 ft x 70 ft wood-covered steel
Arrester wires	9 x 10,000 lb rated @ 60 knots
Hangar	260 ft x 62 ft x 18 ft 9 in
Catapults	1 x H2 7,000 lb @ 60 knots
Aircraft	15 maximum

D78 *Archer*

Ark Royal Fleet Carrier

Builder	Cammell Laird
Machinery	3 x shaft Parsons geared turbines 6 Admiralty 3 drum boilers 102,000 shp = 31 knots
Displacement	22,000 tons standard, 27,720 tons deep load
Dimensions	800 ft overall x 112 ft beam x 27 ft 9 in draught
Armament	8 x twin 4.5 in HA QF 4 x octuple 2pdr Pompom
Endurance	11,200 miles @ 10 knots
Flight deck	720 ft x 95 ft steel
Arrester wires	7 x 11,000 lb rated @ 55 knots, 1 x 11,000 lb rated @ 45 knots
Hangar	Upper 568 ft x 60 ft x 16 ft
	Lower 452 ft x 60 ft x 16 ft
Catapults	2 x BH3 hydraulic 12,000 lb @ 56 knots
Aircraft	60 maximum, 54 normal complement

91 *Ark Royal*

Ark Royal Fleet Carrier

Builder	Cammell Laird
Machinery	4 x shaft Parsons geared turbines 8 Admiralty 3 drum boilers 152,000 shp = 30.5 knots
Displacement	43,060 tons standard, 49,950 tons deep load
Dimensions	808 ft 3 in overall x 158 ft 5 in beam x 35 ft 7 in draught
Armament	8 x twin 4.5 in Mk.6 5 x sextuple 40mm Bofors
Endurance	7,000 miles @ 14 knots
Flight deck	790 ft x 120 ft armoured steel
Arrester wires	6 x 35,000 lb @ 103 knots
Hangar	Upper 364 ft x 67 ft x 17 ft 6 ins
	Lower 364 ft x 53 ft 6 in x 17 ft 6 in
Catapults	2 x BS4 steam 50,000 lbs @ 94 knots
Aircraft	80 normal

R09 *Ark Royal*

Centaur Class Light Fleet Carrier

Builder	Swan Hunter & Wigham Richardson
Machinery	2 x shaft Parsons geared turbines 4 x Admiralty 3 drum boilers 78,800 shp = 28 knots
Displacement	22,000 tons standard 27,800 tons deep load

Dimensions	737 ft 9 in overall x 123 ft beam x 27 ft 10 in draught
Armament	2 x sextuple 40mm Bofors 4x single 40 mm Bofors 1x 3 pdr saluting gun
Endurance	6,000 miles @ 20 knots
Flight deck	732 ft x 84 ft steel
Arrester wires	6 x 30,000 lb rated @ 75 knots
Hangar	274 ft + 55 ft x 62 ft x 17 ft 6 in
Catapults	2 x BH5 hydraulic 30,000 lb @ 75 knots
Aircraft	42 maximum

R06 *Centaur*, RO7 *Albion*, R08 *Bulwark*

Campania Escort Carrier

Builder	Harland & Wolff
Machinery	2 x shafts, 2 x Burmeister and Wain diesels 13,250 bhp = 18 knots
Displacement	13,000 tons standard, 15,970 tons deep load
Dimensions	540 ft overall x 70 ft beam x 23 ft 7 in draught
Armament	1 x twin 4in HA, 4 x quadruple 2pdr Pompom 8 x twin 20 mm Oerlikon
Endurance	17,000 miles @ 17 knots
Flight deck	515 ft x 70 ft steel
Arrester wires	4 x 15,500 lb rated @ 60 knots
Hangar	198 ft x 63 ft 6 in x 17 ft 6 in
Catapults	none
Aircraft	20 maximum

R48 *Campania*

Eagle Fleet Carrier

Builder	Armstrong Whitworth
Machinery	4 x shaft Brown-Curtiss HP Turbines 32 Yarrow boilers 50,000 shp = 24 knots
Displacement	22,600 tons standard 27,500 tons deep load
Dimensions	667 ft overall x 115 ft beam x 26 ft 8 in draught
Armament	9 x 6 in, 5 x 4 in HA, 2 x octuple 2pdr Pompom, 12 x 20 mm Oerlikon
Endurance	3,000 miles @ 17.4 knots

Flight deck	652 ft x 96 ft armoured steel
Arrester wires	6 x 11,000 lb @ 53 knots
Hangar	400 ft x 66 ft x 20 ft 6in
Catapults	none
Aircraft	22 maximum

94 *Eagle*

Eagle Fleet Carrier

Builder	Harland & Wolff
Machinery	4 x shaft Parsons geared turbines, 8 Admiralty 3 drum boilers 152,000 shp = 30.5 knots
Displacement	41,200 tons standard, 49,950 tons deep load
Dimensions	803 ft 9 in overall x 112 ft 9 in beam x 35 ft 7 in draught
Armament	8 x 4.5 in DP, 8 x septuple 40 mm Bofors, 9 x 40 mm Bofors
Endurance	7,000 miles @ 14 knots
Flight deck	800 ft x 112 ft armoured steel
Arrester wires	16 x 30,000 lb @ 75 knots
Hangar	Upper 364 ft + 45 ft x 67 ft x 17 ft 6 in
	Lower 172 ft x 54 ft x 17 ft 6 in
Catapults	2 x BH5 30,000 lb @ 75 knots
Aircraft	100 maximum

R05 *Eagle*

Hermes Fleet Carrier

Builder	Armstrong Whitworth
Machinery	2 x shaft Parsons geared turbines 40,000shp = 25 knots
Displacement	10,850 tons standard, 13,700 tons deep load
Dimensions	600 ft overall 90 ft beam x 26 ft 7 in draught
Armament	6 x 5.5 in LA, 3 x 4in HA 2X quadruple 0.50 in machine guns
Endurance	2,930 miles @ 18 knots
Flight deck	570 ft x 90 ft steel
Arrester wires	4 x 11,000 lb @ 53 knots

Hangar	400 ft x 50 ft x 16 ft
Catapults	none
Aircraft	12 maximum

I95 *Hermes*

Hermes Light Fleet Carrier

Builder	Vickers Armstrong
Machinery	2 x Parsons geared turbines, 4 x Admiralty 3 drum boilers, 76,000 shp = 28 knots
Displacement	24,900 tons standard 27,800 tons deep load
Dimensions	774 ft 3 in overall x 147 ft 11 in beam x 27 ft 10 in draught
Armament	2 x quadruple GWS.22 Sea Cat
Endurance	5,040 miles @ 20 knots
Flight deck	744 ft 6 in x 144 ft 6 in steel
Arrester wires	5 x 35,000 lb @ 103 knots
Hangar	356 ft x 62 ft x 17 ft 6 in
Catapults	2 x BS4 50,000 lb @ 94 knots
Aircraft	28 maximum

R12 *Hermes*

Invincible Class Light Fleet Carrier

Builder	Swan Hunter
Machinery	2 x shafts, 4 x R-R TBM3 Olympus 112,000 shp = 28 knots
Displacement	16,000 tons standard 20,000 tons deep load
Dimensions	677 ft 9 in overall x 104 ft 6 in beam x 29 ft draught
Armament	1 x GWS .30 Sea Dart, 3 x 20 mm Vulcan Phalanx, 3 x 20 mm GAM BO1
Endurance	5,000 miles @ 18 knots
Flight deck	600 ft x 65 ft steel
Arrester wires	none
Hangar	500 ft x 74 ft x 20 ft
Catapults	None – ski jump
Aircraft	22 maximum

R05 *Invincible*, R06 *Illustrious*, R07 *Ark Royal*
L12 Ocean commando carrier version of Invincible class

The one item that made the Invincible class of light carriers a success was the ramp or ski-jump over the bow. As this presented the aircrafts leading edge to the airflow more favourably it was possible to launch aircraft at greater all up weights. (John Ryan Collection)

Nairana Escort Carrier

Builder	John Brown
Machinery	2 x shaft Doxford diesels 10,700 shp = 17 knots
Displacement	13,825 tons standard, 17,210 tons deep load
Dimensions	524 ft overall x 68ft beam x 25 ft 9 in draught
Armament	1 x twin 4 in HA QF, 2 x quadruple 2pdr Pompom, 8 x twin 20 mm Oerlikon
Endurance	13,000 miles @ 16 knots
Flight deck	502 ft x 66 ft steel
Arrester wires	8 x 15,500 lb @ 60 knots
Hangar	231 ft x 61 ft x 17 ft 6 in
Catapults	none
Aircraft	20 maximum

D05 *Nairana*

Ruler Class Assault Escort Carrier

Builder	Seattle-Tacoma Shipbuilding Corp
Machinery	1 x shaft General Electric Geared turbine, 2 x
Foster	Wheeler boilers 8,500 shp = 18.5 knots
Displacement	11,200 tons standard, 15,400 tons deep load
Dimensions	492 ft overall x 108 ft 6 ins beam x 25 ft 5 ins draught
Armament	2 x 5 ins US Mk12 8 x twin 40 mm Bofors, 4 x twin Oerlikon, 25 x single Oerlikon

Endurance	27,500 miles @ 11 knots
Flight deck	450 ft x 80 ft wood covered by steel
Arrester wires	9 x 19,800 lb rated @ 55 knots
Hangar	260 ft x 62 ft x 18 ft
Catapults	1 x H4C 16,000 lb @ 74 knots
Aircraft	30 operational, 90 ferried

D01 *Ameer*, D31 *Arbiter*, D51 *Atheling*, D38 *Begum*, D98 *Emperor*, D42 *Empress*, D62 *Khedive*, D77 *Nabob*, D07 *Patroller*, D23 *Premier*, D19 *Queen*, D10 *Rajah*, D03 *Ranee*, D82 *Reaper*, D72 *Ruler*, D21 *Shah*, D26 *Slinger*, D55 *Smiter*, D90 *Speaker*, D48 *Thane*, D85 *Trouncer*, D09 *Trumpeter*

Argus Fleet Carrier

Builder	Beardmores
Machinery	4 x shaft Parsons geared turbines, 12 x boilers 20,000 shp = 20.2 knots
Displacement	14,000 tons standard, 16,500 tons deep load
Dimensions	560 ft overall x 79 ft 6 ins beam x 22ft 6 ins max draught
Armament	6 x 4ins, 4 x 3 pdr, 13 x 20mm Oerlikon
Endurance	5,200 miles @ 12 knots
Flight deck	470 ft x 85 ft steel later 548 ft x 85 ft
Arrester wires	4 x 11,000 lb rated @ 53 knots
Hangar	350 ft x 68 ft
Catapults	1 x hydraulic 12,000 lb rated @ 66 knots
Aircraft	Max 20 aircraft, 15 carried normally

I49 *Argus*

Attacker Class Assault Carrier

Builder	Western Pipe and Steel Corp. USA
Machinery	1 x shaft General Electric geared turbine, 2x Foster Wheeler boilers 8,500 shp = 18 knots
Displacement	10,200 tons standard, 14,400 tons deep load
Dimensions	491 ft overall x 105 ft max beam x 21 ft max draught.
Armament	2 x 4 ins, 4 x twin Bofors, 8 x twin Oerlikon, 4 x single Oerlikon
Endurance	27,000 miles @ 11 knots

Flight deck	442 ft x 88 ft steel covered wood
Arrester wires	9 x 19,800 lb @ 55 knots
Hangar	262 ft x 62 ft x 18 ft
Catapults	1 x hydraulic rated at 7,000 lb @ 61 knots
Aircraft	20 operational 90 ferry

D02 *Attacker*, D18 *Battler*, D32 *Chaser*, D64 *Fencer*, D80 *Hunter*, D79 *Puncher*, D73 *Pursuer*, D70 *Ravager*, D40 *Searcher*, D91 *Stalker*, D12 *Striker* D24 *Tracker*

Audacity Escort Carrier

Builder	Vulkan
Machinery	1 x shaft Vulkan diesel, 5,200 bhp = 14.5 knots
Displacement	10,200 tons standard,11,000 tons deep load
Dimensions	467 ft 3 in overall x 56ft 3in beam x 21 ft 7 in draught
Armament	1 x 4 in HA QF, 1 x 6pdr, 4 x 2pdr, 4 x 20 mm Oerlikon
Endurance	12,000 miles @ 14 knots
Flight deck	453 ft x 60 ft steel
Arrester wires	3 x 9,000 lb @ 55 knots
Hangar	none
Catapults	none
Aircraft	8 maximum

D10 *Audacity*

Avenger Class Escort Carrier

Builder	Sun Shipbuilding & Drydock Corp
Machinery	1 x shaft, 2 Doxford diesels 8,500bhp = 17 knots
Displacement	12,150 tons standard, 15,700 tons deep load
Dimensions	492 ft overall x 70 ft beam x 26ft 4 in draught
Armament	3 x 4in US Mk.9, 10 x 20 mm Oerlikon
Endurance	14,550 miles @ 10 knots
Flight deck	442 ft x 70 ft
Arrester wires	9 x 8,000 ft rated @ 60 knots
Hangar	190 ft x 47ft x 16 ft
Catapults	1x H2 7,000 lb @ 60 knots
Aircraft	15 maximum

D14 *Avenger*, D97 *Biter*, D37 *Dasher*

Colossus Class Light Fleet Carrier

Builder	Vickers Armstrong
Machinery	2 shaft, Parsons geared turbines 4 x Admiralty boilers 40,000 shp = 25 knots
Displacement	13,190 standard displacement, 18,400 tons deep load
Dimensions	695 ft x 112 ft 6 ins max beam x 23 ft 5 in max draught
Armament	6 x quad 2 pdr Pompom, 11x twin Oerlikon, 10 x Oerlikon
Endurance	8,300 miles @ 20 knots
Flight deck	690 ft x 80 ft steel
Arrester wires	8 x 15,000 lb @ 60 knots
Hangar	275 ft plus 75 ft x 52 ft x 17 ft 6 ins
Catapults	1 x hydraulic 16,000 lb @ 66 knots
Aircraft	42 operational

15 *Colossus* as *Arromanches*, R62 *Glory*, R68 *Ocean*, R51 *Perseus*, R76 *Pioneer*, R64 *Theseus*, R16 *Triumph*, R04 *Venerable*, R71 *Vengeance*, R31 *Warrior*

Illustrious Class Fleet Carrier

Builder	Harland and Wolff
Machinery	3 shaft, Parsons geared turbines, 6 Admiralty boilers, 111,000 shp = 30.5 knots
Displacement	23,207 tons standard, 28,619 tons deep load
Dimensions	740 ft 9 ins x 106 ft 9 ins max beam x 28 ft deep draught
Armament	8 x twin 4 in, 6 x octuple 2 pdr Pompom, 20 x twin Oerlikon, 14 x single Oerlikon
Endurance	14,000 miles @ 12 knots
Flight deck	740 ft x 95 ft 9 in armoured steel
Arrester wires	7 x 11,000 lb @ 55 knots plus 2 x 20,000 lb @ 60 knots
Hangar	456 ft x 62 ft x 16 ft
Catapults	1 x hydraulic 14,000 lb @ 66 knots
Aircraft	54 operational

R67 *Formidable*, R87 *Illustrious*, R92 *Indomitable*, R38 *Victorious*

Furious Fleet Carrier

Builder	Armstrong Whitworth
Machinery	4 shaft, Brown Curtis geared turbines, 18 Yarrow boilers, 90,820 shp = 30 knots
Displacement	22,450 tons standard, 27,165 tons deep load
Dimensions	786 ft 5 ins x 90 ft max beam x 29 ft 11 in deep draught
Armament	6 x twin 4 in, 4 x octuple 2pdr Pompom, 4 x 20mm Oerlikon, 7 x 20mm Oerlikon
Endurance	3,700 miles @ 20 knots
Flight deck	596 ft x 91 ft 6 ins steel
Arrester wires	4 x 11,000 lb @ 60 knots
Hangar	Upper 520 ft x 50 ft x 15 ft
	Lower 550 ft x 50 ft x 15 ft
Catapults	none
Aircraft	33 operational

47 *Furious*, 77 *Glorious:* similar conversion to *Furious*

Courageous Class Fleet Carrier

Builder	Armstrong Whitworth
Machinery	4 shaft, Parsons geared turbines, 18 Yarrow boilers, 90,670 shp = 30 knots
Displacement	22,500 tons standard, 27,560 tons deep load
Dimensions	786 ft 5 in x 110 ft max beam x 28 ft deep draught
Armament	16 x 4.7 in HA QF, 4 x 3 pdr
Endurance	2,920 miles @ 24 knots
Flight deck	530 ft x 91 ft 6 in steel
Arrester wires	4 x 11,000 lb @ 52 knots
Hangar	Upper 550 ft x 50 ft x 16 ft
	Lower 550 ft x 50 ft x 16 ft
Catapults	2 x hydraulic 10,000 lb @ 52 knots
Aircraft	48 operational

Courageous

Modified Illustrious Class Fleet Carrier

Builder	Fairchild Shipbuilding & Engineering Co
Machinery	4 shaft, Parsons geared turbines, 8 x Admiralty boilers, 148,000 shp = 32 knots
Displacement	23,450 tons standard, 32,110 tons deep load
Dimensions	766 ft overall x 131 ft 3 in max beam x 29 ft max draught
Armament	8 x 4.5 in 5x octuple 2 pdr Bofors, 21 x 20 mm Oerlikon, 19 x 20mm Oerlikon
Endurance	12,000 miles @ 10 knots
Flight deck	760 ft x 90 ft armoured steel
Arrester wires	9 x 20,000 lb @ 60 knots, 3 x 20,000 lb @ 60 knots
Hangar	Upper 456 ft x 62 ft x 14 ft
	Lower 208 ft x 62 ft x 14 ft
Catapults	1 x hydraulic 20,000 lb @ 56 knots
Aircraft	81 operational

R86 *Implacable*, R10 *Indefatigable*

Majestic Class Light Fleet Carrier

Builder	Harland and Wolff
Machinery	2 shaft, Parsons geared turbines, 4 Admiralty boilers, 40,000 shp = 24.5 knots
Displacement	15,700 tons standard, 19,550 tons deep load
Dimensions	698 ft overall x 112 ft 6 in max beam x 25 ft max draught
Armament	8 x twin 40 mm Bofors, 14 x 40 mm Bofors
Endurance	8,300 miles @ 20 knots
Flight deck	690 ft x 106 ft steel
Arrester wires	9 x 20,000 lb @ 87 knots
Hangar	275 ft plus 75 ft x 52 ft x 17 ft 6 in
Catapults	1 x hydraulic 20,000 lb @ 56 knots
Aircraft	37 operational

CVL-21 *Magnificent*, CVL-22 *Bonaventure*, R21 *Melbourne*, R17 *Sydney*

Pretoria Castle Trials/ Training Carrier

Builder	Harland and Wolff; conversion carried out by Swan Hunter
Machinery	2 shaft, diesels 16,000 shp = 18 knots
Displacement	19,650 tons standard, 23,450 tons deep load
Dimensions	592 ft overall x 76 ft 4 in max beam x 29 ft 10 in max draught
Armament	2 x 4 in, 10 x twin 20 mm Oerlikon, 2 x quad Pompom
Endurance	16,000 miles @ 16 knots
Flight deck	550 ft x 76 ft steel
Arrester wires	6 x 15,000 lb @ 60 knots
Hangar	354 ft x 46 ft x 17 ft
Catapults	1 x hydraulic 14,000 lb @ 66 knots
Aircraft	21 operational

F61 *Pretoria Castle*

Unicorn Aircraft Repair Ship

Builder	Harland and Wolff
Machinery	2 shaft, Parsons geared turbines, 4 x Admiralty boilers, 40,000 shp = 24 knots
Displacement	14,750 tons standard, 20,300 tons deep load
Dimensions	640 ft overall x 90 ft max beam x 24 ft 10 in max draught
Armament	4 x twin 4 in, 4 x quad 2 pdr Pompom, 5 x twin 20mm Oerlikon, 6 x single Oerlikon
Endurance	7,500 miles @ 20 knots
Flight deck	640 ft x 90 ft armoured steel
Arrester wires	6 x 20,000 lb @ 60 knots
Hangar	Upper 324 ft x 65 ft x 16 ft 6 in
	Lower 360 ft x 62 ft x 16 ft 6 in
Catapults	1 x hydraulic 12,500 lb @ 66 knots
Aircraft	35 operational or 20 under repair

R72 *Unicorn*

Vindex Escort Carrier

Builder	Swan Hunter & Wigham Richardson
Machinery	2 shaft, Doxford diesels, 10,700 shp = 17 knots
Displacement	14,500 tons standard, 17,200 tons deep load
Dimensions	525 ft 6 in overall x 68 ft beam x 25 ft 8 in draught
Armament	1 x twin 4in QF HA, 2 x quadruple 2pdr Pompom, 8 x twin 20 mm Oerlikon
Endurance	13,000 miles @ 16 knots
Flight deck	502 ft x 66 ft steel
Arrester wires	6 x 15,500 lb @ 60 knots
Hangar	231 ft x 61 ft x 17ft 6 in
Catapults	none
Aircraft	20 maximum

R15 *Vindex*

Appendix 2

Aircraft Specifications

Avro Bison Fleet Spotter

Crew: 4
Length: 36 ft (10.97 m)
Wingspan: 46 ft (14.02 m)
Height: 13 ft 10 in (4.22 m)
Wing area: 620 ft² (57.60 m²)
Empty weight: 4,160 lb (1,887 kg)
Max take-off weight: 5,800 lb (2,631 kg)
Powerplant: 1 x Napier Lion II, 450 hp (336 kW)

Performance
Maximum speed: 110 mph (177 km/h)
Range: 340 miles (547 km)
Service ceiling: 14,000 ft (4,265 m)

Armament
1 Lewis gun
Operators: Nos. 421, 421A, 421B, 423, 447 and 448 Flights

Blackburn Dart

Crew: 1
Length: 35 ft 4.5 in (10.78 m)
Wingspan: 45 ft 5.75 in (13.86 m)
Height: 12 ft 11 in (3.91m)
Wing area: 654 ft² (199 m²)
Empty weight: 3,599 lb (1,900 kg)
Loaded weight: 6,383 lb (3,000 kg)
Powerplant: 1 x Napier Lion IIB 12 cylinder, broad arrow piston engine, 450 hp (336 kW)

Performance
Maximum speed: 107 mph (170 km/h) with dummy torpedo at 3,000 ft
Range: 356 nautical miles (410 miles 660 km)
Service ceiling: 12,700 ft (4,000 m)

Armament
Guns: 1 fixed, forward firing Vickers gun (not Mk II) and one Lewis gun
in rear cockpit
Bombs: One Mark VIII or IX, 18 in torpedo or up to two 520 lb bombs
  under each wing
Operators: Nos. 460, 461, 462, 463, 464 and 465 Flights plus No.810
  NAS

Blackburn Blackburn

Crew: 3
Length: 36 ft 2 in (11.02 m)
Wingspan: 45 ft 6 in (13.87 m)
Height: 12 ft 6 in (3.81 m)
Wing area: 650 ft² (60.40 m²)
Empty weight: 3,929 lb (1,786 kg)
Loaded weight: 5,962 lb (2,710 kg)
Powerplant: 1 x Napier Lion 12-cylinder inline engine, 450 hp (346 kW)

Performance
Maximum speed: 122 mph (157 km/h) at 3,000 ft
Service ceiling: 12,950 ft (3,950 m)
Rate of climb: 690 ft/min (210 m/min)
Endurance: 4.25 hours

Armament
Guns: 2 x .303 in (7.7 mm) Lewis guns
Operators: Nos 420, 422,449 and 450 Flights

Blackburn Ripon

Crew: 2
Length: 36 ft 9 in (11.20 m)
Wingspan: 44 ft 10 in (13.67 m)
Height: 12 ft 10 in (3.91 m)
Wing area: 683 ft² (63 m²)
Empty weight: 4,132lb (1,878 kg)
Loaded weight: 7,282 lb (3,310 kg)
Powerplant: 1 x Napier Lion X, XI or XIA 12 cylinder piston engine, 570
  hp (425 kW)

Performance
Maximum speed: 96 knots (111 mph, 179 km/h)
Range: 356 nm (410 miles 660 km)
Service ceiling: 10,000 ft (3,050 m)

Armament
1 x fixed, forward firing Vickers gun (not Mk II) and one Lewis gun in
  rear cockpit
One 18 in torpedo or up to three 530 lb or six 230 lb bombs
Operators: Nos 420,422,449 and 450 Flights

Blackburn Baffin

Crew: 2
Length: 38 ft 3¾ in (11.68 m)
Wingspan: 44 ft 10 in (13.67 m)
Height: 12 ft 10 in (3.91 m)
Wing area: 683 ft² (63 m²)
Empty weight: 3,184 lb (1,447 kg)
Loaded weight: 7,610 lb (3,459 kg)
Powerplant: 1 x Bristol Pegasus I.M3 9-cylinder radial engine, 565 hp (421
  kW)

Performance
Maximum speed: 118 knots (136 mph, 219 km/h)
Range: 426 nm (490 miles 789 km)
Service ceiling: 15,000 ft (4,570 m)

Armament
Guns: 1 x forward firing fixed 0.303 in Vickers gun and one 0.303 in Lewis
  gun in rear cockpit
Bombs: 1 x 1,800 lb 18 in torpedo or 1,600 lb of bombs
Operators: Nos. 810, 811 and 812 NAS

Blackburn Shark

Crew: 3
Length: 35 ft 3 in (10.75 m)
Wingspan: 46 ft (14.02 m)
Height: 12 ft 1 in (3.68 m)
Wing area: 489 ft² (45 m²)

Empty weight: 4,039 lb (1,836 kg)
Loaded weight: 8,111 lb (3,687 kg)
Powerplant: 1 x Armstrong Siddeley Tiger VI 14 cylinder radial, 760 hp (567 kW)

Performance
Maximum speed: 130 knots (150 mph, 242 km/h)
Range: 543 nm (625 miles 1,006 km)
Service ceiling: 15,600 ft (4,760 m)

Armament
Guns: 1 x fixed forward firing 0.303 in Vickers gun and one flexible 0.303 in Vickers K gun
Bombs: 1 x 1,800 lb 18-inch (460 mm) torpedo or 1,600 lb (730 kg) bombs
Operators: Nos 810, 820 and 821 NAS

Blackburn Skua

Crew: 2
Length: 35 ft 7 in (10.8 m)
Wingspan: 46 ft 2 in (14.1 m)
Height: 14 ft 2 in (4.3 m)
Wing area: 312 ft² (29.0 m²)
Empty weight: 5,490 lb (2,490 kg)
Loaded weight: 8,228 lb (3,730 kg)
Powerplant: 1 x Bristol Perseus XII radial engine, 905 hp (675 kW)

Performance
Maximum speed: 225 mph (195 knots, 360 km/h) at 6,500 ft (2,000 m)
Range: 700 nm (800 miles 1,300 km)
Service ceiling: 20,200 ft (6,150 m)

Armament
Guns: 4 x 0.303 in (7.7 mm) forward-firing Browning machine guns
          1 x 0.303 in (7.7 mm) Lewis or Vickers K gun on flexible mount in rear cockpit
Bombs: 1 x 500 lb (230 kg) semi-armour piercing bomb or 1 x 250lb (115 kg) semi-armour piercing/General Purpose bomb and 4 x 40 lb bombs or 8 x 20 lb bombs
Operators: Nos. 800, 801, 803, 806 NAS

Blackburn Roc

Crew: 2
Length: 35 ft 7 in (10.85 m)
Wingspan: 46 ft (14.02 m)
Height: 12 ft 1 in (3.68 m)
Wing area: 310 ft² (29 m²)
Loaded weight: 8,800 lb (4,000 kg)
Powerplant: 1 x Bristol Perseus XII radial engine, 900 hp (670 kW)

Performance
Maximum speed: 170 knots (196 mph, 315 km/h)
Range: 530 nm (610 miles 980 km)
Service ceiling: 15,200 ft (4,630 m)

Armament
Guns: 4 x 0.303 in (7.7 mm) Browning machine guns in power operated
   dorsal turret
Bombs: 8 x 30 lb (14 kg) bombs
Operators: Nos 801, 803 and 806 NAS

The Blackburn Roc was the sea going attempt to create a turret fighter equivalent to the Boulton Paul Defiant. In the event neither machine was particularly successful and both types eventually ended up as target tugs. (NARA)

Blackburn Firebrand TF.5

Crew: 1
Length: 39 ft 1 in (12 m)
Wingspan: 51 ft 3½ in (15.62 m)
Height: ft in (m)
Wing area: 381.5 ft² (35.44 m²)
Empty weight: 11,357 lb (5,150 kg)
Loaded weight: 15,671 lb (7,100 kg)
Powerplant: 1 x Bristol Centaurus IX 18-cylinder radial engine, 2,500 hp
  (1,865 kW)

Performance
Maximum speed: 350 mph (300 knots, 560 km/h)
Range: 1,100 nm (1,250 miles 2,000 km) with torpedo and drop tanks

Armament
Guns: 4 x 20 mm (0.787 in) Hispano Mk.II cannon, two in each wing
Bombs: 1 x 1,850 lb (840 kg) torpedo, or 2x 1,000 lb (450 kg) bombs, one
  under each wing, in place of torpedo
Operators: Nos. 813 and 827 NAS

Blackburn Buccaneer S.2

Crew: 2
Length: 63 ft 5 in (19.33 m)
Wingspan: 44 ft (13.41 m)
Height: 16 ft 3 in (4.97 m)
Wing area: 514.7 ft² (47.82 m²)
Empty weight: 30,000 lb (14,000 kg)
Loaded weight: 62,000 lb (28,000 kg)
Powerplant: 2 x Rolls-Royce Spey Mk 101 turbofans, 11,100 st (49 kN)
  each

Performance
Maximum speed: 645 mph (560 knots, 1,040 km/h) at 200 ft (60 m)
Range: 2,000 nm (2,300 miles 3,700 km)
Service ceiling: 40,000 ft (12,200 m)

Armament
Up to 12,000 lb (5,400 kg) of ordnance carried in the internal bomb bay
  and on four under wing hardpoints
Operators: Nos. 800, 810, 803 and 809 NAS

A dramatic shot of a Buccaneer S.2 catapulting off HMS *Ark Royal*. While the Royal Navy has normally preferred an air defence component aboard its carriers, the current use of RAF Harriers has meant that the Naval Air Wing is ground attack capable only. (BBA Collection)

HSA/BAES Sea Harrier FA.2

Crew: 1
Length: 46 ft 6 in (14.2 m)
Wingspan: 25 ft 3 in (7.6 m)
Height: 12 ft 4 in (3.71 m)
Wing area: 201.1 ft² (18.68 m²)
Empty weight: 14,052 lb (6,374 kg)
Max take-off weight: 26,200 lb (11,900 kg)
Powerplant: 1 x Rolls-Royce Pegasus turbofan, 21,500 st (95.64 kN)

Performance
Maximum speed: 635 knots (735 mph, 1182 km/h)
Combat radius: 540 nm (620 miles 1,000 km)
Service ceiling: 51,000 ft (16,000 m)

Armament
Guns: 2 x 30 mm (1.18 in) ADEN cannon pods under the fuselage
Rockets: 4 x Matra rocket pods with 18 x SNEB 68 mm rockets each

Seen landing aboard one of the RFA support vessels is the first Sea Harrier FRS.1 destined for naval service. (John Ryan Collection)

It was the addition of the ski-jump ramp that improved the take off performance and load carrying capability of the Sea Harrier. (John Ryan Collection)

As the Sea Harrier was an unusual aircraft to fly it came as no surprise that the Royal Navy purchased some two-seat trainers to assist in pilot conversion and training. (John Ryan Collection)

Missiles: AIM-9 Sidewinder, AIM-120 AMRAAM, ALARM, Sea Eagle, Martel missile

Bombs: 5,000 lb (2,268 kg) of payload on four external hardpoints, including a variety of bombs, WE.177 (until 1992), reconnaissance pods, or Drop tanks for extended range

Operators: Nos 800,801,809 and 899 NAS

Chance Vought Corsair

Crew: 1
Length: 33 ft 8 in (10.2 m)
Wingspan: 41 ft 0 in (12.5 m)
Height: 14 ft 9 in (4.50 m)
Empty weight: 9,205 lb (4,174 kg)
Loaded weight: 14,669 lb (6,653 kg)
Powerplant: 1 x Pratt & Whitney R-2800-18W radial engine, 2,450 hp (1,827 kW)

Performance
Maximum speed: 446 mph (388 knots, 718 km/h)
Range: 873 nm (1,005 miles 1,618 km)
Service ceiling: 41,500 ft (12,649 m)

The Chance Vought F4U Corsair IV was viewed favourably by the pilots of the Fleet Air Arm as it was heavily armed, had good performance, a wide track undercarriage and was capable of accepting severe battle damage. (John Ryan Collection)

Armament

Guns: 6 x 0.50 in (12.7 mm) M2 Browning machine guns, 400 rounds per gun or 4 x 20 mm AN/M2 cannons

Rockets: 8 x 5 in (12.7 cm) high velocity aircraft rockets and/or Bombs: 4,000 lb (1820 kg)

Operators: Nos. 1830, 1831, 1833, 1834, 1835, 1836, 1837, 1838, 1841, 1842, 1843, 1845, 1846, 1848, 1849, 1850, 1851, 1852 and 1853 NAS

De Havilland Sea Hornet

Crew: 1

Length: 36 ft 8 in (11.18 m)

Wingspan: 45 ft (13.72 m)

Height: 14 ft 2 in (4.3 m)

Wing area: 361 ft² (33.54 m²)

Empty Weight: 11,700 lb

Loaded weight: 19,550 lb (8,886 kg)

Powerplant: 2 x Rolls-Royce Merlin 130/131 12-cylinder engines, 2,080 hp (1,551 kW) each

Performance
Maximum speed: 472 mph at 22,000 ft (6,700 m) (760 km/h at 6,706 m)
Range: 3,000 miles (4,828 km)
Service ceiling: 35,000 ft (10,668 m)

Armament
Guns: 4 x 20 mm Hispano Mk. V cannon (with 190 rounds per gun) in
   lower fuselage nose
Bombs: 2 x 1000 lb (454 kg) bombs under wing, outboard of engines or 8 x
   60 lb (27 kg) RP-3 unguided rockets
Operators: Nos. 801, 806 and 809 NAS

De Havilland Sea Venom

Crew: 1
Length: 31 ft 10 in (9.70 m)
Wingspan: 41 ft 8 in (12.70 m)
Height: 6 ft 2 in (1.88 m)
Wing area: 279 ft² (25.9 m²)
Empty weight: 9,202 lb (4,173 kg)
Loaded weight: 15,400 lb (7,000 kg)
Power plant: 1 x de Havilland Ghost 103 turbojet, 4,850 st (21.6 kN)

Soon to be made redundant due to ever increasing aircraft approach speeds is the
batsman, seen here guiding a Sea Vampire onto the deck. (Rick Harding Collection)

Seen aboard the carrier HMS *Centaur,* this Sea Venom carried double stacked 60 lbs rockets under the wings. During the development of this method of carriage there were some spectacular failures when the wrong rocket motor ignited or the rocket pair failed to separate correctly. By the time of Suez however these faults had been cured. (Will Blunt Collection)

Sporting Suez striping about its tail booms is Sea Venom WW138. When initially delivered the Venom series of aircraft were not fitted with ejection seats although this was rectified as soon as possible thus ensuring aircrew survival. (Will Blunt Collection

Performance
Maximum speed: 556 knots (640 mph, 1,030 km/h)
Range: 934 nm (1,080 miles 1,730 km)
Service ceiling: 39,400 ft (12,000 m)

Armament
Guns: 4 x 20 mm Hispano Mk.V cannon, 150 rounds per gun
Rockets: 8 x RP-3 60 lb (27 kg) rockets, or;
Bombs: 2 x 1,000 lb (450 kg) bombs
Operators: Nos 808, 809, 831, 890, 891, 892, 893 and 894 NAS

De Havilland Sea Vixen FAW2

Crew: 2
Length: 55 ft 7 in (16.94 m)
Wingspan: 51 ft 0 in (15.54 m)
Height: 10 ft 9 in (3.28 m)
Wing area: 648 ft² (60.2 m²)
Empty weight: 27,950 lb (12,680 kg)
Loaded weight: 41,575 lb (18,860 kg)
Powerplant: 2 x Rolls-Royce Avon Mk.208 turbojets, 11,000 st (50 kN) each

When the Sea Vixen FAW.2 joined the Fleet Air Arm it gave the squadrons a quantum leap in capability, not only was this heavy fighter capable of air defence, it was also plumbed to carry bombs and act as a buddy air refuelling aircraft. (John Ryan Collection)

Performance
Maximum speed: Mach 0.91 (690 mph, 1,110 km/h) at sea level
Range: 790 miles (1,270 km) with internal fuel
Service ceiling: 48,000 ft (15,000 m)

Armament
Rockets: 4 x Matra rocket pods with 18 x SNEB 68 mm rockets each
Missiles: 4 x Red Top or Firestreak air-to-air missiles or Bombs: 2 x 500 lb
  (227 kg) bombs
Operators: Nos. 890, 892, 893 and 899 NAS

Douglas Skyraider AEW1

Crew: 3
Length: 39 ft 3 3/4 in (11.84 m)
Wingspan: 50 ft 0 in (15.25 m)
Height: 15 ft 8 in (4.78 m)
Wing area: 400.31 ft² (37.19 m²)
Empty weight: 10,550 lb (5,430 kg)
Max take-off weight: 25,000 lb (11,340 kg)
Powerplant: 1 x Wright R-3350-26WA radial engine, 2,700 hp (2,000 kW)

Having used the Avenger in the AEW role its replacement was the far more capable
Douglas Skyraider which had proven itself over Korea for the US Navy. (Trevor Jones
Collection)

Performance
Maximum speed: 320 mph (280 knots, 520 km/h)
Cruise speed: 295 mph (256 knots, 475 km/h)
Range: 1,142 nm (1,315 miles 2,115 km)
Service ceiling: 28,500 ft (8,660 m)
Operators: No. 849 NAS

Fairey Campania

Crew: 2
Length: 43 ft 4 in (13.21 m)
Wingspan: 61 ft 7 in (18.77 m)
Height: 15 ft 1 in (4.59 m)
Wing area: 686.6 ft² (63.78 m²)
Empty weight: 3,672 lb (1,757 kg)
Loaded weight: 5,657 lb (2,417 kg)
Max take-off weight: lb (kg)
Powerplant: 1 x Sunbeam Maori II, 260-hp (kW)

Performance
Maximum speed: 74 knots (85 mph, 137 km/h) at sea level
Service ceiling 6,000 ft (1,981 m)

Armament
Guns: 1 x Lewis gun on Scarff ring in rear cockpit. Up to six 116 lb bombs
    under wings and fuselage.
Operators: HMSs *Campania, Nairana* and *Pegasus*

Fairey Flycatcher

Crew: 1
Length: 23 ft 0 in (7.01 m)
Wingspan: 29 ft 0 in (8.84 m)
Height: 12 ft 0 in (3.66 m)
Wing area: 288 ft² (26.8 m²)
Empty weight: 2,038 lb (926 kg)
Loaded weight: 3028 lb (1377 kg)
Powerplant: 1 x Armstrong Siddeley Jaguar IV two row, 14 cylinder
    radial engine, 400 hp (298 kW)

Performance
Maximum speed: 116 knots (133 mph, 214 km/h) at sea level
Range: 270 nm (310 miles 499 km)
Service ceiling: 19,000 ft (5790 m)

Armament
Guns: 2 x two fixed forward-firing Vickers machine guns Provision for
  four 20 lb (9.1 kg) bombs under wings.
Operators: Nos. 401, 402, 403, 404, 405, 406, 407, 408 and 409 Fighter
  Flights No. 801 NAS

Fairey IIIF

Crew: 2
Length: 36 ft 9 in (11.20 m)
Wingspan: 45 ft 9 in (13.95 m)
Height: 14 ft 2 in (4.32 m)
Wing area: 439 ft² (41 m²)
Empty weight: 3,380 lb (1,764 kg)
Loaded weight: 6,041 lb (2,746 kg)
Powerplant: 1 x Napier Lion XI 12-cylinder inline engine, 570 hp (423 kW)

Performance
Maximum speed: 104 knots (120 mph, 192 km/h)
Range: 1,313 nm (1,520 miles 2,432 km)
Service ceiling: 20,000 ft (6,098 m)

Armament
Guns: 1 x forward firing .303 Vickers machine gun, 1 x .303 Lewis
  machine gun in flexible mount for observer, bombs can be carried under
  wings
Operators: Nos. 440, 441, 442, 443, 444, 445, 446, 447, 448, 449, 450 and 460
  Flights plus No. 820, 822, 823 824 and 825 NAS

Fairey Seal

Crew: 3
Length: 36 ft 9 in (11.2 m)
Wingspan: 45 ft 9 in (13.94 m)
Height: 14 ft 1 in (4.32 m)
Empty weight: 3,500 lb (1,588 kg)

Max take-off weight: 5,904 lb (2,679 kg)
Powerplant: 1 x Armstrong Siddeley Panther IIA radial piston engine,
  605 hp (450 kW)

Performance
Maximum speed: 145 mph at 3,000 ft (233 km/h at 915 m)
Range: 600 nm (966 km)
Service ceiling: 22,145 ft (6,705 m)

Armament
Guns: 1 x fixed forward .303 in (7.7 mm) Vickers machine gun, 1 x rear
  .303 in (7.7 mm) Lewis Gun
Bombs: 500 lb (230 kg) or stores carried on lower wing
Operators: Nos 820,821,822,823, 824 and 825 NAS

Fairey Swordfish

Crew: 3
Length: 35 ft 8 in (10.87 m)
Wingspan: 45 ft 6 in (13.87 m)
Height: 12 ft 4 in (3.76 m)
Wing area: 542 ft² (50.4 m²)
Empty weight: 4,195 lb (1,900 kg)
Loaded weight: 7,720 lb (3,500 kg)
Powerplant: 1 x Bristol Pegasus IIIM.3 or XXX radial engine, 690 hp (510
  kW)

Performance
Maximum speed: 138 mph (222 km/h) at 5,000 ft (1,500 m)
Range: 546 miles (879 km)
Service ceiling: 19,250 ft (5,870 m)

Armament
Guns: 1 x 0.303 in (7.7 mm) Vickers machine gun in engine cowling
  1 x 0.303 in (7.7 mm) Lewis or Vickers K machine gun in rear cockpit
Rockets: 8 x 60 lb (27 kg) RP-3 rocket projectiles (Mk.II and later)
Bombs: 1 x 1,670 lb (760 kg) torpedo or 1,500 lb (700 kg) mine
Operators: Nos. 810, 811, 812, 813, 814, 815, 816, 818, 819, 820, 821, 822,
  823, 824, 825, 829, 830, 833, 834, 835, 836, 837, 838, 840, 842 and 860
  NAS

Fairey Albacore

Crew: 3
Length: 39 ft 10 in (12.14 m)
Wingspan: 50 ft 0 in (15.24 m)
Height: 14 ft 2 in (4.62 m)
Wing area: 623 ft² (57.9 m²)
Empty weight: 7,250 lb (3,295 kg)
Loaded weight: 10,460 lb (4,755 kg)
Powerplant: 1 x Bristol Taurus II 14-cylinder radial engine, 1,065 hp (794 kW)

Performance
Maximum speed: 140 knots (161 mph, 259 km/h)
Range: 617 nm (710 miles 1,143 km) (with torpedo)
Service ceiling: 20,700 ft (6,310 m)

Armament
Guns: 1 x fixed forward-firing 0.303 in (7.7 mm) machine gun in starboard wing, 1 x or two Vickers K machine guns in rear cockpit.
Bombs: 1 x 1,670 lb (760 kg) torpedo or 2,000 lb (900 kg) bombs
Operators: Nos. 815, 817, 818, 820, 821, 822, 823, 826, 827, 828, 829, 831, 832, and 841 NAS

Fairey Fulmar

Crew: 2
Length: 40 ft 2 in (12.25 m)
Wingspan: 46 ft 4¼ in (14.13 m)
Height: 14 ft 0 in (4.27 m)
Wing area: 342 ft² (32 m²)
Empty weight: 7,015 lb (3,182 kg)
Loaded weight: 9,672 lb (4,387 kg)
Powerplant: 1 x Rolls-Royce Merlin 30 liquid-cooled inline V-12, 1,300 hp (970 kW)

Performance
Maximum speed: 272 mph at 7,250 ft (438 km/h at 2,200 m)
Range: 780 miles (1,255 km)
Service ceiling: 27,200 ft (8,300 m)

Armament
Guns: 8 x 0.303 in Browning machine guns wing-mounted, and

occasionally 1 x .303 in Vickers K machine gun in rear cabin, 2 x 100 lb (45 kg) or 250 lb (110 kg) bombs
Operators: Nos. 800, 803, 804, 805, 806, 807, 808, 809, 813, 879, 884, 886, 887 and 889 NAS

Fairey Barracuda I-III

Crew: 3
Length: 40 ft 0 in (12.18 m)
Wingspan: 47 ft 6 in (14.49 m)
Height: 15 ft 0 in (4.60 m)
Wing area: 404.94 ft² (37.62 m²)
Empty weight: 9,800 lb (4,445 kg)
Loaded weight: 12,600 lb (5,715 kg)
Powerplant: 1 x Rolls-Royce Merlin 32 liquid-cooled V12 engine, 1,640 hp (1,225 kW)

Performance
Maximum speed: 210 mph (180 knots, 340 km/h) at altitude
Range: 630 nm (725 miles 1,165 km)
Service ceiling: 21,600 ft (6,585 m)

Armament
Guns: 2 x 0.303 in (7.7 mm) Vickers K machine guns in rear cockpit
Hardpoints: 5: (two under each wing and one under the fuselage), with a capacity of 1,620 lb (735 kg), equipped to carry: 1 x torpedo or Bombs or Depth charges or Mines
Operators: Nos. 810, 812, 814, 815, 816, 817, 818, 820, 821, 822, 823, 824, 825, 826, 827, 828, 829, 830, 831, 837, 841, 847 and 860 NAS.

Fairey Firefly Mk.IV

Crew: 2
Length: 37 ft 11 in (11.53 m)
Wingspan: 41 ft 2 in (12.55 m)
Height: 14 ft 4 in (4.37 m)
Wing area: 330 ft² (30.66 m²)
Empty weight: 9,460 lb (4,300 kg)
Loaded weight: 13,200 lb (6,000 kg)
Powerplant: 1 x Rolls-Royce Griffon IIB liquid-cooled V12 engine, 1,730 hp (1,290 kW)

With a deck cargo of Sea Furies and Fireflies aboard HMCS *Magnificent* prepares to depart Britain for Canada. Although the Commonwealth Navies were nominally independent, they were closely allied to Britain therefore they frequently replaced Royal Navy carriers on operations. (John Ryan Collection)

Performance
Maximum speed: 386 mph at 14,000 ft (618 km/h at 4,300 m)
Range: 1,070 miles (1,722 km) with auxiliary tanks
Service ceiling: 28,000 ft (8,530 m)

Armament
Guns: 4 x 20 mm Hispano-Suiza HS.404 cannons
Bombs: 2 x 1,000 lb (450 kg) bomb under wings or 8 pairs of 60 lb (27 kg) rockets
Operators: Nos. 810, 812, 814, 825 and 1840 NAS

Fairey Gannet AEW3

Crew: 3
Length: 44 ft (13.41 m)
Wingspan: 54 ft 4 in (16.57 m)
Height: 16 ft 10 in (5.13 m)
Wing area: 490 ft² (45.5 m²)
Loaded weight: 25,000 lb (11,400 kg)
Powerplant: 1 x Armstrong Siddeley Double Mamba ASMD.4 turboprop, 3,875 hp (2,890 kW) each

Performance
Maximum speed: 250 mph (217 knots, 402 km/h)
Range: 700 miles (609 NM, 1127 km)
Service ceiling: 25,000 ft (7,600 m)
Operators: No. 849 NAS

Departing from *Victorious* is this Fairey Gannet. In this instance the aircraft is no longer utilised in the anti-submarine role having been reworked for the COD, Carrier Onboard Delivery, role. (BBA Collection)

Sitting on the *Ark Royal* catapult is Fairey Gannet AEW.3 preparing to depart on another sortie. With the disappearance of this type of launching the Invincible class carriers required that the radar be carried aloft by Sea King helicopter. (FAAM Yeovilton)

Gloster Sea Gladiator

Crew: 1
Length: 27 ft 5 in (8.4 m)
Wingspan: 32 ft 3 in (9.8 m)
Height: 10 ft 4 in (3.2 m)
Wing area: 323 ft² (30 m²)
Empty weight: 3,553 lb (1,560 kg)
Loaded weight: 4,800 lb (2,205 kg)
Powerplant: 1 x Bristol Mercury IX radial engine, 850 hp (630 kW)

Performance
Maximum speed: 257 mph (414 km/h) at 14,600 ft (4,500 m)
Range: 444 miles (710 km)
Service ceiling: 33,500 ft (10,200 m)
Operators: Nos 800, 801, 802, 804, 805, 813 and 885 NAS

Grumman Martlet/Wildcat

Crew: 1
Length: 28 ft 9 in (8.8 m)
Wingspan: 38 ft 0 in (11.6 m)
Height: 9 ft 2.5 in (2.8 m)
Wing area: 260 ft² (24.2 m²)
Empty weight: 5,760 lb (2,610 kg)
Max take-off weight: 7,950 lb (3,610 kg)
Powerplant: 1 x Pratt & Whitney R-1830-86 double-row radial engine,
  1,200 hp (900 kW)

Performance
Maximum speed: 320 mph (290 knots, 515 km/h)
Range: 670 nm (770 miles 1,240 km)
Service ceiling: 39,500 ft (12,000 m)

Armament
Guns: 6 x 0.50 in (12.7 mm) M2 Browning machine guns, 240 rounds/gun
Bombs: 2 x 100 lb (45 kg) bombs and/or 2 x 58 gal. droptanks
Operators: Nos. 802, 804, 805, 806, 881, 882, 888, 890, 892, 893, 894, 896
  and 898 NAS

The Grumman Martlet/Wildcat series provided the Royal Navy with a small agile fighter that was more than capable of dealing with the Luftwaffe attackers. (BBA Collection)

Grumman Avenger

Crew: 3
Length: 40 ft 11.5 in (12.48 m)
Wingspan: 54 ft 2 in (16.51 m)
Height: 15 ft 5 in (4.70 m)
Wing area: 490.02 ft² (45.52 m²)
Empty weight: 10,545 lb (4,783 kg)
Loaded weight: 17,893 lb (8,115 kg)
Powerplant: 1 x Wright R-2600-20 radial engine, 1,900 hp (1,420 kW)

Also from the Grumman stable came the Avenger which continued to serve with many navies in the immediate post-war period. (BBA Collection)

Performance
Maximum speed: 276 mph (444 km/h)
Range: 1,000 miles (1,610 km)
Service ceiling: 30,100 ft (9,170 m)

Armament
Guns: 1 x 0.30 cal (7.62 mm) nose-mounted M1919 Browning machine
        gun (on early models)
      2 x 0.50 cal (12.7 mm) wing-mounted M2 Browning machine guns
      1 x 0.50 cal (12.7 mm) dorsal-mounted M2 Browning machine gun
      1 x 0.30 cal (7.62 mm) ventral-mounted M1919 Browning machine
      gun
Bombs: Up to 2,000 lb (907 kg) of bombs or 1 x 2,000 lb (907 kg) Mark 13
  torpedo
Operators: Nos. 820, 828, 832, 845, 846, 848, 849, 850, 851, 852, 853, 854,
  855, 856 and 857 NAS

Grumman Hellcat

Crew: 1
Length: 33 ft 7 in (10.24 m)
Wingspan: 42 ft 10 in (13.06 m)
Height: 13 ft 1 in (3.99 m)
Wing area: 334 ft^2 (31 m^2)
Empty weight: 9,238 lb (4,190 kg)
Loaded weight: 12,598 lb (5,714 kg)
Max take-off weight: 15,415 lb (6,990 kg)
Powerplant: 1 x Pratt & Whitney R-2800-10W Double Wasp two-row
  radial engine with a two-speed two-stage supercharger, 2,000 hp (1,491
  kW [29])

Performance
Maximum speed: 330 knots (380 mph, 610 km/h)
Combat radius: 820 nm (945 miles 1,520 km)
Service ceiling: 37,300 ft (11,370 m)

Armament
Guns: either 6 x 0.50 in (12.7 mm) M2 Browning machine guns, with 400
  rounds/gun, (All F6F-3, and most F6F-5) or 2x 20 mm cannon, with 225
  rounds/gun and 4x 0.50 in (12.7 mm) Browning machine guns with 400
  rounds/gun (F6F-5N only)
Rockets: 6 x 5 in (127 mm) HVARs or 2 x 11¾ in (298 mm) Tiny Tim
  unguided rockets

Bombs: up to 4,000 lb (1,800 kg) full load, including: Bombs or Torpedoes:
(Fuselage mounted on centreline rack)
Operators: Nos. 800, 804, 808, 881, 885, 888, 889, 891, 892, 896, 898, 1839,
1840, 1844 and 1847 NAS

Hawker Nimrod

Crew: 1
Length: 26 ft 6 in (8.09 m)
Wingspan: 33 ft 7 in (10.23 m)
Height: 9 ft 10 in (3.00 m)
Wing area: 300 ft² (27.96 m²)
Empty weight: 3,110 lb (1,413 kg)
Max take-off weight: 4,050 lb (1,841 kg)
Powerplant: 1 x Rolls-Royce Kestrel VFP inline piston engine, 525 hp (391
kW)
Performance
Maximum speed: 168 knots (194 mph, 311 km/h)
Service ceiling: 28,000 ft (8,535 m)

Armament
2 x forward firing fixed .303 (7.7 mm) machine guns
4 x 20 lb (9 kg) bombs on underwing racks
Operators: Nos. 402, 408, 409 Flights plus Nos. 801 and 802 NAS

Hawker Osprey

Crew: 2
Length: 29 ft 4 in (8.94 m)
Wingspan: 37 ft 3 in (11.36 m)
Height: 10 ft 5 in (3.18 m)
Wing area: 349.5 ft² (32.5 m²)
Empty weight: 2,530lb (1,150 kg)
Max take-off weight: 4,596 lb (2,089 kg)
Powerplant: 1 x Rolls-Royce Kestrel IB water-cooled V12 engine, 510 hp (380
kW)

Performance
Maximum speed: 161 knots (185 mph, 298 km/h) at 13,000 ft
Range: 374 nm (430 miles 692 km)
Service ceiling: 22,800 ft (6,950 m)

Armament
Guns: 1 x synchronised forward firing .303 in Vickers machine gun, 1 x
  Lewis gun on Scarff ring in rear cockpit
Bombs: Up to 500lb (227 kg) bombs under wings.
Operators: Nos 403, 406, 407, 443, 444, 447 Flights plus Nos. 800, 801, 802
  and 803 NAS

Hawker Sea Hurricane

Crew: 1
Length: 32 ft 3 in (9.84 m)
Wingspan: 40 ft 0 in (12.19 m)
Height: 13 ft 1½ in (4.0 m)
Wing area: 257.5 ft² (23.92 m²)
Empty weight: 5,745 lb (2,605 kg)
Loaded weight: 7,670 lb (3,480 kg)
Max take-off weight: 8,710 lb (3,950 kg)
Powerplant: 1 x Rolls-Royce Merlin XX liquid-cooled V-12, 1,185 hp (883
  kW) at 21,000 ft (6,400 m)

Performance
Maximum speed: 340 mph (547 km/h) at 21,000 ft (6,400 m) [27]
Range: 600 miles (965 km)
Service ceiling: 36,000 ft (10,970 m)

Armament
Guns: 4x 20 mm Hispano Mk II cannon
Bombs: 2 x 250 lb or 500 lb bombs
Operators: Nos. 800, 801, 802, 803, 804, 806, 811, 813, 824, 825, 835, 877,
  883, 885, 889, 891, 895 and 897 NAS

Hawker Sea Fury

Crew: 1
Length: 34 ft 8 in (10.6 m)
Wingspan: 38 ft 4¾ in (11.7 m)
Height: 16 ft 1 in (4.9 m)
Wing area: 280 ft² (26 m²)
Empty weight: 9,240 lb (4,190 kg)

Max take-off weight: 12,500 lb (5,670 kg)
Powerplant: 1 x Bristol Centaurus XVIIC 18-cylinder twin-row radial
  engine, 2,480 hp (1,850 kW)

Performance
Maximum speed: 460 mph (740 km/h) at 18,000 ft (5,500 m)
Range: 700 miles (1,127 km) with internal fuel; 1,040 miles (1,675 km)
  with two drop tanks
Service ceiling: 35,800 ft (10,900 m)

Armament
Guns: 4 x 20 mm Hispano Mk V cannon
Rockets: 12 x 3 in (76 mm) rockets or Bombs: 2,000 lb (908 kg) of bombs
Operators: Nos. 801, 802, 803, 804, 805, 806, 807, 808, 811, 871 and 898 NAS

Hawker Sea Hawk

Crew: 1
Length: 39 ft 8 in (12.09 m)
Wingspan: 39 ft 0 in (11.89 m)
Height: 8 ft 8 in (2.64 m)
Wing area: 278 ft² (25.83 m²)
Empty weight: 9,278 lb (4,208 kg)
Loaded weight: 13,220 lb (5,996 kg)
Powerplant: 1 x Rolls-Royce Nene 103 turbojet, 5,200 st (23.1 kN)

The Hawker Sea Hawk was the first jet aircraft to give the Royal Navy a positive
fighter and attack aircraft. Here a Sea Hawk prepares to touch down, of note is the
plane guard Whirlwind helicopter in the background. (FAAM Yeovilton)

Performance
Maximum speed: 600 mph (965 km/h)
Range: 480 miles (770 km)
Service ceiling: 44,500 ft (13,564 m)

Armament
Guns: 4 x Hispano-Suiza 20 mm cannons (200 rounds per gun, 800
    rounds total)
Bombs: 4 x 500 lb (227 kg) bombs
Rockets: 2 x 3 in (76 mm) unguided rockets, 16 x 5 in (127 mm) unguided
    rockets
Drop tanks: 2 x 100 gallon-410 l jettison drop tanks
Operators: Nos. 800, 801, 802, 803, 804, 806, 807, 811, 831, 895, 897 and 898
    NAS

McDonnell Douglas Phantom FG.1

Crew: 2
Length: 57 ft 7 in (19.2 m)
Wingspan: 38 ft 4.5 in (11.7 m)
Height: 16 ft 6 in (5.0 m)
Wing area: 530.0 ft² (49.2 m²)
Empty weight: 30,000 lb (13,757 kg)
Loaded weight: 56,000 lb (18,825 kg)
Powerplant: 2 x Rolls Royce Spey 201 Turbofans rated at 12,250 lb dry
    thrust each, reheat 20,515 lb

The Omega symbol on the fin of this FAA Phantom signifies the Royal Navy's
acceptance that the F-4 and Buccaneer would be the last catapult launched aircraft for
the service. (Trevor Jones Collection)

Performance
Maximum speed: Mach 2.23 (1,472 mph, 2,370 km/h) at 40,000 ft (12,190 m)
Cruise speed: 506 km (585 mph, 940 km/h)
Combat radius: 367 nm (422 miles 680 km)
Ferry range: 1,403 nm (1,615 miles 2,600 km) with 3 external fuel tanks
Service ceiling: 60,000 ft (18,300 m)
Operators: No.892 NAS

Short Type 184

Crew: 2
Length: 40 ft 7 in (12.38 m)
Wingspan: 63 ft 6in (19.36 m)
Height: 13 ft 6 in (4.11 m)
Wing area: 688 ft² (63.9 m²)
Empty weight: 3,703 lb (1680 kg)
Powerplant: 1 x Sunbeam Gurkha (74 units), Sunbeam Maori, 260 hp (194
   kW)

Performance
Maximum speed: 88 mph (142 km/h)
Service ceiling: 9,000 ft (2,745 m)

Armament
Guns: 1 x Lewis gun in rear cockpit
Bombs: 1 x 14-inch (356 mm) torpedo or up to 520 lb (236 kg) of bombs
Operators: Nos. 219, 229, 233, 234 235, 237,239, 240, 241, 242, 243, 244, 245,
   248, 249, 251, 252, 253, 254, 255, 257, 260, 269 and 271 Squadrons after
   April 1918

Sopwith Baby

Crew: 1
Length: 23 ft 0 in (7.01 m)
Wingspan: 25 ft 8 in (7.82 m)
Height: 10 ft 0 in (3.05 m)
Wing area: 240 ft² (22.30 m²)
Empty weight: 1,226 lb (557 kg)
Loaded weight: 1,715 lb (779 kg)
Powerplant: 1 x Clerget rotary engine, 110 hp (82 kW)

Performance
Maximum speed: 87 knots (100 mph, 162 km/h) at sea level
Service ceiling: 10,000 ft (3,050 m)
Endurance: 2.25 hrs

Armament
Guns: 1 x Lewis gun
Bombs: 2 x 65 lb (28 kg) bombs
Operators: All RNAS Stations plus numerous warships of the Grand
    Fleet

Sopwith 1½ Strutter

Crew: 2, pilot and observer
Length: 25 ft 3 in (7.7 m)
Wingspan: 33 ft 6 in (10.21 m)
Height: 10 ft 3 in (3.12 m)
Wing area: 346 ft² (32.14 m²)
Empty weight: 1,260 lb (570 kg)
Loaded weight: 2,149 lb (975 kg)
Powerplant: 1 x Clerget 9B rotary engine, 130 hp (97 kW)

Performance
Maximum speed: 102 mph (164 km/h)
Range: 350 miles (565 km)
Service ceiling: 13,000 ft (3,960 m)

Armament
Guns: 1 x .303 in (7.7 mm) forward-firing Vickers machine gun with Ross
            interrupter gear
        1 x .303 in (7.7 mm) Lewis gun in observer's cockpit
Bombs: Up to 224 lb (100 kg) bombs
Operators: Nos 2,2,5,7 and 8 Squadrons RNAS, A,B,C,D,E and F
    Squadrons RNAS plus coastal stations and warships of the Grand Fleet

Sopwith Pup

Crew: 1
Length: 19 ft 3¾ in (5.89 m)
Wingspan: 26 ft 6 in (8.08 m)
Height: 9 ft 5 in (2.87 m)

Wing area: 254 ft² (23.6 m²)
Empty weight: 787 lb (358 kg)
Loaded weight: 1,225 lb (557 kg)
Powerplant: 1 x Le Rhone air-cooled rotary engine, 80 hp (60 kW)

Performance
Maximum speed: 97 knots (111½ mph, 180 km/h) at sea level
Service ceiling: 17,500 feet (5,600 m)
Endurance: 3 hours
Operators: No.1 Wing RNAS, Nos 3,4,8,9 and 12 Squadrons RNAS plus
  coastal stations and warships of the Grand Fleet

Sopwith 2F.1 Camel

Crew: 1
Length: 18 ft 9 in (5.71 m)
Wingspan: 26 ft 11 in (8.53 m)
Height: 8 ft 6 in (2.59 m)
Wing area: 231 ft² (21.46 m²)
Empty weight: 930 lb (420 kg)
Loaded weight: 1,455 lb (660 kg)
Powerplant: 1 x Clerget 9B 9-cylinder Rotary engine, 130 hp (97 kW)

Performance
Maximum speed: 115 mph (185 km/h)
Range: 300 miles ferry (485 km)
Service ceiling: 21,000 ft (6,400 m)
Operators: aircraft carriers HMS *Argus, Eagle, Furious* and *Pegasus* plus
  coastal stations

Supermarine Walrus

Crew: 3-4
Length: 33 ft 7 in (10.2 m)
Wingspan: 45 ft 10 in (14.0 m)
Height: 15 ft 3 in (4.6 m)
Wing area: 610 ft² (56.7 m²)
Empty weight: 4,900 lb (2,220 kg)
Loaded weight: 7,200 lb (3,265 kg)
Powerplant: 1 x Bristol Pegasus VI radial engine, 680 hp (510 kW)

Performance
Maximum speed: 135 mph (215 km/h) at 4,750 ft (1,450 m)
Range: 600 miles (965 km)
Service ceiling: 18,500 ft (5,650 m)

Armament
Guns: 2 x Vickers K machine guns
Bombs: 760 lb (345 kg) of bombs and depth charges
Operators: Nos. 702, 711, 712, 714, 715, 718 and 720 Catapult Flights plus
  Nos 700, 701, 710, 711, 712, 714 and 715 Catapult Squadrons

Supermarine Sea Otter

Crew: 4
Length: 39 ft 10¾ in (12.2 m)
Wingspan: 46 ft 0 in (14.0 m)
Height: 15 ft 1½ in (4.61 m)
Wing area: 620 ft² (56.7 m²)
Empty weight: 6,805 lb (3086 kg)
Loaded weight: 10,000 lb (4536 kg)
Powerplant: 1 x Bristol Mercury XXX, 965 hp (720 kW)

Performance
Maximum speed: 163 mph at 4,500 ft (262.3 km/h at 1371 m)
Range: 600 miles (1110 km)
Service ceiling: 17,000 ft (5181 m)

Armament
Guns: 1 x Vickers machine gun and twin Vickers K machine guns
Bombs: 4 x 250 lb (112 kg) bombs
Operators: Nos. 1700, 1701, 1702 and 1702 NAS

Supermarine Seafire LF.III

Crew: 1
Length: 30 ft 2½ in (9.21 m)
Wingspan: 36 ft 10 in (11.23 m)
Height: 11 ft 10 in
Wing area: 241.97 ft² (22.48 m²)
Empty weight: 6,204 lb (2,814 kg)
Max take-off weight: 7,640 lb (3,565 kg)
Powerplant: 1 x Rolls-Royce Merlin 55M liquid-cooled V-12, 1,585 hp (1,182
  kW)

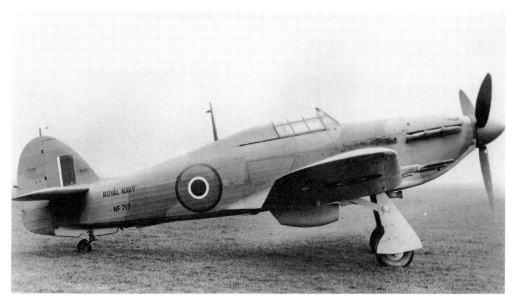

Even in its sea going form the Hurricane seemed to be overshadowed by the seemingly more glamorous Seafire, even if the former was the more capable machine for carrier operations. (FAAM Yeovilton)

One of those pictures that give the Seafire a bad name as FIII LR856 tips over on its nose and proceeds to wreck its propeller. This kind of accident happened more aboard the smaller escort carriers, this being HMS *Khedive* while the operating unit was No.899 Sqdn. (FAAM Yeovilton)

Proving that not all Seafire landings ended up nose down on the deck as this aircraft made a successful landing. (Rick Harding Collection)

Performance
Maximum speed: 348 mph (560 km/h) at 6,000 ft (1,830 m)
Range: 513 miles (825 km) with drop tanks
Service ceiling: 24,000 ft (7,315 m)

Armament
Guns: 2 x 20mm cannon 4 x .303 cal machine guns
Rockets: 4 x 3.5 in 60 lb (27 kg) rockets
Bombs: 1 x 500 lb (227 kg) bomb
Operators: Nos. 801, 805, 807, 809, 816, 833, 834, 842, 879, 880, 884, 885,
    886, 887, 889, 894, 895 and 897 NAS

Supermarine Attacker

Crew: 1
Length: 37 ft 1 in (11.3 m)
Wingspan: 36 ft 11 in (11.25 m)
Height: 9 ft 6.5 in (2.9 m)
Wing area: 227,2 ft² (21 m²)
Empty weight: 8,426 lb (3,822 kg)
Loaded weight: 12,211 lb (5,539 m)
Powerplant: 1 x Rolls-Royce Nene turbojet, 5,000 lb st (2,313 kg)

Performance
Maximum speed: 590 mph (950 km/h)
Range: 1,200 miles (1,900 km)
Service ceiling: 45,000 ft (13,716 m)

Armament
Guns: 4 x 20 mm Hispano Mk. V cannon in wings (125 rounds per gun,
    500 rounds total)
Bombs: 2 x 1,000 lb bombs or 4 x 300 lb rocket projectiles under the wings
Operators: Nos. 800, 803, 890, 1832, 1833, 1834 and 1836 NAS

Supermarine Scimitar

Crew: 1
Length: 55 ft 4 in (16.87 m)
Wingspan: 37 ft 2 in (11.33 m)
Height: 15 ft 3 in (4.65 m)
Wing area: 485 ft^2 (45.06 m^2)
Empty weight: 21,000 lb (9,525 kg)
Loaded weight: 34,200 lb (15,515 kg)
Powerplant: 2 x Rolls-Royce Avon 202 turbojets, 11,250 st (50.0 kN) each

Performance
Maximum speed: 710 mph (1,145 km/h) at sea level
Range: 600 miles (965 km)
Service ceiling: 50,000 ft (15,200 m)

Armament
Guns: 4 x 30 mm ADEN cannons
Hardpoints: 4 with a capacity of 4 x 1,000 lb (450 kg) bombs or 4 x AGM-
    12 Bullpup or AIM-9 Sidewinder missiles or Pods with 8, 16, or 24 3 in
    (76 mm) Semi Armour-Piercing (SAP) or HE unguided rockets
Operators: Nos. 800, 803, 804 and 807 NAS

Westland Wyvern S.4

Crew: 1
Length: 42 ft 3 in (12.88 m)
Wingspan: 44 ft 0 in (13.42 m)
Height: 15 ft 0 in (4.57 m)
Wing area: 355 ft^2 (33 m^2)
Empty weight: 15,608 lb (7,095 kg)

Having forged a partnership with Sikorsky the Westland Aircraft Company would become a licensed producer of their designs albeit altered to suit British requirements. One of the first successes of this partnership was the Dragonfly seen here in its rescue guise as the winch above the cabin door reveals. (John Ryan Collection)

One of the most unusual and under rated aircraft used by the FAA was the Westland Wyvern. Powered by a turboprop driving a contra rotating propeller assembly, the Wyvern was a very effective ground attacker. (BBA Collection)

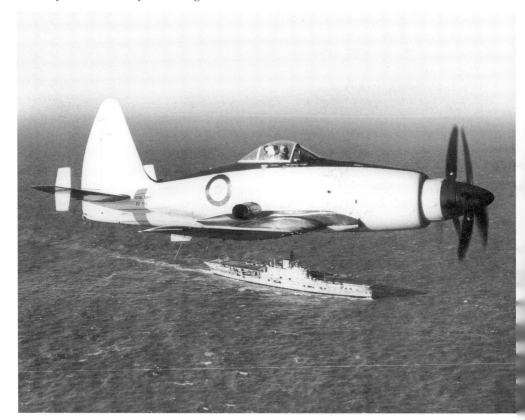

Loaded weight: 21,200 lb (9,636 kg)
Powerplant: 1 x Armstrong Siddeley Python 3 turboprop, 3,667 hp (2,736 kW)

Performance
Maximum speed: 383 mph (613 km/h)
Range: 904 miles (1,446 km)
Service ceiling: 28,000 ft (8,537 m)

Armament
Guns: 4 x 20 mm Hispano Mk. V cannons in the wings
Bombs: 1 x 1,850 lb (840 kg) torpedo, 16 x under wing rockets or up to 3,000 lb (1,364 kg) of bombs or 1 x Mk-15/17 torpedo or sea mine
Operators: Nos. 813, 827, 830 and 831 NAS

Westland Whirlwind HAS.7

Crew: 3 pilots
Length: 41 ft 9 in (12.71 m)
Rotor diameter: 53 ft 0 in (16.15 m)
Height: ft in (m)
Disc area: 2,205 ft² (205 m²)
Empty weight: lb (kg)
Loaded weight: lb (kg)
Powerplant: 1 x Alvis Leonides Major 9-cylinder radial, 750 hp (559 kW)

The Wessex followed the Whirlwind into Royal Navy service and was utilised in many roles. This aircraft was used for transporting troops, of note is the rocket pod mounted on the undercarriage leg. (John Ryan Collection)

Performance
Maximum speed: 104 mph (167 km/h)
Range: 334 miles (534 km)
Service ceiling: 9,400 ft (m)

Armament
Guns: 1 x torpedo (carried in place of dipping sonar)
Operators: Nos. 814, 815, 820, 824, 825, 829, 845, 846, 847 and 848 NAS

Westland Wasp HAS.1

Crew: 2
Capacity: up to 3 passengers
Length: 40 ft 4 in (12.29 m)
Rotor diameter: 32 ft 3 in (9.83 m)
Height: 8 ft 11 in (2.72 m)
Empty weight: 3,452 lb (1,566 kg)
Loaded weight: lb (kg)
Powerplant: 1 x Rolls-Royce Nimbus 103 turboshaft, 1,050 shp (783 kW)

Performance
Maximum speed: 120 mph (193 km/h)
Range: 303 miles (488 km)
Service ceiling: 13,400 ft (m)

Armament
Bombs: 2 x Mk 44/46 torpedoes or 2 x Mk 44 depth charges or 4 x SS-11
    replaced by 2 x AS.12 missiles.
Operators: Nos. 829, 845 and 848 NAS

Westland Wessex HU.5   app15

Crew: 2
Capacity: 16 troops or 8 stretchers
Length: 65 ft 8 in (20.03 m)
Rotor diameter: 56 ft 0 in (17.07 m)
Height: 16 ft 2 in (4.93 m)
Empty weight: 8,304 lb (3,767 kg)
Loaded weight: lb (kg)
Powerplant: 2 x Rolls-Royce Gnome turboshaft, 1,535 shp (1,150 kW)
    each

Performance
Maximum speed: 133 mph (212 km/h)
Range: 480 miles (772 km)
Service ceiling: 14,100 ft (m)
Operators: Nos. 845, 846, 847 and 848 NAS

Westland Sea King HAS.5 app16

Crew: 4
Length: 54 ft 9 in (16.69 m)
Rotor diameter: 61 ft 0 in (18.90 m)
Height: 16 ft 10 in (5.13 m)
Empty weight: 13,672 lb (6,202 kg)
Loaded weight: 21,000 lb (9,525 kg)
Powerplant: 2 x Rolls-Royce Gnome H1400-2 turboshafts, 1,660 shp
  (1,238 kW each) each

Due to be fully replaced by the Merlin, the Sea King first entered service in the A/S role, here an early model drops a homing torpedo. (BBA Collection)

Performance
Maximum speed: 144 mph (232 km/h)
Range: 764 miles (1,230 km)
Service ceiling: 10,000 ft (3,050 m)
Operators: Nos. 820 and 825 NAS

Westland Lynx

Crew: 2
Length: 15.24 m (50 ft)
Rotor diameter: 12.80 m (42 ft)
Height: 3.67 m (12 ft 0.5 in)
Empty weight: 3,291 kg (7,255 lb)
Max take-off weight: 5,330 kg (11,750 lb)
Powerplant: 2 x Rolls-Royce Gem turboshafts, 835 kW (1,120 shp) each

Performance
Maximum speed: 324 km/h (201 mph)
Cruise speed: km/h (mph)
Range: 328 miles (528 km)

Armament
2 x torpedoes or 4 x Sea Skua missiles or 2 x depth charges.
Operators: Nos. 815 and 829 NAS

Bibliography

Thetford, Owen, *British Naval Aircraft since 1912*, Putnam.

Hobbs, Commander David, MBE RN, *Aircraft Carriers of the Royal and Commonwealth Navies*, Greenhill.

Sturtivant, Ray, *The Squadrons of the Fleet Air Arm*, Air Britain.

Sturtivant, Ray; Burrow, Mick; Howard, Lee, *Fleet Air Arm Fixed-Wing Aircraft*, Air Britain.

Index